# SPOKEN SIBE
## MORPHOLOGY OF THE INFLECTED PARTS OF SPEECH

VERONIKA **ZIKMUNDOVÁ**

CHARLES UNIVERSITY IN PRAGUE
KAROLINUM PRESS
2013

Reviewed by:  Bayarma Khabtagaeva-Kempf, Ph.D.
              Cheng Zhi, PhD.

CATALOGUING IN PUBLICATION – NATIONAL LIBRARY OF THE CZECH REPUBLIC

Zikmundová, Veronika
Spoken sibe : morphology of the inflected parts of speech /
Veronika Zikmundová. – 1st ed. – Prague : Karolinum Press, 2013
Published by: Charles University in Prague
ISBN 978-80-246-2103-6

811.512.223 * 81'42 * 81'366
– Sibo language
– spoken language
– morphology (linguistics)
– inflection
– studies

494 – Altaic, Uralic languages [11]

ISBN 978-80-246-2103-6

# CONTENTS

# LIST OF ABBREVIATIONS

| | | |
|---|---|---|
| ACC. | – | Accusative case suffix |
| ACT. | – | Actualizing particle |
| BEN. | – | Benedictive |
| CC. | – | Conditional converb suffix |
| CI. | – | Imperfective converb |
| CP. | – | Perfective converb |
| CT. | – | Terminative converb |
| DL. | – | Dative-locative |
| DOUB. | – | Doubling |
| ECHO | – | Echo doubling |
| EMP. | – | Emphatic vowel |
| F. | – | Foregrounding particle |
| GEN. | – | Genitive |
| GEN.II | – | Genitive form used to appropriate sb. or sth. to a person or object which itself is appropriated to sb. |
| IMP. | – | Praesens imperfecti |
| IMPER. | – | Imperative |
| INC. | – | Inceptive verbal form |
| IS. | – | Instrumental-sociative |
| LAT. | – | Lative case suffix |
| LIM. | – | Limiting particle |
| NEG. | – | Particle of negation |
| NEG.EX. | – | Negative existential |
| NI.II | – | Imperfective verbal noun II |
| NI. | – | Imperfective verbal noun |
| NP. | – | Perfective verbal noun |
| NP.II | – | Perfective verbal noun II |
| NPROG.II | – | Progressive verbal noun II |
| MOD. | – | Suffix with the meaning of modulation and slight emphasis |
| ONOM. | – | Onomatopoetic expression |
| PERF. | – | Perfective verb (finite form) |
| POSS. | – | 3rd person enclitic possessive pronoun |
| PROB. | – | Particle of probability, suggestion etc. |
| PROG. | – | Progressive verb |
| S.G. | – | Suffix of a separately standing genitive form |
| QUEST. | – | Interrogative particle |
| QUOT. | – | Quotation particle |

# 0 INTRODUCTION

In the present work I attempt to describe one of the subsystems of the grammatical structure of the Sibe language, the morphology of the flexible parts of speech, to the extent and depth as the collected material and my own experience with the language has allowed. In the course of the description I have attempt, when possible, to put the given idiom into the context of literary Manchu and Mongolian, and to perceive it within the context of communication. I also discuss some problems of interpretation, mainly the classification of parts of speech.

Sibe is a Tungusic language closely related to classical Manchu. The Jungarian Sibes, who at present live in the north-west of Xinjiang, are in fact the last speakers of the Manchu language. Although around 20 thousand Sibes still speak their language, Sibe deserves to be labelled as an endangered language for a number of reasons. Several descriptions of the basic grammatical structure of spoken Sibe have been published, and parts of grammar have been studied in detail. Still, there is a persistant need of a thorough description of the language as a whole, which is becoming more urgent with the decreasing level of its knowledge among the Sibe speakers themselves.

The present description is based mainly on authentic language material gathered during my fieldwork among the Sibes in Xinjiang. I have focused on the description of the two most clearly defined parts of vocabulary, previously analyzed in depth in the context of various Altaic languages – the nouns and the verbs.

In addition to this main contribution I also give the brief general characteristics of the morphology of spoken Sibe, and I attempt a tentative classification of the parts of speech and their syntactical characteristics. All of the described features are accompanied by examples drawn from the language material collected in the course of my fieldwork in Xinjiang.

A sample of texts in spoken Sibe with translations is appended. It is intended to supplement the description presented here of the language with characteristics of higher than the morphosyntactical level – the text structure, idiomaticity, some poetical and other special means of expression, humour, etc.

Comparison with Mongolian suggests itself for a few reasons: Above all spoken Sibe and its historical predecessors have repeatedly been subjected to the strong influence of the Mongolic languages, and all levels of the language show remarkable typological correspondences with Mongolian. Since there is not enough space for systematic comparison in this work, I attempt to point out parallels and analogies, as well as differences, between spoken Sibe and Khalkha Mongolian in the course of the description.[1]

Apart from the structure of the language I attempt to describe its use in communication as well. I comment on the pragmatics of the oral language and on the various conditions and background of its actual usage. This is a result of the observation that while Sibe is the main and fully functional means of communication for the older generation of speakers, competence in the language rapidly decreases with age. It is very likely that in the course of the next few decades spoken Sibe will be on the verge of extinction, and it is therefore important to record it in as much detail as possible in its full form existing at present, together with the communication context which undergoes changes as drastically as the language itself.

## The Sibe people and their language

The self-appellation of the Sibe people is pronounced *Sivə*,[2] the official Chinese term is *Xibo*, in Russian literature the terms **sibin'ci** / **šibin'ci** are used, while in the English works the name '**Sibe**' has been established, which corresponds to the written form. The Jungarian Sibes are part of the larger Sibe ethnic group, whom the earliest records situate in south-eastern Manchuria (the Changbaishan mountain range). At present the Manchurian Sibes live mostly in the provinces of Girin (Jilin) and Mukden (Shenyang), numbering around 100,000 persons.[3] These Sibes lost the Sibe language at the beginning of the 20th century. In 1764, a segment of the of the Sibe population was commanded by the Emperor Qianlong to settle in the Ili area of Xinjiang, which had been depopulated by the Jungar wars. The descendants of these Sibes now number around 30,000 individuals, and the greater part of them have retained their traditions and use the Sibe language as their mother-tongue.

The language of this ethnic group, which I refer to as spoken or oral Sibe, may be considered one of the Manchu dialects. Since the Manchu language of Manchuria is on the verge of extinction, the Sibe people are the only heirs to the Manchu language and culture.

The spoken Sibe language, despite its unique position as an oral form of Manchu, has been the subject of relatively little research. Most of the fieldwork conducted among the Sibe people has been focused on various aspects of their culture, in particular the Sibe folklore, music, literature and religion. Apart from a few grammatical descriptions, several publications of materials of the spoken language and dictionaries have significantly contributed to the study of spoken Sibe. Complex descriptions and deep analyses of the grammar, however, are still lacking.

---

[1]  I take Khalkha Mongolian as the basis for comparison, because it is the only codified oral form of Mongolian and I do not have sufficient knowledge of any other Mongolian dialect. For further comparative work it will be necessary to work with the Khorchin dialect of Mongolian, which historically was in close contacts with Sibe during certain periods and which forms the main source of Mongolian loanwords in both Manchu and Sibe. The differences between the Mongolian dialects are not crucial for the typological correspondences, but are relevant for the study of vocabulary, idiomatics and communicative behaviour.

[2]  For the details of transcription see the section No. 1.2 Questions of transcription.

[3]  According to L. M. Gorelova, in Heilongjiang province there are Sibes who may still have some knowledge of their language (Gorelova 2002, p. 31).

# Brief summary of the history of the Sibes[4]

The early history of the Sibe people is subject to speculation. Following their language and cultural closeness to the Manchus, the Sibes were originally regarded as one of the Jurchen tribes (An, Wu, Zhao pp. 21–23). Modern Sibe historians have advanced a theory about the Xianbei afilliation of the Sibe tribe (An, Wu, Zhao, pp. 13–58).[5] This change of view, however, seems to have a certain political background.

The earliest historical records, which can be unambiguously identified with the present-day Sibe ethnic group, date from the 16th century, when the Sibe people were living as a vassal tribe of an eastern Mongolian group, the Khorchins. At that time the Sibes were settled in the Changbaishan mountains (Ma. Golmin šanggiyan alin) in south-eastern Manchuria. Those Sibe historians, who suggest the Xianbei origin of the Sibes, suppose that in the earlier stages of their history the Sibe tribe lived in Western Manchuria, in the region known today as Hölönbuir (An, Wu, Zhao, pp. 57–60).

During the reign of the Emperor Kangxi, the Sibes were persuaded by the Manchus to separate from the Khorchins. In the following period they were resettled from the Changbaishan mountains (allegedly due to their unruly character) and divided among Manchu administration centres – Girin, Mukden and Guihua (present Hohhot). According to the Sibe tradition, they were valued by the Manchu Emperors for their warlike character and courage in battle. The Sibe banners became a part of the New Manchu military formation. In 1764, following a decree of the Emperor Qianlong, a group of the New Manchus, consisting mostly of the Sibe banners, moved to the newly conquered areas of the former Dzungar Khanate. The movement to Xinjiang, which dispersed families and clans, the hard journey through Mongolia and other aspects of the whole event subsequently found a rich reflection in the Sibe popular history, folklore and written narratives. After a year-long journey and several resettlements inside Dzungaria the New Manchus settled along the left bank of the Ili River in an area known as Chabchal (Mo. Čavčaal, Chin. Chabuchaer). The Sibe soldiers were put in charge of the border fortresses along most of the north-western border of Xinjiang, and were also compelled to man the Imperial garrisons in the Uighur cities of the Tarim basin.

During the next two hundred years the Sibe banners played an important role in the suppression of the anti-Manchu (in the last case anti-Chinese) rebellions of the local people. During the 19th century smaller detachments of the Sibe soldiers were moved to other places in the vicinity of Ili, the most distant being that of Tarbagatai (Mo. Tarbagatai, Uig. Čöčäk, Chin. Tacheng).[6] During the 20th century many Sibes settled in Ghulja city.

The Ili valley forms part of the former Jungar Khanate and of the geographical unit called the Jungar basin, therefore the local Sibe enclave has been generally known as the Jungarian Sibes.

---

[4]  To my knowledge, so far the most detailed study on Sibe history is the book *Sibe uksurai šolokon suduri* by native scholars (An, Wu, Zhao 1985). Among Western scholars, L. M. Gorelova (2002, pp. 32–45) and Lebedeva discuss the subject extensively.

[5]  The only possibility to trace the Sibe history to earlier times is to admit their relationship to the Shiwei tribal union. More on this topic see in e.g. Gorelova 2002, Janhunen 1996.

[6]  The Sibe enclaves outside Chabchal, namely those of Huocheng (Iče Gazn), Gongliu, Nilka and Tarbagatai, have been under a stronger influence of the neighbouring peoples, mostly the Khazakhs. After the massive exodus of the Khazakhs to Khazakhstan in 1962, the Khazakh cultural heritage was gradually overcome by the ever-present Chinese influence.

The river Ili separates the Chabchal region from the city of Ghulja,[7] which was one of the traditional administrative centres of Jungaria as a whole. The western border of Chabchal is formed by the mountain range of Usun,[8] which forms the border with Khazakhstan. The Ili valley is, thanks to its relatively moist climate, the most fertile part of Xinjiang. Chabchal, irrigated by the Chabchal canal[9] with the water from Ili, has been an important agricultural area.

Until the middle of the 16th century, when the Manchus conquered Jungaria and the Tarim basin and created a new administrative unit with a military government, corresponding to the present-day Xinjiang, the mountain pastures of the Ili region were inhabited by the remnants of the western-Mongolian Oirat tribes (mainly the Choros, Khoshuud, Dörbet, Torghuut and Khoit). During Manchu rule the ethnic composition of the inhabitants in Ili greatly changed. Muslim farmers were moved from the Tarim oases to provide food supply for the Manchu army.[10] Part of the Chakhar Mongols was moved from southern Mongolia to Xinjiang and settled near Lake Sayram on a plateau above the Ili valley. During the 18th and 19th centuries nomadic Kazakh and Kirghiz as well as Uzbek farmers moved gradually to the area. As the result of the Russian conquest of Siberia many Russian, Tatar, Nogai and Central Asian Jews gradually resettled in Ili. The Russian influence in the Ili area culminated during the rule of Sheng Shicai (1933–1944)[11] and the Second East Turkestan Republic (1944–1949).

This multiethnic and multi-cultural milieu existed until the 1950s, when after the entry of the Maoist army, cruel repressions of all non-Han inhabitants began to be enforced. During the Cultural Revolution it was forbidden to teach the Sibe language and the Manchu script, the shamans and Buddhist monks were persecuted and the artifacts and religious and cult implements were destroyed. The Cultural Revolution caused an entire generation of the Sibes grow up without knowledge of the Manchu script and with a limited knowledge of spoken Sibe.

Thus during the past 400 years, the Sibe people changed their abodes, language and cultural environment several times. Sibe culture has absorbed a large number of influences, which can be seen today in their folklore and literature.

## Contacts and influences

The oldest roots of Sibe culture are presumed to lie in the ethnically and culturally diverse milieu of the half-settled hunters, fishermen and herders of Middle Manchuria. The Sibe scholars, judging from information in the oldest layer of folklore, place the ancestral homeland[12] of the tribe to the forested mountains of the Hinggan range. In any case the importance of clans, the role of shamans, the cults of wild and domestic animals and veneration

---

[7] Uighur *Ghulja*, Mongolian *Ili hot* and Chinese *Yi ning shi*.

[8] Ma. *Usun alin*, Uighur *Uzun tagh*, Chin, *Wusun shan*.

[9] The Chabchal canal was dug in the year 1808, 44 years after the arrival of the Sibe people to Ili, by the amban Tukšan. After their arrival the Sibes were settled on the left bank of the Ili, which was fertile and suitable for farming, but was lacking water. Therefore the beginnings in Chabchal were hard for the newcomers. In 1802 the amban Tukšan, followed by his clan members, started to dig the irrigation canal. For four years they wdug, with their own hands, the canal which transformed Chabchal into a uniquely fertile area and which ultimately turned the Sibe enclave into one of the richest places in Xinjiang. The amban Tukšan – known as Tu amban – has become one of the nation's heroes.

[10] This Uighur population became known as the Taranči – an Oirat-Mongolian word for a farmer.

[11] Sheng Shicai exercised pro-Soviet policy until 1942, when he expelled the Soviet advisors.

[12] *ba na* lit. 'place earth', interpreted as the 'ancestral homeland' by native scholars, seems to be an important concept even in the oldest folk songs (Zhonglu, personal communication 2002).

of numerous spirits link the Sibe culture to that of the Manchus and the Daghurs.[13] There are two folksongs,[14] which are perceived by all Jungarian Sibes as the most ancient ones – the songs *Yačina* (the meaning of the title is unclear) and *Domdoqŭn učun* ('The Butterfly Song'). The lyrics of these songs recall the lifestyle of forest hunters and fishermen and is not fully comprehensible to modern Sibes. It is also not clear on what occasions they were originally performed. Their melody and rhythm considerably differ from most of the later songs.

Similarly, the lullaby used by all Sibes, as well as some of the shaman songs, seem to come from the most ancient layer of the cultural heritage of the Jungarian Sibes.

Later, in the times of their vassalage to the Khorchins, the Sibes absorbed some features of the Khorchin shamanic cult, which, it appears, developed a previously non-existing stratification and hierarchy under the influence of Buddhism. They also adopted Buddhism in the earliest stage of its spread among the Khorchins, with Classical Mongolian as a liturgical language.[15] The influence of the Khorchin Mongols was in many respects more direct and profound on the Sibes than on the Manchus. One part of Sibe folklore is thought to bear[16] traces of Mongolian influence, as some wedding songs and many shaman songs, melodies for the traditional dance known as *bəylən* (cf. Mo. *bielgee*) etc.

After the Sibes left the Changbaishan mountain and re-settled in the great Manchu garrison cities, they came into intensive contact with the Chinese-influenced Manchu culture. This led to the emergence of a clear-cut and important layer of culture.[17]

After their arrival to Xinjiang, the position of the Sibes as a garrison of the army of occupation significantly hindered the possibility of contact with the local inhabitants, particularly the settled Muslim farmers. In fact the first significant contacts with the Uighurs do not date to earlier than to the beginning of the 20th century. After the arrival of the tribe to Xinjiang, the Sibe culture underwent an interesting development. Some parts of their cultural heritage, which they brought to their new home, were gradually lost, while others were intentionally handed down and developed in new directions.

The relatively modern layer in the traditional Sibe culture has formed after the arrival to Xinjiang, when the separation from the homeland and relatives, the wars with the Uighurs during various rebellions[18] and the Russian occupation of Ili[19] became the main motives in their folklore. A specific literary form, typical for the Jungarian Sibes, is the *julən* (Lit. Ma. *julun*), an extensive epic poem on mostly historical topics.[20] Among the most famous *juləns*

---

[13] As it follows from studies of Manchurian ethnic history (e.g. Janhunen 1996), great ethnic diversity had existed in the region until the beginning of the Manchu expansion. Investigations of the modern remnants of this plurality show that the languages and cultures of the various tribes and ethnic groups experienced considerable cross-contact, forming a distinct cultural complex of which the Sibes were an integral part.

[14] A valuable study of the Sibe folk music has been published by the British ethnomusicologist Rachel Harris (Harris 2005).

[15] Sibe Buddhism seems to be one of the least studied topics whithin the Sibe culture. The last Sibe Buddhist monk, who left the monastery when he was 14, died in 1999. When I interviewed him in 1994, he recited to me several short texts in Classical Mongolian and wrote a mantra in Mongolian and Sanscrit. It seems that Classical Mongolian played here a role similar to the role of Tibetan in the Mongolian Gelugpa tradition.

[16] I have heard this 'periodization' of the Sibe folklore heritage from several members of the Sibe language community, and I consider it to be part of a tradition which, dealing with the relatively recent past, may have a certain historical value.

[17] The native scholars believe, that before this the Sibe tribe lived beyond the reach of Chinese influence and that all the important Sino-Manchu features in their culture date from the 16th century and later.

[18] Especially the great Muslim rebellion in the 2nd part of 19th century.

[19] An almost ten year period in the 70s of the 19th century.

[20] A similar literary form is found among the Manchurian Daghurs (Bilid, Soijim, Bilig, 1987: *Dayur ulamjilal-tu uran jokiyal*. Hohhot).

are the *Gurinjihe učun* ('The Song of Resettlement'), *Kašgar-i učun* ('The Song of Kashgar') and *Lasihiyantu-i učun* ('The Song of Lasihiyantu').[21] Many *juləns*, namely the earlier ones, have developed from folk songs, but many, especially those more recent, have been authorial compositions. Famous *juləns* were handed down the families, but generally the composition of *juləns* seems to have been a widespread form of art, and chanting the *juləns* used to be a common entertainment for winter nights.[22]

A special chapter in the Sibe history are the contacts with Russians, which, although hostile in the beginning (Russians were in fact the invaders against which the border had to be defended), by the end of the 19th century turned into an intensive trade relationship and cultural exchange. The main traded goods were pigs,[23] bred by the Sibes and sought by the Russians, and, from the Russian occupation on, opium[24] as well. The city of Ghulja was in fact built by the Russians and some Russian settlers lived in Chabchal itself. The Sibe community in Ghulja is imporant from the point of view of cultural syncretism. Starting from the end of the 19th century, members of rich and influential Sibe families lived in this mainly Russian and Uighur, city; they formed a kind of secondary aristocracy. These Sibes, who valued education and culture as much as material wealth and military skills, maintained contacts above all with the Russians, the Tatars and the Nogais, but also with the Uighur aristocracy.[25] Through these contacts elements of Russian and other cultures began to spread among the Sibe people.

## Dialectal position of spoken Sibe

The problem of the position of spoken Sibe among the dialects of Manchu has been discussed only rarely,[26] clearly for the reason of the lack of available comparative material of oral Manchu. Materials of great interest relevant to this topic have been published by Chao Ke and Zhao Aping in the book *Heilongjiang xiandai Manyu yanjiu – Sahaliyan ula ne bisire manju gisun be sibkihe bithe* (*Study of the present-day Manchu language in the Amur region –* Chao Ke, Zhao Aping 2001). This publication presents samples of materials of four Manchu dialects, designated as Alecuha, Bala, Lalin and Sanjiazi (Ilan boo). The linguistic material shows that the Sanjiazi dialect is the closest to literary Manchu, while the other three dialects display divergences which the authors place into the context of the surrounding Tungusic languages and of Jurchen (the most striking being the system of teens in Alečuha numerals, which resembles the Jurchen teens[27] – pp. 70–72). The areal position of the dialects seems to support the idea that the dialects Bala, Alecuha and Lalin, besides being under the influence of other Tungusic languages, also retained some archaic features of the Jurchen language. On the other hand the Sanjiazi dialect is spoken in an area close to the traditional Sibe homeland.

---

[21] The *juləns* mentioned above have been translated by Prof. Stary into German.

[22] Even at present reports are heard that one or another old man has written a *julən*, and occasionally even young people know how to read and chant them.

[23] Not only the Xinjiang Muslims, but also the nomadic Mongols of the Ili area neither bred nor ate pork.

[24] The growing and subsequent use of opium became a threat for the whole Sibe population and had to be forceably stopped at the beginning of the 20th century.

[25] Descendants of these families are known for their multilingualism, which caused the spread of a reputation of the Sibe people as polyglots.

[26] L. M. Gorelova mentions the opinion of the Sibe scholar An Jun that spoken Sibe is particularly close to the Ilan Boo (Sanjiazi) dialect of Manchu.

[27] For teens in Jurchen and Manchu cf. Janhunen 1993.

I had been told previously by a Sibe scholar who visited Sanjiazi that he was able to communicate in his native language with the Manchu speakers.[28] I had the same experience in 2007, when I was able to converse with a Manchu speaker in Sanjiazi using Sibe. Taking into account the somewhat limited language competence of the speaker caused by the fact that she had not used Manchu in everyday communication for a long time, the difference between the Sanjiazi Manchu and the Jungarian Sibe of the octogenarian speakers was minor and should be partly ascribed to the Chinese influence being heavier in Sanjiazi than in Chabchal.

Since the main body of Manchu upon which the literary language was based had ceased to exist before the start of the field research in China[29] and all materials available at present come from the margins of the Manchu language area, it may be justified to assume that the Sibe language, which is apparently close to literary Manchu, is the descendant of the central or official Manchu dialect.

Another indirect source of information concerning the relationship of Manchu and Sibe may be the account of a Daghur soldier from Manchuria, who came to Ili during the great Muslim rebellion, and described his first meeting with the Sibes saying, that he suddenly heard several people talking in 'our Manchu language' (Donjina 1989, p. 31).

It may be concluded that spoken Sibe, except for the strong influence of Khorchin Mongol manifested mainly on the lexical level, is most likely a descendant of the Manchu coinée.

## Previous research of spoken Sibe

Various aspects of the Sibe language and culture have been explored by researchers in China by both ethnic Sibe and Chinese scholars. All of them are to be found in the bibliography of Manchu Studies by G. Stary. Here I would like to mention the 'classical' reference books for Sibe studies – the Sibe Ethnography (Ma. *Sibe uksurai an tacin*) and the Short history of the Sibe nation (Ma. *Sibe uksurai šolokon suduri*).[30] An important study of Sibe shamanism was published by Kicešan (Qicheshan 2011) and a monumental collection of Sibe folklore by Zhonglu is hopefully forthcoming.

Outside China, Russia has the longest tradition in Sibe studies, which started with the phenomenal collection of Sibe folk texts by Fedor Muromskij (Kałużyńsky 1977). This work has been further developed by the Manchurologists Tatiana Pang, Liliya M. Gorelova, Konstantin S. Yahontov and others.

In Japan the tradition of Sibe studies begins with Kengo Yamamoto in the 1960s; similarly, several young Japanese scholars have been conducting research into Sibe last years. A Sibe scholar living in Japan – Kicengge (Chengzhi) – has published several studies of Manchu and Sibe history based on early Qing documents.

In Europe, the Italian Manchurologist Professor Giovanni Stary is the most deserving of praise due to his extensive research and publication activities concerning the Sibe nation. Besides numerous specialized articles, mainly on Sibe literature and history, and several overviews of Sibe studies, Professor Stary translated most of the relevant texts in written

---

[28] Kicengge, personal communication, 1999.

[29] During several years immediately preceding the Cultural revolution extensive field research was pursued among the non-Han nationalities in Northern China and valuable materials of the minority languages were recorded. Thanks to this effort, records of Manchu spoken by that time in the marginal areas, namely Heilongjiang, have been preserved in China.

[30] The last book has been translated and published by G. Stary.

Sibe published in Xinjiang into European languages. His monumental bibliography of Manchu studies contains all works concerning the Sibe ethnic group, published both in and outside China.

Aspects of Sibe culture have been studied by Alessandra Pozzi[31] (Italy) and Rachel Harris (UK).[32]

As mentioned before, spoken Sibe has been viewed either as a Manchu dialect, or as an oral variation of Manchu proper. Until recently the living Sibe language had been the object of relatively little study and complex descriptions of grammar have yet to be published. The majority of the publications relevant to spoken Sibe are dictionaries and editions of commented and analyzed texts of the oral language.

The oldest source for spoken Sibe is the *Man'čžurskaja chrestomatia* (Manchu Reader) by A. O. Ivanovskij (Ivanovskij 1895), which contains two oral Sibe texts. A collection of spoken language materials, unique in content as well as a linguistic document, are the texts which were recorded in Chabchal by F. Muromskij at the beginning of the 20th century and later published by the Polish scholar S. Kałużyński (1977).

Several oral Sibe texts have been published during the last decades. The most important of these are the record of a folktale 'The Young Man and the Fairy' with parallel literal and free translations and a list of nominal and verbal formants by the Chinese scholar Li Shulan (1986), and two works by the Sibe author Jin Ning, particularly the edition of the 'Legend of blackening the face' in transcription and translation into literary Manchu and English (Jin Ning 1991) and the *Sibe-English Conversations*, which contains an abundant selection of phrases used in daily communication (Jin Ning 1993).

The Sibe-English dictionary by K. Yamamoto including a detailed phonetic analysis has not yet been surpassed. Among several dictionaries published in China the most important and useful is the monolingual dictionary published in Urumchi in 1987 (*Sibe 'manju' gisun-i buleku bithe*, 1987).

The linguistic research of 'real'[33] spoken Sibe in the West began, for all intents and purposes, with the description by Jerry Norman (Norman 1974). His informants were the members of a Sibe family living in Taiwan. The work of Prof. Norman includes a detailed description of the phonology and morphology of the spoken language and, with minor divergences caused mainly by the different age of the informants, precisely fits with my experience with the Sibe speakers. The part concerning morphology is limited to the list and characteristic of the nominal and verbal suffixes.

The collective work of Chinese and Sibe authors Li Shulan, Zhongqian and Wang Qingfeng (Li Shulan 1984), comprises a detailed phonetic, phonological and morphological description with examples and a Sibe-Chinese vocabulary. The description is based on rich material collected by fieldwork. Apparently the material was collected among speakers with high competency in literary Manchu and some of the forms found in the work would not be typical for the speech of less educated speakers.

The Polish linguist S. Kałużyński, who edited the unique materials collected by F. Muromskij, later published a brief morphological description of the language of these

---

[31] For the first detailed study on Sibe shaman beliefs, see Pozzi 1992.

[32] The recently published book by Rachel Harris presents rare materials of Sibe folk and especially shaman songs and an important study of the Sibe folk culture in general (Harris 2005).

[33] Some authors in speaking about Sibe, refer not to the Sibe vernacular, but to the pronunciation of the written language by the Sibes which only slightly differs from written Manchu.

materials (Kałużyńsky 1987). According to the interpretation of contemporary Sibe scholars (Kicengge 1994 – personal communication) the records of F. Muromskij seem to reflect the pronunciation of the written language[34] and not of the contemporary spoken language, which could not be so different from the modern vernacular. In his interesting and unconventional Manchu reader the Polish Manchurologist Jerzy Tulisow uses constructions of the living language and every-day communication, which makes the grammatical thinking of Manchu accessible to the reader. The author has also visited the Jungarian Sibe.

The Chinese scholar Wang Xiaohong and the Sibe author Guo Meilan published an analysis of the phonological structure of the oral Sibe language (Wang, Guo, 1985).

Among Manchurological works which apply to Sibe I would mention the Manchu reader with an overview of grammar and explanation of idiomatics by Gerthraude Roth-Li, which contains texts of modern Sibe. The comprehensive Manchu Grammar by L. M. Gorelova presents useful historical and demographic information about the Sibe ethnic group, and uses comparative material of Evenki, Nanai, literary and spoken Sibe in addition to literary Manchu.

I would also like to draw attention to an interesting publication by Zhang Bo, which, though it does not concern spoken Sibe, is a unique and remarkable attempt. This textbook of spoken Manchu, written by a young ethnic Manchu, is not a record of the existing spoken language but an original work meant to 'revive' Manchu by basing its analysis on the written form and inventing new expressions when possible and needed. This publication, though striking by intentionally not taking into account any existing vernacular related to Manchu, is the admirable and courageous effort of a talented young linguist.

Finally, a description and analysis of the grammar – phonetics, phonology, morphology, and syntax – of both spoken and written Sibe has recently been published by the Korean scholar Jang Taeho. The author, in addition to using modern methods of Western linguistics, utilizes as well his linguistic insight as a native speaker of Korean, a language whose grammar is in some ways close to that of Manchu and Sibe. Jang Taeho's work is a result of 10 years of the study of oral Sibe, during which he has gained an active command of the language. Jang Taeho's book is at present the only existing complex description of spoken Sibe written with the use of Western linguistic approaches. Unfortunately for many Western linguists, the main part of the book is written in Chinese. A textbook of spoken Sibe has been recently published in Tokyo (Kubo 2011).

In writing the present work I relied, in addition to the above-mentioned works and the collected language materials, upon older Manchurological literature, mainly the works by I. Zaharov – the Manchu Grammar (Zaharov 1879) and the Manchu-Russian dictionary (Zaharov 1875). In addition to the classical Altaistic literature (Ramstedt 1957, Poppe 1960) I used comparative Tungusologic works, above all the exhaustive and critical monographs by O. P. Sunik dealing with verbs (Sunik 1962) and nouns (Sunik 1982) in the Tungusic languages.

Among descriptive works dealing with particular languages, the description of the Chakhar dialect of Mongol by the Inner Mongolian linguist B. Sechenbaatar (2003) has been very inspirational for my work. I acquired this book while writing my dissertation and the solutions concerning some problems of the application of the European language categories on the Altaic languages have been particularly helpful for the description of Sibe. Certain questions

---

[34] Like Mongolian, Sibe has a particular method of enonciating written texts which does not exactly reproduce the written form, but preserves the main differences from the oral language.

concerning parts of speech in Chahar (which can be applied to all Mongolian dialects) are dealt with in an especially innovative way. Since the use of grammatical methodology is practically identical in Mongolian and Sibe, I followed Sechenbaatar's classification in some crucial points of the classification of the Sibe parts of speech.

## Sources of data, methods of work

The material for this description was collected among Sibe speakers mostly in Chabchal and Urumchi. During my first study period I concentrated on gaining an active knowledge of spoken Sibe and endeavoured to obtain a deeper understanding of Sibe culture and history, an acquisition rendered possible due to the kindness of my teacher Mr. Kicengge, who taught me intensively for one year and allowed me to follow him on his field research in Chabchal. Later I spent more time collecting language material for description. Part of the records used in this work were completed by Mr. Kicengge.

The material was collected during study periods and shorter visits in Xinjiang in the course of approximately 10 years (1992–2002). Several important and high quality recordings (approximately 280 minutes of folktales, readings of the *julən* etc.) were made by Mr. Kicengge in the winter of 1995. The collected material contains approximately 70 hours of tape recordings, and approximately 10 hours of digital data.

Most of the material actually used in the description was collected during a study period in Urumchi during 1999–2000. For gathering of the language data I used two methods – writing notes by hand and recording onto tape. The first method proved to be the more suitable for acquiring full paradigms of morphological descriptions. Sometimes writing notes by hand was the only way to take down accounts or expressions which the speakers were for some reasons not willing to have tape-recorded. I also concentrated on fixed expressions, idioms, jokes and other properties of the informal communication. The second method was used for recording longer accounts, the topics of which were chosen in advance according to the interest of the speakers. Often the speaker chose the topic himself based upon what he considered to be important to relate about the Sibes. Most of the recordings concern about history, military matters, shamans, ghosts and spirits and everyday life in the past.

I discussed the paradigms, variants etc. with the speakers after a preliminary classification. The help and support of my informants enabled me to complete some larger units of material for the grammatical description.

In the course of the following description I attempted to choose examples which are either typical for everyday speech, or which show some exceptional features of the spoken language. Whenever it seemed meaningful, I have added notes to the examples, mostly to frame the immediate communication context or morphosyntactical peculiarities of the given example, but sometimes also to provide cultural or historical context. This variance reflects my wish to transmit the live speech material as fully as possible and to avoid potential misunderstandings.

## Notes on the literal translations of examples

Among the many possibilities of morphological glossing I have chosen one of relatively medium specificity. In view of the relatively simple morphological structure of spoken Sibe, I try to gloss the greater part of the morphemes with grammatical meaning and some of the particles with grammatical meaning. Since most of the derivational suffixes are not dealt with in the present work, I do not mark them in the literal translation. Zero suffixes, in view of their great frequency, are glossed only when it is relevant to the grammar in the given explanation. Glossing of particles is slightly more complicated and for several I rather use a fixed lexical translation, which does not vary according to the context. I do the same in the case of some adverbials. This concerns mainly the following expressions:

*o-* (translated as 'to become'), an existential verb functionally similar to the Mongolian verb *bol-*, used mostly to express indentity, with a wide range of usage developed from the basic meaning: 'to become', 'to be possible', etc.

*gəɹ* (translated as 'still'), lexical meaning 'still, also, too; any',[35] also used in negative constructions as 'nothing, never, nowhere', etc.

*su/šu* (translated as 'ultimately') is an emphatic particle, which usually designates high degree of quality or high intensity of an action; sometimes it is used in proximity to a superlative.

*dači* (translated as 'originally') is an expression used to determine mainly verbs. It is composed of the noun *da* 'root, base' etc. and the case suffix *-či*, (ablative in lit. Manchu and lative in Sibe). The meaning of the expression varies between 'originally', 'formerly' and 'long ago'.

Another problem was posed by the word *ňi*, which, being originally an enclitic third person possessive pronoun, is also frequently used as a particle for marking the topic, emphasis or foregrounding of the noun which it follows. In some cases it might be appropriate to translate it by a definite article or a demonstrative pronoun (Khalkha Mongolian uses the third-person possessive enclitic pronoun *n'* in an analogical way). In the literal translation I decided to mark these two functions separately and while the pronoun in its original function is glossed as POSS., in the function of a foregrounding particle or a topic marker it is marked as F.

---

[35] A particle of similar function seems to exist in the entire linguistic sphere of Inner Asia (Mongolian *c'*, Uighur *mu*, Mongghul *da*, Mandarin Chinese *ye*, Tibetan *yang* etc.). In Manchu the word *geli* is apparently a more recently grammaticalized expression).

# 1 CHARACTERISTICS OF SPOKEN SIBE

This chapter contains more general information, which is important for the understanding of the detailed explanations that follow. It concerns phonetics, phonology, the lexicon and the definition of the parts of speech.

## 1.1 Notes on the phonetics and phonology

### 1.1.1 Problems of the phonological description of Sibe

The phonetic and phonological structure of spoken Sibe has been the subject of relatively little research. The greatest obstacle to clarifying the Sibe phonemic system in a way that would encompass the overall present situation is the great variance among groups of speakers and the fluidity in the pronunciation of the spoken language. The problems concern above all the distribution of allophones, which significantly differs in dependence on the age of the speakers, and, to some extent, on their adherence to one or another dialectal group.

The local variants of Tarbagatai, Nilqa, Gongliu and Ice Gašan are marked mostly on the levels of prosody, syntax and vocabulary. They concern mostly the older generation, because among the middle-aged and young speakers the knowledge of the Sibe language is considerably less frequent than in Chabchal.

Concerning the age of the speakers, the situation is more complicated and applies more to phonetics. Despite the fact that the language is currently undergoing changes and despite the variability of the mentioned idiolects, it is possible to define roughly two major varieties of spoken Sibe, which are considered to be correct by the speakers while differing from each other. Their origin is closely connected with the the cessation of the use of the Manchu script. Knowledge of written Manchu prevails among speakers born roughly before 1955.[1] Among younger speakers, who grew up during the time when teaching and using Manchu script was forbidden, the number of those who can use it for recording of their own language is around a hundred people. (Kicengge, personal communication 2012)

The overall impression given by the present situation is that the spread of literacy constrained the natural tendencies in the development of the language, and the later loss

---

[1] The relatively high level of literacy (compared to the contemporary Manchu speakers) is a result of educational reform that took place among the Jungarian Sibes during the first two decades of the 20th century.

of literacy among the bulk of the people accelerated phonetic changes, which then took place within one single generation. It is therefore possible to speak about the language of the 'older generation', which would include speakers born before 1955, and that of the 'younger generation', which would comprise speakers born approximately between 1955 and 1975[2].

Generally it is possible to say that in the speech of the older generation forms that are phonetically closer to the written language occur together with purely oral forms,[3] while the younger generation employs only the oral forms. An illustration may be given by the expression meaning 'ended, finished': its written form is *wajiha*, with the equivalent oral form *vašq*, in addition to which the forms *vajĭχ, vačχ, vačqa, vačq* (and possibly more) may occur among speakers of the older generation.

It often happens that a word has either fallen out of use or has never been used as 'colloquial' by a certain group of speakers and is known to them only in the written form, while another group of speakers uses its oral variant. One example is provided by the general expression for 'fruits', Lit. Ma. *tubihe*, which was presented to me as a literary word for what is commonly known as *suʌвo jaq*, lit. 'apple thing', by my Chabchal informants; only recently, however, I heard, in oral expression, the word *tüvɣø* from a 60-year-old speaker whose mother came from Tarbagatai.

## 1.1.2 Previous research of the Sibe phonemic system

The phonemic system of genuine[4] spoken Sibe has been described several times. Probably the earliest description comes from Yamamoto Kengo as a part of his famous dictionary (Yamamoto 1969), followed by separate chapters in the two basic works on Sibe grammar: the classic of spoken Sibe studies by Jerry Norman (Norman 1974, pp. 163–164) and the description of spoken Sibe by Li Shulan et al. (Li Shulan 1984). Further there is a important article by Guo Meilan and Wang Xiaohong. Various details and aspects of the phonology of spoken Sibe have been discussed by native and Chinese scholars during the last 20 years. The most detailed description of the phonetic and phonological system of both spoken and written language (including a synchronic and diachronic comparative analysis) has been presented by Jang Taeho in his recently published book (Jang 2008, pp. 6–95).

J. Norman describes the Sibe phonemic system as follows:

Consonants:

|  | labials | alveolars | alveopalatals | velars | uvulars |
|---|---|---|---|---|---|
| fortis stops | p | t | c | k | Q |
| lenis stops | b | d | j | g | G |
| nasals | m | n |  | ŋ | *G* |
| fricatives | f | s | (š) | x | H |

---

[2]  This was the year of birth of the youngest of my informants.

[3]  According to Kicengge, the main features which characterize the phonetic shape of spoken Sibe as opposed to written Manchu must have developed quite early, most probably before the beginning of the 20th century (Kicengge, personal communication 1995).

[4]  Besides the analyses of the live speech there are several works based on the earlier records of Sibe, which in fact are records of recitation of the literary language, a tradition which survives in Chabchal up till the present day (Kaluzynski 1977, 1987).

| semivowels and liquids | v | l/r | y | | |
|---|---|---|---|---|---|

Vowels:

| | front | central | back |
|---|---|---|---|
| high | i ü | | u |
| mid | ε | ə | o |
| low | | a | |

Diphthongs:

| ai | əi | | oi | ui |
|---|---|---|---|---|
| au | əu | | | |
| ia | | iε | io | |
| ua | | üε | | |

The description of the phonemic system by Li Shulan (pp. 5–7) generally resembles that of J. Norman but lists more consonantal sounds among phonemes than the latter.

| | bilabial | labio-dental | appical | retroflex. | dorsal | radical | epiglottal |
|---|---|---|---|---|---|---|---|
| voiceless stops | b | | d | | | g | oɪ |
| voiceless aspir. stops | p | | t | | | k | ĸ |
| voiceless affricates | | | z | zh | j | | |
| voiceless aspir. affricates | | | c | ch | q | | |
| voiceless fricatives | | f | s | sh | x | h | h |
| voiced fricatives | | v | | | | | |
| nasals | m | | n | | | ng | |
| laterals | | | l | | | | |
| | | | r | | | | |
| semivowels | w | | | | y | | |

The differences concern mostly back and front variants of sibilant affricates and fricatives (Norman: *c* [middle č] – Li Shulan: *ch* [back č] vs. *q* [front č]. These differences seem to be conditioned by the fact that, while J. Norman's informants were an emigrant Sibe family who had left China in the 1940s, Li Shulan is a Chinese linguist, and her informants were most probably bilingual in Mandarin Chinese in which front and back sibilants are separate phonemes.

The detailed study by Guo Meilan and Wang Xiaohong agrees in most parts with that of J. Norman, except for the two varieties of sibilants, accepted by them as phonemically distinct.

Wang Xiaohong and Guo Meilan present the following table of the Sibe consonantal phonemes:

| | | Labial | | appical | | | | lami-nal | dorsal | | radical | |
|---|---|---|---|---|---|---|---|---|---|---|---|---|
| | | *bilab.* | *labio-dent.* | *inter-dent.* | *front app.* | *mid-dle app.* | *back app.* | | *Front* | *mid-dle* | *radi-cal* | *epi-glottal* |
| stops | voiceless aspired | p | | | | t | | | | | k | q |
| | voiceless unasp. | p' | | | | t' | | | | | k' | q' |
| | voiced | | | | ts | | tʃ | | tɕ | | | |
| affricates | voiceless aspired | | | | | | tʃ' | | tɕ' | | | |
| | voiceless unasp. | | | | | | | | | | | |
| | voiced | | | | | | | | | | | |
| nasals | | m | | | | n | | | | | ŋ | |
| | voiced | | | | | r | | | | | | |
| | | | | | | | | | | | | |
| later. | | | | | | l | | | | | | |
| frica-tives | voiceless | | f | | s | | ş | | | | x | χ |
| | voiced | | f | | | | | | | | | |

To give an example of the present linguistic situation, in the speech of the oldest speakers[5] there is no phonemic opposition between back and front sibilant affricates and the back and front variants are allophones conditioned by the following vowel, whereas the middle and younger generation perceives the two variants as separate phonemes and considers that there is a phonemic distinction between them.

In general, any investigation into the Sibe phonology is complicated by the fact that part of the speakers recognize written Sibe or written Manchu as the written standard of their speech, while the other part does not. For the first group it is natural to perceive the oral forms of words as realizations of their written forms, while the phonemic structure of the language of the second part relies only on the oral forms.[6]

---

[5]  The way of pronunciation differs not only according to the age of the speakers, but often due to family tradition and other considerations. Pronunciation of the middle š usually occurs in the speech of Sibes born approximately before 1940.

[6]  While it is difficult to prove this theory, there are some important indicators to support it. One of them may be the way in which speakers illiterate in Sibe transcribe their language into Chinese characters, or the way the speakers familiar with romanized alphabets of the non-Chinese languages use them for spoken Sibe. In most such transcriptions which I have been able to observe the characteristics of spoken Sibe become very evident.

## 1.1.3 List of sounds in spoken Sibe

In view of the precarious linguistic situation I do not attempt a phonological description of my own, and instead I list the sounds used in spoken Sibe and comment on their usage.

**The vowels of spoken Sibe:**

| | | Front | | Central | | Back | |
|---|---|---|---|---|---|---|---|
| | | *non-labial* | *labial* | *non-labial* | *Labial* | *non-labial* | *Labial* |
| high | higher | i | ü | | u | | |
| | lower | ï | | | | | |
| mid | higher | | ø | e | | | |
| | lower | | | ə | | | o |
| low | higher | ɛ | | | | | ů |
| | lower | | | | | a | |

The vowels *a, ɛ , ə, e, o, ø, u, ü, ů, i* and *ï* occur in stressed syllables, and the vowels *o, u, ů, ə, i* and *ï* occur in unstressed syllables.

### *Palatal vowels*

The palatal vowels are not noted in written Manchu. In Sibe they mostly occur in the vicinity of an *i*. The palatal vowels often merge with diphthongs: Lit. Ma. *amargi*, Si. *ɛmirgi/ ɛⁱmirgi* 'northern'; Lit. Ma. *dobi*, Si. *døf/düəf* 'fox'; Lit. Ma. *turi*, Si. *türⁱ*).

Sometimes the palatal vowels occur in words without an *i* as in the cases of an elided *k* before consonants (Lit. Ma. *sakda*, Si. *saⁱt/sɛt/set* 'old'). In some cases the palatalisation results in a change of the vowel quality (Lit. Ma. *fonji-*, Si. *fienji-* 'to ask').

### *Diphthongs*

The diphthongs which are probably indigenous to spoken Sibe are the closing diphthongs *ai, oi, ůi, ei* and opening diphthongs *ia, io, iu, ie, u a, ao*. In loan-words the diphthong *ui* is common.

The diphthong *ue* (written as *uwe*) of literary Manchu does not exist in spoken Sibe (Lit. Ma. *kuwesi*, Si. *kuźi* 'knife') and a secondary diphthong ao has developed by the elision of *k* before consonants (Lit. Ma. *akdun*, Si. *aoduⁿ* 'firm, secure'; Lit. Ma. *akjan*, Si. *aojuⁿ* 'lightening' ).

Further, the opening diphthongs in Sibe often correspond to the closing diphthongs of literary Manchu (Lit. Ma. *gayi-*, Si. *gia-* 'to take'; Lit. Ma. *bayi-*, Si. *bia-* 'to ask, to look for'; Lit. Ma. *boihon*, Si. *bioʁůⁿ* 'dust, earth').

In some cases there is a palatal diphthong in spoken Sibe corresponding to a simple vowel in written Manchu (Lit. Ma. *foholon*, Si. *fioʁůlůⁿ/føʁůlůⁿ* 'short').

On the whole, it seems that palatal diphthongs and palatal vowels in spoken Sibe are often interchangeable and their use varies individually.

**The consonants of spoken Sibe:**

| | | bilab. | labio dental. | alveol. | retroflex. | alveopalat. | palat. | velar. | uvul. |
|---|---|---|---|---|---|---|---|---|---|
| stops | voiced | b | | d | | | | g | ɢ |
| | lenis voiceless | ḅ | | ḍ | | | | g | ɢ̥ |
| | fortis | p | | t | | | | k | q |
| affricates | voiced | | | | ǰ | j | | | |
| | lenis voiceless | | | | ǰ | j | | | |
| | fortis | | | | č | ź | | | |
| fricatives | voiced | | v | z | | ź | | ɣ | ʁ |
| | lenis voiceless | | v̥ | z̥ | | ź̥ | | | |
| | fortis | | f | s | š | ś | | x | χ |
| resonants | laterals | | | | l | λ | | | |
| | medials | | | | ɹ | r | y | | |
| | nasals | m | | n | | | | ŋ | ɴ |

The phonemes /g/, /k/, /x/ and /ŋ/ have velar and uvular allophones, which are distributed according to the place of articulation (uvulars in the vicinity of back vowels and velars in the vicinity of front vowels) the velar fricative [ɣ] and the uvular fricative [ʁ] are allophones of either the phoneme /g/or the phoneme /x/ in an intervocalic position.

The voiced consonants [v], [z], [ź] are allophones of /f/, /b/, /s/ and /š/ occurring both between vowels and in the initial position.

The sounds [j] and [ǰ] may be either the realization of the phonemes /j/ and /ǰ/, or allophones of /ć/ and /č/ in intervocalic positions.

Below I append several comments on the most characteristic features and developments in spoken Sibe.

### *1) Vowel harmony*

Vowel harmony, which is present to some degree in most Uralic-Altaic languages, as well as in others and which is strictly observed in written Manchu, is relatively less consistent in spoken Sibe, especially in the younger generation. Still it is possible to state that vowel harmony is an effective principle of the spoken language.

The articulatory positions are, as in Mongolian, two – back and front. The back vowels are /a/ and /o/, the front row is represented only by /ə/, while /i/ and /u/ are treated as neutral. In fact, /u/ has two allophones – back and front – and it seems that in most words containing /a/ or /o/, especially in those with uvulars, the back allophone [ů] is pronounced. Exception are words with an initial /u/, which is mostly pronounced as [u] in words without uvulars. This, however, requires a detailed phonetic examination to clarify the precise phonetic qualities of the sounds.

The vowel /i/ generally retains its front vowel qualities, although a slightly lower and backer allophone occurs in the vicinity of uvulars.[7] /i/, in its turn, has a strong palatalizing effect on the sounds in its vicinity.

## 2) Reduction of vowels

One of the most intensive changes that is currently taking place in the spoken language is the strong reduction of vowels in unstressed positions, which in some cases results in their loss.[8]

Approximately three degrees of reduction may be distinguished.

The first (lowest) degree concerns the vowels *o*, *u* and *i* in unstressed positions, which have a shorter pronunciation without qualitative changes (e.g. *foro$^n$* 'peak', *gətku$^n$* 'intelligent', *jaqǔ$^n$* 'eight', *χoñi$^n$* 'sheep').

The second (middle) degree of reduction affects the vowels *a* and *e* in unstressed positions, where they are pronounced as a short medial [ə] (e.g. *yaχčə$^n$* 'puppy', *aməɹ* 'after', *samə$^n$* 'shaman').

The third (maximum) degree of reduction occurs in some unstressed positions, mostly in the word ending, in the second syllable of three-syllable words and in the first syllable after the unvoiced sibilant [s] and [š]. All vowels can be reduced in this way. In these positions vowels often lose their syllabicity and are difficult to reconstruct except from Manchu/Sibe orthography or from other grammatical forms. In the younger generation's speech these vowels tend to be dropped altogether (e.g. *čiśkə* Lit. Ma. *cecike* 'sparrow, little bird'; *ś$^i$qa*, Lit. Ma. *sika* 'horsehair'; *gəɹɣ$^ə$i*, Lit. Ma. *gələhə* 'be afraid-PERF.' *arχ* 'way to do' *arʁəf* 'way to do-ACC.' etc.).

## 3) Vowel length and stress

The length of vowels is not phonologically distinctive and it is accompanied by stress.

In most cases the first syllable is stressed, and only some words beginning with unvoiced speech sound(s) have stress on the second syllable. In some words there is an additional stress on the last syllable. Apart from this, the last syllable of a prosodic unit is usually stressed, and in slow and distinct speech the last syllable of every emphasized word is stressed. In some cases of strong emphasis prolonged pronunciation of a vowel is accompanied by a glottal constriction or stop (e.g. *yavma$^ʔ$aq duth$^ə$i* lit. go-CP. lie-PERF. 'goes on and on').

## 4) Alternation of occlusives and fricatives

The lenis stops /b/, /g/ and /ɢ/ in the medial and final positions are, with some exceptions, pronounced as fricatives [v], [ɣ] and [ʁ] respectively (e.g. Lit. Ma. *sarganjui*, Si.- *saʁənč* 'daughter, girl'; Lit. Ma. *abala-*, Si. *avələ-* 'to hunt').

The fortis fricatives /s/ /(š)/, /x/ and /χ/ in an medial position (in the case of /s/ and /(š)/ sometimes even at the word beginning, are pronounced as lenis by most of the speakers (e.g.

---

[7] In Li Shulan's phonemic transcription /i/ sometimes corresponds to /a/ of written Manchu (e.g. Si. *asirem* < Ma. *asarambi*). In my opinion this vowel, much lower and backer than /i/ after an uvular, should be treated as a variant of /e/.

[8] J. Norman (1974, p. 163) makes the following observations on vowel reduction: "When unstressed, the vowels /i/, /u/ and /e/ are drastically reduced, especially in final position: /i/ in this position is realized as a palatalization of the preceding consonant, /u/ as a rounding of the preceding consonant and /e/ as a neutral or centralized release. When the same vowels are unstressed in other positions, they are reduced but generally retain their syllabicity. Such unstressed vowels become voiceless when they occur between fortis stops and/or fricatives."

Lit. Ma. *tafa-*, Si. *tavənə-* 'to ascend'; Lit. Ma. *gisuⁿ*, Si. *gizun* 'word, language'; Lit. Ma. *se-*, Si. *zə-* 'to say' vs. Lit. Ma. *sa-*, Si. *sa-* 'to know'); Lit. Ma. *siden*, Si. *śidəⁿ* 'between'; Lit. Ma. *indahūn*, Si. *yindaʁûⁿ* 'dog'; Lit. Ma. *ehelinggū*, Si. *əɣəliŋ* 'ugly, wicked').

### 5) Assimilation of lenis consonants

The lenis consonants are mostly pronounced as voiced in the medial position, before vowels, resonants and other voiced consonants, and as unvoiced before fortis consonants and in the final position (e.g. Lit. Ma. *abka*, Si. *afqa* 'sky, heaven'; Lit. Ma. *afahabi*, Si. *avʁəi* 'fight-PERF'; Lit. Ma. *gajiha*, Si. *ɕaškəi* 'bring-PERF'; Lit. Ma. *gajimbi*, Si. *ɕajəm* 'bring-IMP.')

### 6) Dissimilation of affricates

The affricates **č** and **j** before stops are realized as the fricative **š**. This is an increasingly frequent phenomenon due to the current process of reduction and elision of interconsonantal vowels and formation of the cluster *-čk-*. In the speech of the older generation the variants *-čk/čq-* and *-šk/šq-* occur, while middle-aged and younger speakers mainly pronounce *–šk/šq-* (e.g. Lit. Ma. *tacikū*, Si. *tačqû > tašqû* 'school').

### 7) Medial allophone of /l/

The lateral /l /has a retroflex medial allophone [ɻ], which occurs at the end of a syllable . More and more laterals currently change into this medial as a result of vowel elision (e.g. Lit. Ma. *gelehe*, Si. *gəɻɣəi* 'fear-PERF').

### 8) Nasal /n/

The nasal /n/ in word final position is usually realized as a nasalisation of the preceding vowel.

### 9) Alternation of the prothetic 'n' with prothetic 'y' before an 'i' in word initial position

In the initial position /i/ has two variants of pronunciation – either with a glottal stop, or without it. In the latter case a prothetic [y] is pronounced in the beginning of the word, which often alternates with a prothetic [n], for example Lit. Ma. *nikan*, Si. *yiqaⁿ* 'Chinese'; Lit. Ma. *inenggi*, Si. *ňinəŋ* 'day'; Lit. Ma. *niyehe*, Si. *yiɣə* 'goose'. This phenomenon is encountered in some words beginning with palatal vowels as well (Lit. Ma. *umiyaha*, Si. *ňimaχ* 'beetle'; Lit. Ma. *umiyesun*, Si. *ňumzuⁿ* 'belt').

### 10) Alternation of 'l' with 'n'

I have registered this alternation only in two cases of homophonic words (Lit. Ma. *nei*, Si. *li* 'sweat'; Lit. Ma. *nei-*, Si. *li-* 'to open'), though a certain regularity cannot be excluded.

In the modern spoken language many changes of the **sandhi type** are encountered. The following changes are the most common:

The words which end in a stressed syllable (e.g. *aʁa* 'rain', *afqa* 'sky', *solo* 'freedom', *čiškə* 'sparrow, little bird', *muku* 'water', *uči* 'door') usually retain the final vowel, while in words which do not have stress on the final syllable the final vowel is reduced and eventually tends to disappear (Lit. Ma. *gala*, Si. *gaɻ* 'hand'; Lit. Ma. *uju*, Si. *uj* 'head'; Lit. Ma. *kara*, Si. *qar* 'black (horse)'; Lit. Ma. *bəthə*, Si. *bətk* 'foot'). All of these words, however, have an emphasized variant of pronunciation, in which the last syllable is stressed and a vowel, usually medial *ə*, is pronounced (*ɕalə, ujə, bətkə*).

The same can be said about the suffixes ending in a vowel. Most of the suffixes behave like an unstressed word-ending; some, however, tend to be stressed. For example the DL. suffix Lit. Ma. *-de* is reduced to *-t* in spoken Sibe, unless emphasized (*ərin-t* 'time-DL'., *ərin-də* 'time-DL'. emphasized), but the CC suffix *-či* retains its full syllabic form, unless it is reduced before a voiceless consonant (*gən-či* 'go'-CC, *gən-š* da CC ACT.).

All words, which end in a primary or secondary consonant, except resonants, are liable to a voiced/voiceless assimilation – when followed by a pause or a voiceless consonant, they are pronounced as voiceless (sometimes fairly voiced – lenis) – e.g. *ɕaχ* 'crow', *as* 'net', *čeňinj* 'the day before yesterday'; when followed by a vowel or a voiced consonant, most consonants except **k/q** become voiced – e.g. *ɕaʁ-ə-f* 'crow-ACC.', *az-ə-f* 'net -ACC.', *čəňinj-ə-i* 'the day before yesterday-GEN.'

Epenthetic vowels are usually inserted before suffixes or particles beginning with consonants.

## 1.2 Questions of transcription

Among the works presenting the materials of spoken Sibe or analyzing them, J. Norman and Li Shulan use phonemic transcriptions based on the respective phonemic systems which they have described.

Guo Meilan and Wang Xiaohong use a rather narrow IPA based phonetic transcription to record the phonetic shape of the Sibe words.

Among the works of 'western' provenance, the richest material of the spoken language has been published by Jin Ning (Jin Ning 1991, 1993).

In her works Jin Ning employs a phonetic transcription based on the IPA, which she describes as 'a kind of blend one between the broad and the narrow transcriptions' (Jin Ning 1993, p. 9). The set of IPA symbols used in her work seems to serve the purpose of transmitting the acoustic shape of the spoken Sibe language very well.

A comparison of the above-mentioned works demonstrates major differences, which, however, concern those features of spoken Sibe that are currently in process of change, in particular vowel reduction and elision, palatalization of vowels and assimilation/dissimilation of consonants. Undoubtedly some of the differences are also conditioned by the authors' personal phonemic experience (e.g. the perfective verb suffix syllable centre is treated as a single vowel by J. Norman, which corresponds to my own experience, while scholars working in a Chinese-speaking environment tend to hear a diphthong).

| Written Manchu | Norman | Li Shulan | Wang-Guo | Jin Ning | my material |
|---|---|---|---|---|---|
| torhombi | tüɛrhume | torhum | | tœrʁ im | tiørʁ um, tüɛrʁ um |
| genehebi | gənĕhi | genhei | kɯnɣɯi | gənɣəj | gənɣʾi |

The transcription used by Guo Meilan and Wang Qingfeng reflects the real shape of the language with great accuracy. I have elected, however, to follow the example of Jin Ning and note only the more remarkable distinctions in order to make the texts more accessible. The main feature which distinguishes Jin Ning's method from the phonemic transcriptions is the marking of the voiced fricative allophones of velar and uvular *g/h*, which is one of the most outstanding differences between the written and oral languages. In my transcription I add a sign for the retroflex allophone of the phoneme *l*, which occurs at the end of syllables. I have also elected to use top index letters to mark some typical features of the spoken language connected to the reduction of certain sounds, namely the letter [u/ŭ] to mark labialized pronunciation of syllable-closing consonants caused by elision of a labial vowel (e.g. aq[ŭ]< aqŭ *negative existential* ); similarly I use the sign [i] to mark the strongly reduced but partially syllable-forming /i/which often appears after /s/ (e.g. s'[i]qa<s'iqa *horsehair*), as well as the sign [n] for the strongly reduced /n/ in some word endings, which is pronounced as a nasalisation of the preceding vowel (e.g. mori[n]<morin *horse*). In the latter case, in order to avoid too many forms, I have chosen a more phonemic principle and use the basic form [n] for for the other two sandhi variants as well – *n* before dental consonants and *m* before *m, v* and *f*.

As for the time being there is no codified orthography in transcribing spoken Sibe, and as in the former works I have consulted the actual shapes of the particular words differ considerably, I have transcribed the words as I was able to hear them, using the IPA signs.

## 1.3 Remarks on the Sibe vocabulary

The basic layer of the Sibe vocabulary is clearly of Tungusic origin, and is virtually identical with Manchu. Among the modern living Tungusic languages Nanai (Gold) is closer than others to Sibe. The opinion of some native scholars that the Sibes were originally a Mongolian tribe is not supported by the lexical material.[9]

The expressions of Tungusic origin contain many terms connected with life in forests and at riversides – plants, forest animals, fishes, deities and spirits of forests and water, etc. Part of the agricultural terminology, expressions connected with household, food, some of the kinship terms, numerals and most basic verbs are Tungusic.

A relatively large section of the Sibe lexicon is formed by loanwords from Mongolic languages. Although most of these loanwords are identical with the Mongolic loanwords in literary Manchu,[10] there is still a significant amount of words, which were probably borrowed directly into Sibe from the Khorchin Mongol dialect at the time, when the Sibes were a vassal tribe of the Khorchins. These words do not occur in written Manchu and most of them are

---

[9] The only trace seems to be provided by the tradition comcerning 'jivš gizun', a different language that is reported to have been used by one of the Sibe banners till the end of the 19th century, and is said to be 'the original Sibe language' by some Sibes. The word 'jivš' is probably related to the denomination of the Barghu-Mongolian tribe of Chipchins, and the scanty information regarding the entire problem suggests a different type of language contact than is reported by Sibe tradition. Most probably a part of the Chipchin tribe was incorporated into the Sibe banners and assimilated by the Sibes.

[10] Apart from the apparent cultural borrowings from the Mongolic to Manchu languages datable to at least two historical periods (the Jurchen state and the early period of the Manchu expansion) there is an enormous amount of related words which seem to be partly the result of borrowing between Mongolic and Tungusic languages. This phenomenon has been noted as occurring in both directions and at varying time periods, and so thus may partially have developed from the hypothetical common basis (cf. Janhunen 1996, p. 252).

expressions connected with religion, cattle-breeding, horse-herding and expressions of everyday life.[11] Very few of the Mongolian loanwords in spoken Sibe seem to originate from the contacts with the Oirat and Chahar Mongols that occurred after their resettlement to Xinjiang.

Compared to literary Manchu more loanwords from Chinese are used in spoken Sibe. The main cause of this is probably the fact that many words of literary Manchu were created artificially and were never used in speech. In modern spoken Sibe, part of agricultural terminology, some of the expressions for household equipment and food and practically the whole vocabulary connected with technical goods have been taken directly from Chinese. As is the case with many other non-Han languages in China, the use of Chinese loanwords dramatically increases among the middle and younger generation and the experience of hearing a sentence composed of Chinese words with Sibe suffixes is by no means an exception. The first expressions to be replaced by Chinese loanwords are usually loanwords from other languages – Mongolian, Kazakh, Uighur and Russian[12].

A remarkable difference between written Manchu vocabulary and the vocabulary of spoken Sibe is the latter's tendency to use analytic expressions instead of the synthetic expressions or specialized terms found in the former. This concerns both verbs and nouns. The Manchu synthetic verbal forms formed by the derivational suffixes with the exception of several petrified forms such as *ɕajə-* 'to bring' (Ma. *ga-ji-* < *ga-* 'to take' + *-ji-* 'to come'), are replaced by verbal phrases (e.g. Ma. *ala-na-* 'to go and tell' × Si. *aɪm gən-* 'telling go' or *gənəm al-* 'going tell'; Ma. *nima-ra-* 'to snow' < *nimanggi* 'snow' + *-ra* deriv. suffix x Si. *ňimaŋ da-* lit. 'snow + to have relationship'= 'to snow'). A somewhat similar difference is seen in nouns, as when synthetic forms of the written language, such as Ma. *abalasi* 'hunter' < *abala-* 'to hunt' + *-si* (agent suffix) are replaced by analytic forms, e.g. Si. *avələr nan* lit. 'hunting person' = 'hunter'. Specialized or abstract terms of the literary language are often abandoned in favour of complex expressions formed by means of everyday use (e.g. Ma. *tubihe* 'fruits' Si. *suɪʁo jaq* lit. 'apple thing' = 'fruits').

Due to contacts with the Russians, which became particularly close during the Russian occupation of the Ghulja area in the 2nd half of the 19th century and lasting till relatively recent times (one entire generation of the Sibe people of Ghulja grew up under the strong influence of the local Russian community), a certain amount of Russian words were borrowed into Sibe. These loanwords are mostly modern technical terms, particularly those connected with the military, but include as well many terms from Russian culture, for example, words for household equipment and food, which were assumed by the Sibes along with the objects they denote. Most of the Russian loanwords are used alternatively with Chinese loanwords and are particularly favoured by older speakers from Ghulja and Tarbagatai. The most frequently cited example is the word for 'tomato' – *famdor* (< Ru. *pomidor*).

---

[11] This layer of Sibe vocabulary is still unexplored and its extent is unknown. Most of these expressions exist in Sibe as synonyms of indigenous Sibe-Manchu words (e.g. Si. *amre-* <Mo. *amra-* 'to take a rest', as a synonym to the Sibe-Manchu *erge-* 'to take a rest'). According to my informants many of these synonyms occur in the speech of the older generation and are either unknown to the middle and younger generations, or do not form a part of their active vocabulary.

[12] E.g. the word for 'girlfriend', which in the middle generation of Chabchal used to be *padruga* (<Ru. *podruga*), but nowadays has been replaced either by the older Chinese expression *duixiang* – which now sounds archaic to Chinese native speakers – or the more modern Chinese form *nü pengyou*.

## 1.3.1 Personal names

The religious and social life of the traditional Sibe community was based on the clan system, which remains unchanged until present. Originally 38 clans (Lit. Ma. *hala*, Si. *χaᴊ*) existed among the Sibes in Manchuria. Representatives of 24 clans came to Xinjiang (Heling, Tong Kiri 1989, pp. 22–24). Most of the clan names are to be traced to the Manchurian ethnic and language milieu (*Gorgia, Ujala, Hǝyer, Gioro, Nara* and others), some, like the clans of *Tumurči* and *Korči*, seem to be of Mongolian origin, while some are originally Chinese clan names incorporated into the Sibe system. Chinese surnames such as *Wang, Xu, Liu, Zhang* and others are found among the Sibes.

At present, in official communication, the first syllable of the clan name in an approximate (but fixed) transcription by Chinese characters is used. In modern times the clan structure has remained significant mainly for the purpose of marriage: the rule of exogamy is strongly observed.[13]

Despite the fact that during the entire 20th century Chinese personal names were in frequent use, the tradition of the Sibe personal names has survived until present and has even been re-gaining popularity. Many of the young Sibes have a Chinese name, which they use in communication outside the Sibe community, and a Sibe name.

As in literary Manchu, the Sibe personal names are usually derived by several specialized literary suffixes, of which the most frequent are *-ngga/-ngge*, *-su*, *-bu*, *-tai*, *-bai*, *šan/šen* and *-tun/-cun* for men's names, and the suffix *-ji* or *-ju* for women's names. Generally it seems that Chinese names are given more often to girls than to boys.

In recent times Sibe personal names have been given in accordance with the Sino-Manchu tradition, which primarily emphasizes spiritual qualities and abilities. Examples of such names are *kičǝŋǝ* (*kicengge*)[14], *kičǝsu* (*kicesu*), *kičǝbu* (*kicebu*), *kičǝšǝn* (*kicešan*) from *kičǝ-* 'to be diligent or thoughtful'; *mutǝbu* (*mutebu*), *mutǝsu* (*mutesu*), *mutǝšǝn* (*mutešan*) from *mutǝ-* 'to be able, to master, to overcome'; *jalůна* (*jalungga*) from *jalu-* 'full'; *saracun* (*saracun*) from *sa-* 'to know' etc. Examples of female names are *mǝrgǝnji* (*mergenji*) from *mǝrgǝn* 'wise, clever; *aodunji* (*akdunji*) from *aodun* 'firm, stable' etc.

In modern times substantives in their original form become more frequently used as personal names. The general tendency in the meanings of the names has also changed (e.g. *ǝrǝčun* 'hope', *qaltari* 'diamond', *arslan* 'lion', *yiᴊвa* 'flower', *tana* 'pearl').[15]

All Sibe names are pronounced very closely according to their literary form and there are no diminutive or familiar forms of the names. Sometimes the first syllable of the name followed by a title is pronounced (e.g. *tu amban* 'the amban Tu' for the amban whose name was *tukšan*). This is a widespread method of creating an honorific, originating in Chinese culture but known as well to many Inner Asian ethnicities.

---

[13] For most other requirements of modern social life, such as establishing the order of visiting relatives during New Year celebrations and suchlike, units smaller than clans, which can be probably designated as "broader family", are important. With the partial revival of shamanism, however, the clan structure re-gains some of its importance.

[14] Forms in brackets are transliterated literary Manchu forms.

[15] A case illustrating the attitude to personal names is that of a boy whose first name was Arslan (Lion). After it was realized that the boy was mute his parents were advised to change the name. The new name was Sarasu (Knowledge).

## 1.3.2 Children's expressions

Spoken Sibe, as in most languages, has a group of special words used for communication with infants. In Sibe the 'children's vocabulary' is comparatively rich and covers all the important topics of basic communication. These words are most often one-syllable words and are usually reduplicated. Examples of such expressions are (*ji*)*jii* 'to urinate' *bobo* 'bread', *ajii* 'to hug', *jüjü* 'clothes, *guoguo* 'shoes', *qaqa* 'hot' and others. The expressions for actions are always followed by the auxiliary verb *ze-* 'to say', e.g. *ajii zə*! 'Hug it!'

## 1.3.3 Vicarious expressions

Spoken Sibe has vicarious words for all the nominal categories and also for verbs.

The greater part of the vicarious expressions (except personal pronouns) is derived from five roots, which are the apparently phonetic variants of two roots: The proximate reference expressions have the roots *ə-*/*u-*/*i-* while the distant reference expressions are derived from the roots *tə-*/*tu-*. Besides these five basic roots there is the stem *mə*/*mu-* of Mongolian origin, whose basic meanings may be defined as foregrounding (*mər* 'preciously this, exactly this') and identification with a previously known or mentioned object or fact (*mətər nan* 'that same person'). Interrogative vicarious expressions are mostly derived from the roots *ya-* or *a-*.

The nominal vicarious words can be divided into several subclasses according the parts of speech they substitute. Thus we can distinguish vicarious nouns (pronouns), adjectives, temporal nouns, spatials, numerals and verbs. Since vicarious expressions have the same morphological characteristics as the parts of speech they represent and a corresponding semantic field, I deal with every subclass within the respective part of speech individually.

A special chapter is dedicated to the substitutes for nouns – the pronouns in view of their greater formal and semantic variety, resulting mainly from the specific semantics of personal pronouns.

The vicarious verbs have the morphological properties of verbs, I analyze them, therefore, in chapter 4 (Verbs).

## 1.4 Remarks on syntax – negation

In the present work there is not sufficent space to deal with the Sibe syntax in its entirety. Subsequently, I have limited myself to an explanation of the system of negation, which is important to understand morphological as well as for syntactical relations.

As in other Altaic languages, Manchu and Sibe have two basic types of negation. B. Sechenbaatar defines the two types of negation in Chakhar Mongol as negating either 'nominal existence' or 'nominal identity' (Sechenbaatar 2003, p. 184). This definition expresses the essence of the difference between the two types of negation and is applicable to spoken Sibe as well. Still, in many other specific instances, it is difficult to establish precisely the basis upon which one or the other type has been used.

It may be helpful to bear in mind that while in both Chakhar and Sibe (unlike modern Khalkha) the former type of negative particle is in fact a negative existential (Sechenbaatar

2003, p. 184), whereas the latter negative particle in Sibe is semantically connected with the meaning 'erroneous, incorrect, improper' etc. Similar use of this 'identity negating particle' is attested in Khalkha Mongolian.[16]

## 1.4.1 The negative particle aqᵘ̊

The function of this particle roughly corresponds to that of the Mongolian negative particle (*ü*)*güi*, which B. Sechenbaatar designates as a 'negative existential' (2003, p. 184). The word *aqᵘ̊*, as *ügüi* in most Inner Mongolian dialects, functions as the negative equivalent of the existential verb *bi* (Mo. *bii/bai-*). Its lexical meaning is therefore 'non-existence', 'non-being', or 'absence'. As in most Altaic languages, the semantic field of the existential verbal pair present/absent (*bi-aqᵘ̊*) also includes, in addition, the expression of possession and non-possession. Both of the negative particles behave grammatically as nouns.[17]

The first type of negation, expressed by the particle *aqᵘ̊* (Lit. Ma. *akū*), negates either the existence or the presence of the object, fact, matter etc., expressed by a noun (a), or, when following a verbal noun, forms a negative verbal expression (b). When used as a separate clause, it can negate the entire utterance (c).

### a) Negation of nominal existence

Ex. 1:  *daivə ǹi ta-maq **ǹuŋk aqᵘ̊** zəm.*
Lit. Doctor F. look-CP. **disease absent** say-IMP.
The doctor examined her and said that she **was not ill** (**had no disease**).

Ex. 2:  *kəčən-dəri ta-ʁəɴ **əm naⁿ gəɹ aqᵘ̊.***
Lit. Wall-ABL. look-NP.II. **one person still absent.**
He looked around from the top of the wall, but **there was nobody**.

Ex. 3:  *əva-dəri **aqᵘ̊-ʁᵘ̊i** (< aqᵘ̊ oʁᵘ̊i).*
Lit. Here-ABL. **absent-become-PERF.**
He **is not here any more**.

Ex. 4:  ***aqᵘ̊-dəri śieⁿ.***
Lit. **Absent-ABL.** good.
Better **than nothing**.

Ex. 5:  *təsk laft jiʁa mi-n-d **aqᵘ̊.***
Lit. Thus much money 1s-DL. **absent.**
**I do not have** that much money.

---

[16] Cf. phrases in the colloquial language of the type *neg l biš* 'somehow improper, incorrect' etc.

[17] Besides being frequently used as an attribute, both of the negative particles can take case suffixes, e.g. *aqᵘ̊ dəri sieⁿ* lit. NEG.-ABL. good 'better than nothing', or *vaqəf mənjaɴ zəm* lit. not-ACC. true say-IMP. 'he says about something that is not so that it is so'.

### b) Negative verbal forms

Ex. 1:  *čəksə bi gənə-m **mut-qa-q$^ŭ$**.*
   Lit. Yesterday 1sg. go-CI. **can-NP.-NEG.**
   **I could not** visit you yesterday.

Ex. 2:  *bi **sa-r** χaň **aq$^ŭ$**.*
   Lit. 1sg. **know-NI.** least **NEG.**
   **I do not** even **know** about it.

Ex. 3:  *taqŭ-q$^ŭ$ nan-maq əm gizər.*
   Lit. **Know-(NOM.IMP).-NEG.** person-S. PROH. speak-(NI.).
   Do not speak with people you do **not know**.

### c) The word aq$^ŭ$ as an independent clause.

Used as a clause, the word *aq$^ŭ$* either has the same meaning as explained above (non-existence, absence), or it negates a verbal expression.

Ex. 1:  ***aq$^ŭ$**.*
   Lit. **Absent.**
   **He is not here.**
   Note: Usually summarizing the result of search or a reply to a question about presence, possession of somebody or something.

Ex. 2:  *ər baitəf śi aɹmbuʁŭ ba? – **aq$^ŭ$**.*
   Lit. This matter you tell-CI.-give-NP. PROB. – **NEG.**
   It was you who told (him) about it, wasn't it ? – **No (it was not me).**

## 1.4.2 The negative particle vaq

The particle *vaq* (Lit. Ma. *waka*) usually negates a statement in terms of its quality, essence, or identity of what is expressed by the noun. Its function is similar to that of the Mongolian particle *biš*, which is designated as a 'negative copula' by Sechenbaatar. The expression *vaq* is a negative counterpart to the expression *mənjaʁ* 'indeed, true, the same'. The lexical meaning of the word *vaq* is 'wrong, erroneous, not that' etc. It may determine a noun or a verb (*vaq jŭʁŭ$^n$* 'the wrong way', *vaq vaq učulum* 'he sings out of tune'). Owing to its lexical meaning the Sibe expression *vaq* has broader use and more functions than the Mongolian particle *biš*; it is a frequent and stylistically favoured expression.

### a) Negation of a quality or identity expressed by a noun

Ex. 1:  *mi$^n$ ər ašta paka zəči davɹ **tarʁŭ$^n$ vaq**.*
   Lit. 1sg.-GEN. this youngster short say-CC. too **fat not.**
   I am short but **not** so **fat.**
   Note: From a contemporary song.

Ex. 2:   *huis mim-(b) ta-mə* **huis gəɹ vaq, yiqaⁿ gəɹ vaq**, *ai uksurə: zəm bodə-m.*
Lit. Uighur 1sg.-ACC. look-CI. **Uighur still not, Chinese still not**, what nationality say-CI. think-IMP.
The Uighurs, seeing me, wonder: **She is neither Chinese, nor Uighur**, what nationality could she be?

### b) The particle vaq *as a separate clause*

When used as a separate clause, the particle *vaq* has either the same meaning as above (Ex. 1), or it negates the statement, implying that some part of the statement is wrong.

Ex. 1:   *ər śi-n jaq na? –* **vaq**.
Lit. This 2sg.-GEN. thing QUEST. – **Not**.
Is this yours? – **No (it belongs to someone else)**.

Ex. 2:   **vaqa**, *set, torə-nə-f bia-vŭ-qŭ.*
Lit. **Not**, old man, abuse-NI.II.-ACC. ask-CAUS.-(NOM.IMP).-NEG.
**Oh no**, man, there is no need to abuse them.

# 1.5 Word classes in spoken Sibe

The discussion about the existence and character of parts of speech in the Altaic languages generally oscillates between two strongly opposing views. According to the first one, adhering to strictly formal criteria, it is not possible to classify words in Altaic languages into word classes; it is possible only to distinguish between inflected and non-inflected words, and then to divide the inflected words into nouns and verbs according to the variations in their inflexion. The opposing standpoint is based upon semantic criteria and finds in the Altaic languages most of the word classes as defined for Indo-European languages. This approach is widespread in Russian linguistics largely employing linguistic material drawn from the Turkic and Tungusic languages found within the territory of the former Soviet Union.

G. J. Ramstedt maintains that within the Altaic languages one cannot speak about parts of speech in the sense in which they are understood in the Indo-European linguistic context. He distinguishes only two main categories – inflected and non-inflected words. Inflected words are further divided into nouns, pronouns, numerals and verbs (Ramstedt 1957, p. 26).

N. A. Baskakov, commenting on Ramstedt's analysis, opposes this view: 'Even if we completely ignore semantic criteria in defining the nominal parts of speech and base our analysis solely on formal marking, we still have to admit that modern, at least Turkic languages have specific formants for particular nominal word classes: Nouns, adjectives, adverbs, numerals and pronouns ...' (Ramstedt 1957, p. 31).

Ivan Zaharov uses traditional Manchu grammars for his description of Manchu and tries to find a way to convey their conception of the language by means of Russian grammatical terminology. 'Following the example of the Russian language', he finds eight parts of speech: nouns, pronouns, verbs, adverbs, postpositions, conjunctions, interjections (including onomatopoetic words), and particles. Zaharov then immediately divides the above-mentioned parts of speech into three categories: words which are declined (nouns, numerals and pronouns), inflected (verbs) and the non-inflected words (Zaharov 1879, pp. 68–9).This division corresponds to that of the traditional Chinese grammars, which served as a model for the Manchu grammars (Zaharov 1879, p. I–V).[18] E. Haenisch lists eight parts of speech in his Manchu Grammar (1986) – substantives, pronouns, adjectives, numerals, postpositions, final particles, adverbs and verbs. This classification (in particular, the absence of interjections and onomatopoeia) seems to reflect an approach grounded in European tradition.

In her extensive Manchu Grammar L. M. Gorelova, before embarking upon an extremely detailed explanation of the functions and use of various lexical categories, states that "it is difficult to divide all Manchu words into parts of speech because the notion 'parts of speech' itself requires the existence of well developed morphological devices corresponding to certain grammatical functions. Because of weak differentiation of parts of speech, parts of sentence assume greater importance in the organization of the Manchu utterance." (Gorelova 2002, p. 123)

All attempts to classify the parts of speech in Manchu using the terminology of Latin and other European grammars demonstrate that it is possible to describe Manchu employing these designations. Similar criteria as in the European languages can be used, without significant objection, for nouns, pronouns, numerals and verbs, whereas concepts such as adjectives, adverbs and all types of non-inflected expressions have always been much more problematic. If the aim of the description is to grasp the external shape of the language and describe it from the synchronous point of view, then it may be well achieved by means of this terminology. The question remains, however, as to what degree these abstract categories, which are reflected in the European classification of parts of speech, correspond to indigenous language thinking of the East-Asian languages.

To my knowledge, to date there is no modern alternative description of the Manchu parts of speech according to different critieria than that of the morphological and syntactical classifications followed by European linguistics.

From the 1960s onward in China, a new school in description of Altaic languages, Mongolian in particular, was formed. The pioneer of this school, Prof. Chinggeltei, himself inspired by the Mongolian linguist Sh. Luvsanvandan, relies upon Western descriptive linguistics, but tries to find solutions for the discrepancies between the instruments of Western linguistics and the inner structure of Altaic linguistic material.

In their description of spoken Sibe, Li Shulan, Zhongqian and Wang Qingfeng seem to be inspired by this linguistic school. Their classification of the parts of speech in spoken Sibe contains twelve word classes: 1) **substantives**, 2) **adjectives**, 3) **numerals**, 4) **pronouns**, 5) **verbs**, 6) **adverbs** 7), **imitatives**, 8) **postpositions**, 9) **conjunctions**, 10) **auxiliary words** (= syntactic particles), 11) **modal words** (= modal particles), 12) **interjection**s. In his morphological description of the Chakhar dialect, B. Sechenbaatar (2003) combines the Chinese and Mongolian linguistic approach with Western methods and introduces new methodologies of classification, previously not considered by Western scholars, into the sphere of Mongolian studies. Among his most important alternative classifications, I would list the definition of **temporal nouns** as a separate subgroup of nouns, the definition of **spatials** as a nominal part of speech, the creation of **imitatives** as a specific category, and the narrower division of non-inflected words of adverbial character, namely the definition of **modals** in addition to adverbs.

---

[18] The traditional Chinese grammars distinguish *shi ci* ('concrete words') a *xu ci* ('empty words') – words with grammatical meaning. This classification was to a certain extent applied in the grammars of some agglutinative languages such as Japanese, Korean and Manchu.

In spoken Sibe two classes of inflected words may be easily defined by means of morphological criteria – **nouns** and **verbs**. Among the words which are nouns as defined by the main morphological criterion (taking case suffixes), several groups can be distinguished by specific syntactical properties and semantic fields, and in some cases by distinct morphological formants as well: **pronouns, numerals, spatials**, and **qualitative nouns**. Apart from these basic word classes various groupings of non-inflected expressions are also present. Their classification is as problematic as in the other Altaic languages. Morphologically these expressions are words of differing origin (verbal or nominal forms as well as non-inflected root words) and the main criteria for their classification has been their syntactical function. These words have been usually described as **adverbs, imitatives, particles, interjections** and **postpositions**.

In the present work I focus on the **basic inflected parts of speech** (**nouns, adjectives, pronouns, numerals, spatials** and **verbs**) and leave aside the non-inflected classes.

## 1.5.1 Brief characteristics of the parts of speech

### Basic inflected parts of speech

1. Nouns are defined through the main morphological criterion of the category of case. This definition therefore also includes verbal nouns. Since, however, verbal nouns have both verbal and nominal characteristics and are traditionally classified as verbs, I adhere to this classification and discuss them in the chapter describing verbs. Nouns are further divided into the following subgroups:

1a. The basic nominal class is formed by **nouns** in the proper sense, which by their semantical properties correspond to the Indo-European category of **substantives**. Besides the category of case, another important category, the category of number, also applies. Nouns distinguish as well the categories of concreteness and of rationality, both of which are manifested on morpho-syntactic level. On the morpho-syntactic level the distinction between countable and uncountable nouns is seen.

1b. **Qualitative nouns** are a subgroup of nouns which have conventionally been labelled as 'adjectives'. The Sibe qualitative nouns are a subgroup of nominal words which like other nouns have the categories of case and number; they are, however, marked by several peculiarities on the semantic and syntactic levels (the meaning of quality, constructions with a particle expressing a certain degree of quality). The qualitative nouns occur particularly often as verb-determinants, a function which is not contradicted for other nouns, but is very rare for them.

1c. **Pronouns** form a subgroup of nouns, which take suffixes of case and number like other nouns. They differ, however, from other nouns by their anaphoric semantics and other grammatical categories. Personal pronouns have the category of person; demonstrative pronouns have the category of actualization and distinguish proximate and distant deixis. The limited number of pronominal roots is connected with their partially grammatical functionality.

1d. **Numerals** are a specific subgroup of nouns, distinguished both semantically and morphologically. In spoken Sibe the system of numerals is simplified due to their limited function and a single specific morphological formant is employed.

1e. **Spatials** in Manchu and Mongolian are essentially nouns which denote a certain point in space existing in a certain relation to the speaker or to another object. Several nouns of this group are used for determination of time as well. Sibe spatials are derived from a limited number of roots by a group of specific derivational suffixes. In addition to the common case suffixes, their inflectional paradigm includes some partially productive specific suffixes. Spatials in Manchu and Sibe occur in three basic functions: as attributes of nouns, as determinants of verbs and as postpositions.

2. **Verbs** are the second separate part of speech defined according to morphological criteria. Verbs are morphologically the most complex part of speech, and in grammatical structure, the most prominent.

The verbal system of Manchu and spoken Sibe corresponds by its main features to the verbal systems of other Altaic languages. In his description of verbs in Chakhar Mongol B. Sechenbaatar (2003, p. 116) summarizes the main properties of verbs in Mongolian.

"The principal morphological categories of verbs are voice, aspect, mood, tense, person, nominalization, and converbialization. As a result, verbs show more morphological inflexions than any other part of speech. Verbal stems have also inherent characteristics, such as transitivity (intransitive, transitive and ditransitive verbs), which are manifested at the morphosyntactic level. From the point of view of semantic content, morphological behaviour, and functional roles, verbs can be classified into a number of types (full verbs, pronominal verbs, auxiliary verbs and others). Verbs are intimately connected with some distinctions expressed by sentence-final particles (interrogative, negative, copular, modal, and others)."

Using an analogical paradigm to characterize the Sibe verb, we may list tense, person and mood as the main morphological categories. Derivational suffixes expressing meanings close to voice and aspect rather can be interpreted as forming one general category. Transitivity, as in Mongolian, forms an inherent characteristic of verbal stems. The principal groups of verbal stems to be distinguished are full verbs, vicarious verbs and modal/auxiliary verbs. As in Mongolian, particles often form an inseparable part of verbal expressions.

In comparison with Mongolian and the other Altaic languages, Manchu and Sibe contain a notably smaller number of verbal forms, fewer case suffixes are used with verbal nouns, and the variation of suffixal formations is lesser. Spoken Sibe differs from literary Manchu by a tendency to analytic expression of actions, making it closer to Mongolian in this respect.

Manchu and Sibe distinguish four basic types of verbal expressions, which differ one from another by their morphological and syntactical properties:

**finite verbs** (including optative and imperative forms),
**verbal nouns** (participles),
**verbal nouns II** (participles with a nominalizing suffix) and
**converbs**.

### Other parts of speech

In addition to the above-mentioned, morphologically clearly differentiated parts of speech, a number of other kinds of expressions exist in Manchu and Sibe, as well as in Mongolian and other Altaic languages. These expressions do not precisely fit into the definitions of the parts of speech outlined above, and traditionally they are classified, according to Indo-European criteria, as adverbs and postpositions. Apart from these, at least one group of expressions may be defined as morphologically, semantically and syntactically coherent – the imitatives. The status of the expressions of temporal and spatial determination is problematic when traditional European criteria are applied.

A solution to the question of these parts of speech, some of which are defined solely on syntactical grounds and other on semantical criteria without consideration of their morphology, will require more detailed research and above all, more documentation. In his description of Chakhar Mongol B. Sechenbaatar makes crucially important progress in this direction by defining the expressions for spatial and temporal determination as subgroups of the nominal class, and by creating a classification for the special part of speech formed by the imitatives.

I do not deal with these parts of speech in detail in the present work; they are, therefore, listed here with the general statement that these groups of expressions are defined on different grounds and a different level than the main inflected parts of speech.

1. **Adverbs**. Among varying linguistic traditions, there are substantial differences concerning the question of defining adverbs in the Mongolic and Tungusic languages. Many Russian and European authors (Zaharov, Haenisch, Sunik), using a functional methodology, classify all words which occur in the adverbial function and position, regardless of their origin, as adverbs. Adverbially used qualitative nouns, spatials, temporal nouns and numerals are thus classified as adverbs. Scholars emerging from the Chinese tradition (Sechenbaatar, Li Shulan) take into account the morphological properties of the word and regard only inflexible adverbial expressions as adverbs. The concept of adverbs is thus confined to a small group of words of various origins, which share the traits of non-inflectedness and a pronounced grammatical meaning. While the former definition reproduces the classifications of Indo-European linguistics, the latter solves the problem of description by using the term 'adverb' for a limited group which is marginal among Indo-European adverbs themselves.

After separating out root words and imitatives, a small group of expressions remains both in Mongolian (e.g. *maš* very, *tun* immensely) and Sibe (*əli* still more, *əza* quite, significantly), which at first glance does not seem to fit into any of the categories mentioned above and thus to correspond to the common definition of adverbs.

The content of the term 'adverb' in Mongolic and Tungusic grammars may be subject to further analysis. Among the related expressions in Sibe and Manchu, groups of expressions with common features can be observed, as in the case, for example, of the words defined as 'root words'.

2. **Root words**. As in Mongolian, in Manchu and Sibe two types of adverbial expressions exist, which may be generally termed as 'root adverbs'. The importance of these expressions in the language is proven by their frequency in speech. They are often onomatopoeic to some degree, and the boundary between imitatives and root adverbs is somewhat unclear.

From the morphological point of view root adverbs constitute two groups:

2a) **Root words proper** are monosyllabic root expressions that in all but a few instances function only to bind with the verb immediately following, the meaning of which is then modified in the sense of the result or aspect of the respective verbal action. The root adverbs are often productive roots, from which largely verbs are derived (e.g. Si. *čaq* 'in a broken way' – *čaqaj-* 'to be broken').

Other examples of root adverbs in spoken Sibe are *boɹq* 'vehemently', 'completely', *aɹč* 'stuck in an upright position', *fus* 'through', *χaf* 'ultimately, thoroughly', *fita* 'airtight, impervious', *χŭa* 'in a tearing way', *luk* 'firmly, inseparably'.

2b) **Paired** modal expressions are less frequent in Sibe than in Mongolian and often the Sibe expressions are likely to be loanwords from Mongolian. The paired expressions are formed by monosyllabic or disyllabic words, often with a unified ending, which, however, seems to be more a result of reduplication than a common morphological formant, e.g. *qaɹt muɹt* 'quickly, smoothly, superficially' (< Mo. *hal't möl't* smoothly, superficially), *śider χodur* 'indivisibly, in close friendship'.

3. **Imitatives**. This category of expressions, which exists in many Asian languages, has often been classified as adverbs by European linguistic analysis, while traditional Asian grammars usually treat them as a separate part of speech. Imitatives are a morphologically, syntactically and semantically coherent group of expressions, which describes the reality by specific means (evoking sensual perceptions). Their morphological peculiarities differ among the individual languages. While, for example, in Mongolian mostly imitative verbal forms are used, in Manchu and Sibe non-inflected, mainly reduplicated or paired imitative expressions are favoured. We can cite the following examples of imitatives in Sibe: *giliŋ giliŋ* 'shiningly, cleanly, totally'; *foq foq* 'consistence of a dried apple or cucumber'; *χŭalar χŭalar* 'a great waterstream, an extrovert and talkative character'; *čir čir* 'a pointy object, a stitching pain'.

4. **Particles**. Like many other East Asian languages, Manchu and its oral varieties are rich in particles. From the etymological point of view the origin of particles is twofold:

4a) 'Primary' particles which roughly correspond to the term 'clitics' ('bound words which are added to adjective phrases, noun phrases, and adverb phrases, and to entire predications, either verbal or nonverbal' – Bright 1958, p. 45, in: Vacek 2002, p. 152). The meaning of this type of particles is mostly modal: 'Clitics express certain presuppositions on the part of the speaker towards the hearer and the speech act.' (Krishnamurti 1998, p. 226, in: Vacek 2002, p. 153). In Sibe, for example, the interrogative particle *na*, the limiting particle *li*, the particle of probability *ba*, the emphatic long vowel and others belong to this type.

4b) In the Altaistic tradition a broader definition of particles is common. Particles are mainly monosyllabic words with grammatical meaning, originating in another word class or occurring simultaneously in a different word class. In Manchu and Sibe many particles fit this definition, like the particle *da*, which simultaneously has the meaning of 'root, base, essence, chief' etc.

Many words with grammatical meaning are, definitionally speaking, actually located on the boundary between the categories of particle and postposition or adverb, as in the word *gaɹ* 'still, also, any'. Similarly, they may also be situated on the boundary between the categories of particle and grammatical suffix, as in the instance of the suffix or particle *deri* (ablative). The abundance of these ambiguous expressions seems to be a feature typical for the relatively analytic and isolative grammatical thinking of spoken Sibe.

5. **Interjections**. As in many languages, spoken Sibe has several expressions containing no specific lexical or grammatical meaning. These serve mainly to attract the attention of the interlocutor (e.g. *ei!*, *-re!*) or to express emotions (the interjection of nodding *eng*, the sigh *ere*, the interjection of astonishment *uňu* and others).

# 2 THE NOUN

According to G. J. Ramstedt (1957, p. 26, p. 31) the nouns, adjectives, adverbs, numerals and pronouns of the Altaic languages form a single word class which cannot further be divided by morphological criteria.[1] In his Manchu Grammar, I. Zaharov distinguishes words that can be declined, such as nouns, adjectives, numerals and pronouns (Zaharov 1989, p. 69). In his monograph on the noun in the Manchu-Tungusic languages O. P. Sunik (1982, p. 4) treats the noun as a separate word class, distinct in its 'substantivity' from verbs, as well as from other word classes (adjectives and adverbs), which function as attributes. 'Though nouns can function not only as determinans, but also as determinatum, not only as subject, object or predicate but also as nominal determinata or adverbs, having at the same time their own grammatical meanings and forms, they do not automatically pass to the general and broad class of adjective words or their subgroups (according to their syntactical functional characteristics). They remain substantive words even though having certain attributive functions.'[2]

The authors of the 'Xibo yu kouyu yanjiu' treat nouns, adjectives, numerals and pronouns separately, without placing them into the broader class of 'nouns'.

In the case of both written Manchu and spoken Sibe defining nouns as a part of speech with only slightly distinguished sub-classes seems to be a useful starting point for the purposes of description.

## 2.1 The category of number

The concept of grammatical number in Manchu and Sibe is very close to that of other Tungusic languages (Sunik 1982, pp. 115–137). The marked and unmarked forms have similar functions in Mongolic and in some Turkic languages as well. Most scholars use the terms 'plural' and 'singular' to describe the opposition between the marked and unmarked

---

[1] 'Zdes' ne suščestvuet osobyh fleksij, specifičnyh tol'ko dlja imen suščestvitel'nyh ili tol'ko dlja imen prilagatel'nyh, tak kak eti klassy v grammatičeskom otnošenii nerazgraničimy: oni vmeste obrazujut jedinyj klass imen, k kotoromu otnosjatsja takže mestoimenija.'

[2] 'I hoťa suščestvitelnye tože mogut funkcionirovať ne tol'ko v roli opredeljajemyh, no i opredelenij, ne tol'ko v roli podležaščego, dopolnenija, skazuemogo, no i substantivnogo opredelenija ili obstojatel'stva, oni, imeja pri etom svoi osobye častnogrammatičeskie značenija i formy, ne perehodjat avtomatičeski (po funkcional'no-sintaksičeskomu priznaku) v obščij i širokij klass adjektivnyh slov ili v ih podklassy, ostavajas' slovami substantivnymi, hoťa pri etom imejut opredelionnye atributivnye funkcii.'

forms, usually adding commentary concerning the differentiation of their functions as opposed to that of Indo-European languages. B. Sechenbaatar employs the term 'indefinite number' for the unmarked form and 'definite number' for the marked form (Sechenbaatar 2003, p. 23).

The terms '**partial number**' (suffixed form) and '**generic number**' (without suffix), used by Vacek and Luvsandorj for Mongolian (Vacek, Luvsandordž 1979, p. 12), seem to agree with the usage of the two forms in Sibe. This division, like that of Sechenbaatar, points to the category of 'general' as opposed to the 'particular'.

The unmarked form, called 'generic' here, usually designates an entire category of objects, beings etc., referred to by one word, without specifying its number, or every single object or being of that category (e.g. *nan jim*, lit. '**person** will come' means either 'one person' or 'some people'). A statement about a single object, being etc., is usually marked by the numeral *əm* 'one, some, a'. When speaking about a particular object or being, it is necessarily specified by deictic ,personal, or other pronouns, e.g. *ər nan* 'this person', *nan ňi* lit. 'his/its person, the person' etc.).

The form with a partial number suffix usually denotes a concrete, exactly defined group of rational beings who can be designated by the same noun. This group is most often specified by deictic words (*tər χaвəjus* – 'those boys') or delimited by other lexical means such as attributes (*čafčaɹ χafsə ňi* 'the bosses in Chabchal'). When a group is defined by a numeral, irrespective whether concrete or general, the unmarked form is used (*sunja haвəč* 'five boys', *tər laft tačiš* 'those many schoolchildren'). As Manchu and Sibe, with several exceptions, have no grammatical agreement, the deictic pronouns specifying the group of beings are always in the unmarked form.[3]

This type of opposition between the marked and unmarked forms, in which spoken Sibe resembles spoken Mongolian, is slightly different from literary Manchu, where the marked form is often used to designate an entire category of beings (*Manjusa* 'the Manchus', *niyalmasa* 'people generally').

In the category of number in Manchu and Sibe we can observe a distinction between what may be called 'rationality' and 'irrationality' of the object denoted by the nominal word. The marked form is used only for beings that may be labelled as 'rational' – i.e. people, deities, ghosts, spirits, and so on, and words used figuratively to refer to rational beings (e.g. *jaq* 'thing, figuratively person'). Unlike Mongolian, the suffixed form in Sibe is almost never used to designate things or animals.

It is possible to say that, analogically with the Mandarin Chinese plural marker '*men*' and the Mongolian partial number/plural marker '*nar*', the Sibe partial number suffix '-*s*' essentially points to human or other rational beings, and when used it frequently may imply respect or reverence.

## 2.1.1 Generic number

The generic number is a basic, unmarked form of a nominal word, which mostly denotes a single being, a category of beings or a large, undefined group.

---

[3] With some words, however, the marked form is used idiomatically in the spoken language (*saвənč* 'a daughter, a girl' is used mainly to denote a single girl, while the marked form *saвanjus* may mean either a concrete group of girls or girls in general.

Ex. 1:  *śivə **naⁿ** dači ňonʁůⁿ yeɹ jə-qů̓*.
Lit.: Sibe **person** originally dog meat eat-(NOM.IMP).-NEG.
The Sibe **people** formerly did not eat dog meat.

Ex. 2:  *əva **naⁿ** da təraŋ naⁿ*.
Lit.: Here person ACT. like.this person.
The people of this place are just like this.

Ex. 3:  *śivə **naⁿ** dači gum č̓ůaχ*.
Lit.: Sibe person originally all soldier.
In the past, all the Sibe people used to be soldiers.

### Category of number with nouns denoting irrational beings and objects

In the case of animals and inanimate objects, the category of number is morphologically not distinguished in spoken Sibe. The unmarked form is used regardless of the categories of the particular versus the general and the single versus the many. These categories are either expressed by lexical means or understood from the context.

Ex. 1:  *ɢazn-t gənə-mə, ər gia-t dəyi-r **čiškə** gəɹ śivə mədaⁿ daʁə-v-m*.
Lit.: Village-DL. go-CI. this street-DL. fly-NI. **bird** also Sibe melody follow-CAUS-. IMP.
When you go to the Village (Chabchal),[4] even the **sparrows**[5] flying in the streets sing with the Sibe accent.

Ex. 2:  *dači śomoχoɹ-t χačχačiⁿ **ňimʁa**, **məih**, **čiškə** bi*.
Lit.: Originally mill.valley-DL. kind-DOUB. **fish, snake, bird** is.
Earlier there used to be all kinds of **fish, snakes and birds** in the Mill Valley.

Ex. 3:  *ɢazn **ňonʁům-f** gum yiqaⁿ jə-m vaš-kᵊi*.
Lit.: Village **dog-ACC**. all Chinese eat-CI. finish-NP.
The Chinese have eaten all the **dogs** in Chabchal.

Ex. 4:  *urumči **gia-t** səjəⁿ li čaŋ*.
Lit.: Urumchi **street-DL**. cart LIM. full.
In the **streets** of Urumchi there is nothing but a lot of cars.

## 2.1.2 Partial number

The partial number often denotes a more precisely specified group of rational beings, although, in some cases, it may also refer to an entire category of beings.

---

[4]  The word '*Gazn*' (Gašan in written Manchu) refers mainly to somebody's birthplace or home, but can be also used for any village. The Jungarian Sibe, saying '*Gazn*', usually mean Chabchal which is the birthplace to most of them.
[5]  '*čiškə*' means a small bird, but is often used specifically for a sparrow.

43

In spoken Sibe there are two suffixes of the partial number: -s (with allomorphs) and -t. The suffix -s (-sə, -zə) is more frequent, and is the only productive suffix of the partial number, which occurs in three sandhi variants. While written Manchu distinguishes three variants of this suffix according to vowel harmony -se/-sa/-so, in colloquial Sibe, these three variants have merged into one with the neutral vowel 'ə' which tends to disappear in present-day pronunciation, and is preserved only in emphasized positions or before a morpheme beginning with a consonant, which then needs to be separated by a vowel from the preceding suffix.

In the latter case, when the suffix is attached to a vowel stem, voicing of the medial consonant takes place and the resulting form is -zə.

The partial number suffixes are attached to the nominal stem. The nominal suffix -n, and in rare cases other suffixes like -r of ər/tər, are dropped (*e.g. ər – əs, χavə$^n$ – χafs, yiqa$^n$ – yiqas*).

Examples of the forms with the suffix -s:

Ex. 1:  **yiqa-s** *uču$^n$ učulu-m bana-q$^{\mathring{u}}$, qaičim li.*
Lit.: **Chinese-PART.N.** song sing-CI. can (NI.)-NEG., shout IMP. LIM.
**The Chinese (PART.)** can not sing, they just scream.
Note: A statement about differing preferences in entertainment.

Ex. 2:  **ju-s da-zə-f** *χ$^{\mathring{u}}$azə-v-m ǔ*ɴ*an da-f śie$^n$ giɲul!*
Lit.: **Child- PART.N. base-PART.N.** grow-CAUS.-CP. elders base ACC. good serve-IMPER.
Bring up your **children** and take good care of your parents-in-law.
Note: Fragment of a fairy-tale. *Jus* is an irregular partial number form of the noun *ji* child.

Ex. 3:  *tər gizu$^n$ dənji-maq ta ər čavčaɪ* **mamə-s** *gum inšk aɪdə-v-ʁ$^ə$i.*
Lit.: This word hear CP. ACT. this Chabchal **grandmother-PART.N.** all laughter lose-CAUS.-NP.
When the **old women** from Chabchal heard this, they all burst out laughing.

Examples of the forms with the suffix -sə:

Ex. 1:  *čavčaɪ* **χaf-sə** *ňi erk li emi-m baʁənə-m.*
Lit.: Chabchal **chief-PART.N.** F. liquor-LIM. drink-CI. can-IMP.
**The bosses** in Chabchal know only drinking.
Note: χavə$^n$ at present refers to any kind of leader; during the time of the Qing dynasty it was used for higher state officials.

Ex. 2:  *ju,* **maf-sə**, *bi son-t jaq aram-bu-ʁ$^ə$i.*
Lit.: Come-IMP. **ancestor-PART.N.**, 1.sg. you-DL. thing make.CP.-give-PERF.
Come here, **you two**, I have prepared the food for you.
Note: The word *maf* 'ancestor, forefather, old man' is often used as a familiar term, caring but humorous, addressed to a family member, a relative or a friend.

Ex. 3: *əmdaⁿ gən-ɣəŋ, gum aji **jaq-sə**.*
Lit.: Once go-NP.II. all small **thing-PART.N.**
When I went there once, there were only young **children**.
Note: The speaker talks about his own inadequacy, as an adult visiting a disco-bar.

Examples of forms with the suffix -*ze:*

Ex. 1: *uɣuri **gučú-zə-f** iza-v-maq əm diovr iv-ɣᵊi.*
Lit.: All **friend-PART.N.-ACC.** gather-CAUS.-CP. one night play-NP.
He gathered all his **friends** and they were partying the whole night.

Ex. 2: *bi **śivə-zə-maq** davɹ yavŭ-qᵘ.*
Lit.: 1sg. **Sibe-PART.N.-SOC.** exceedingly go-(NI.)-NEG.
I do not have many contacts with **Sibe people**.

2) The suffix -*te* occurs only with some forms, mostly with kinship terms.

Ex.: ***gəh-tə** ňi afqa-či dəyi-maq yav-ʁᵊi.*
Lit.: **Sister-PART.N. POSS.** heaven-LAT. fly-CP. go-PERF.
**Her sisters** flew to the sky.

## 2.1.3 Specific forms of the use of the partial number

### *Honorific use of the partial number suffix*

The partial number suffix is often used in a polite address, which can be, to some extent, compared to the use of honorific plural in Slavonic languages, but also as a polite appellation in the third person (mostly in the presence of the person being referred to).

Ex. 1: ***əčə-s** tə!*
Lit.: **Uncle-PART.N.** sit.IMP.
Please take a seat, **uncle**.
Note: In Manchu and Sibe kinship terms (except for 'mother' and 'father') are used for polite address to unrelated people as well as relatives. In the case of unrelated people, usually the term for the speaker's own relative of the corresponding age is used, but the use of a term suggesting a more advanced age is always more polite.

Ex. 2: ***dəɣəmə-s** bait-aqᵘ na?*
Lit. **Aunt-PART.N.** matter-no QUEST.
How are you, **Aunt**?

Ex. 3: ***əyi-zə** śieⁿ yila-ʁə na?*
Lit.: **Grandfather-PART.N.** well stay-NP. QUEST.
Are you doing well, **Grandfather**?

Ex. 4:  *miⁿ əňi-s jiɣⁱi.*
        Lit.: **My mother-PART.N.** come-PERF.
        **Mother** came.

### *Specifying a group of people connected to a certain person*

This suffix is further used to denote a group of people who are in some way connected to a particular person. Similar patterns are used, for example, in Mongolian, where the suffix *nar* is used in a similar manner, or in Chinese – by means of the expression *ta men*.

Ex. 1:  **yiŋhua-z** *jiɣⁱi.*
        Lit.: **Yinghua-PART.N.** come-PERF.
        **Yinghua and her friends** came.

Ex. 2:  **guočiŋ-zə** *bo-t ut naⁿ bi?*
        Lit.: **Guoqing-PART.N.** house-DL. how many person is?
        How many people live at **the Quoqings'**?
        Note: Such a formulation suggests that the house does not belong only to Guoqing, but probably to his family. If the partial number suffix had not been used, the question would have probably implied that strangers were staying in a house which belongs only to Guoqing.

Ex. 3:  **hara-zə** *gurunbo-t ai jaq jə-mie?*
        Lit.: **Hara-PART.N.** country-DL. what thing eat-IMP.
        **Hara**, what does one eat in your country?
        Note: When talking to a foreigner, an expression of the type XY-*ze gurunbot* 'in XY's country' means 'in your country' and sounds more polite than the common expressions like *son təvat* 'at your place' or *son gurunbot* 'in your country'.

Ex. 4:  *tər əm učur bi* **yiktan-zə-maq** *məji laft yav-ʁⁱi.*
        Lit. That one period I **Yiktan-PART.N.-IS.** little much go-PERF.
        At that time I was more often in contact with **Yiktan and his friends**.

## 2.1.4 Expressing plurality through lexical means

As is clear from the examples above, the suffix of the definite number is not the most frequent means to express plurality. Listed below are several instances of using lexical means to denote the meaning of 'many', these being suppletive forms (mainly the word *guruⁿ* 'folk, people'), numerals and other expressions.

### *The word* guruⁿ *(folk, people)*

The word *guruⁿ*, originally meaning 'a people', 'a state' or 'an empire', has become a suppletive form for the partial number/plural of the word *naⁿ* 'man, person', for which there is no regular form in the colloquial language (written Manchu has a regular plural form of the word *niyalma-niyalmasa*).

Ex. 1: *śivə **həh guruⁿ** daməŋ ɢŭči-qᵘ̌, set mamə-s li ɢŭči-m.*
Lit.: Sibe **woman** folk tobacco suck-(NI.)-NEG., old grandmother-PART.N. LIM.
suck -IMP.
The Sibe **women** do not smoke, only old women do.

Ex. 2: *so-n təva **guruⁿ** gum suyeⁿ ba?*
Lit.: 2pl.-GEN. there **folk** all yellow PROB.
In your country all **people** are fair-haired, aren't they?

Ex. 3: *məzəliaŋ **ašta guruⁿ** gum śivə hərɣəⁿ baʁəna-qᵘ̌.*
Lit.: Like.us **youngster folk** all Sibe letter can-(NOM.IMP.)-NEG.
**Young people** like us do not know the Sibe script.

Ex. 4: ***set guruⁿ** li gənɣᵊi.*
Lit.: **Old folk-LIM.** go-PERF.
Only **old people** went there.

### Numerals

When the definite number is expressed by numerals and other nouns denoting number, the partial number suffix is never used.

Ex. 1: ***nadəⁿ saʁənč** əm čiškə bətkə-f jə-m vajə-qᵘ̌.*
Lit.: **Seven girl** one sparrow leg-ACC. eat-CI. finish-(NI.) NEG.
**Seven girls** together cannot finish one sparrow leg.
Note: A saying which ridicules girls who are shy and squeamish in public.

Ex. 2: *ənəŋ gia-t **naⁿ laft.***
Lit.: Today street-DL. **man many**.
Today there are **many people** in the streets/outside.

### The word χačiⁿ 'kind'

The word *χačiⁿ* 'kind, type' is often used to express plurality. This expression has, among other functions, a function close to the numerative (*ju χačiⁿ bitkə* lit. 'two kind book' = 'two different books').
When expressing plurality, the word *χačiⁿ* is usually reduplicated, either fully or by means of echo doubling ( e.g. *χač χačiⁿ, χala χačiⁿ*), or determined by another word with the meaning of number, most often the word *gərəⁿ* 'all'. [6]
Sometimes, as in Ex. 2, the second member of these reduplicated constructions is dropped.

Ex. 1: ***χačačiⁿ nanᵊ-maq** yav-m.*
Lit.: **Kind-ECHO person-IS.** go-IMP.
(He) makes friends **with many people/all sorts of people**.

---

[6] These constructions are used both adnominally and adverbially in the spoken language.

Ex. 2: *χačiⁿ jaq gia-m.*
**Kind thing** take-IMP.
(She) is buying **lots of things**.

Ex. 3: *χačačiⁿ gizərə-m.*
Lit.: **Kind-ECHO** talk-IMP.
(He) talks **a lot**, different things etc.

### Imitative expressions

Both written Manchu and spoken Sibe are rich in imitative expressions, which, similarly to onomatopoeia, describe various qualities, circumstances etc. Some of these can serve as figurative expressions of number or plurality.

Ex. 1: *bazar-t gən-ɣəŋ naⁿ šu da saq saq.*
Lit.: Market-DL. go-NP.II. man completely ACT. *saq saq* (an image of dense and intertwined tree branches).
I went to the market and there was a **tangle** of people.

Ex. 2: *dači Ili bira-t ňimвa dəvər dəvər.*
Lit.: Formerly Ili river-DL. fish *dəvər dəvər* (an image of boiling water)
Earlier there used to be **lots of fish** in the Ili river.

## 2.2 The category of case

In the opinions of the scholars cited above, the number of cases in the Altaic languages varies between five and eighteen, and the terminology is not uniform (Sunik 1982, p. 146). Among the Tungusic languages, Evenki is reported to have the most complicated system of cases, while the simpliest one is that of literary Manchu (Zaharov 1879, p. 126).

One of the traditional problems of description of cases in the Altaic languages is the relatively vague distinction between a case suffix on one hand and a particle or a postposition on the other. This problem mainly concerns the cases with directional meaning, but also the sociative and instrumental cases.

Following traditional Manchu grammars, I. Zaharov maintains that the Manchu nouns are inflexible and the cases are expressed by particles or postpositions (Zaharov 1879, p. 125).[7] According to Zaharov, there are four case formants in written Manchu (the particles *-i*, *-be* and the postpositions *-de*, *-či*). Thus the cases in written Manchu are five in total (Zaharov 1879, p. 126).

In spoken Sibe, four case suffixes are similar to literary Manchu, while three others are different. These differences, especially the use of an instrumental case suffix, make the Sibe case system closer to that of Mongolian.

---

[7] This conception is probably connected with traditional Manchu orthography, i.e. writing the suffixes separately from the stem which does not change.

1. **The nominative (N.)** is, as in written Manchu, an unmarked case. (An unmarked form of a noun may, however, be a zero form of another case).
2. **The genitive (GEN.)** is, as in written Manchu, formed by the suffix *-i*.
3. **The dative-locative (DL.)** has, similarly to written Manchu, the suffix *-d/-t*.
4. **The accusative (ACC.)** is formed by the suffix *-f/-və* or *-bə* which corresponds to *-be* of written Manchu.
5. **The ablative (ABL.)** is formed by the suffix *-dəri*, which is found as a postposition in written Manchu.
6. **The lative (LAT.)** is formed by the suffix *-či*, which has an ablative function in written Manchu.
7. **The instrumental-sociative (IS.)** is formed by the suffix *-maq*, which has no correspondence in written Manchu.

Table of case suffixes in Manchu, Sibe and Mongolian:

|  | genitive | dative-locative | accusative | ablative | directive | instrumental | sociative |
|---|---|---|---|---|---|---|---|
| Manchu | *-i* | *-de* | *-be* | *-či* | – | *(-i, -be)* | – |
| Sibe | *-i* | *-d(ə)/-t* | *-f/və* | *-dəri* | *-či* | *-maq* | *-maq* |
| Mongolian | *-i/-iin* | *-d/-t* | *-iig* | *-aas⁴* | *-ruu* | *-aar⁴* | *-tai³* |

### Unmarked forms of indirect cases

In spoken Sibe, the usage of zero grammatical forms is particularly frequent. In some cases, the constructions with zero forms correspond to written Manchu, but in many others the spoken language uses unmarked forms where written Manchu requires forms with suffixes. The most remarkable types of constructions with zero forms of indirect cases are the following:

### Genitive – attribute

Unlike written Manchu, where proper nouns and attributive pronouns occur almost regularly with the genitive suffix, in spoken Sibe, proper nouns often form an attribute in their unmarked form.

Ex. 1:  *ɢaʐn saʁənjuzˀ-**maq** gizərə-r gizuⁿ baʁə-qᵘ.*
       Lit. **Village-0GEN. girls-IS.** speak-NI. word find(NI.)-NEG.
       I have nothing to talk about with **village girls**.

Ex. 2:  *soⁿ təva moriⁿ gum ambu ba?*
       Lit. **2pl.-GEN. there-0GEN. horse** all big PROB.
       In **your place all horses** are big, aren't they?

### Dative-locative – temporal determination

A clearly defined group of nouns with temporal meaning regularly functions as verb determinants in their unmarked form. B. Sechenbaatar designates a similar group of nouns in Chakhar Mongol 'temporal nouns' and treats them as a coherent subgroup within nouns. The situation in spoken Sibe resembles that of Mongolian. The group includes a limited number of simple or complex expressions with the meaning of a temporal determinant, including the interrogative noun *aitiŋ* 'when'.However, since these temporal nouns likewise fall into various nominal sub-classes (proper nouns – e.g. *čimar* 'tomorrow', qualitative nouns – e.g. *ərt* 'early', spatials – e.g. *aməɹ* 'after', it seems to be more proper to speak of an idiomatic noun usage. As certain other nouns in a similar function take the dative-locative (e.g. *tər ərin-t* Lit. that time-DL.'at that time'), the unmarked forms may be rendered as zero dative-locative.

**Examples:**

Ex. 1:  *aitiŋ ji-ɣʲye? čəksə ji-ɣʲi.*
Lit. **When** come-PERF. **yesterday**-0DL. come-PERF.
**When** did you arrive? I arrived **yesterday**.

Ex. 2:  *aməɹ gəɹ bo-či ňi bədərə-m yav-ʁʲi.*
Lit. **After-0DL.** still house-LAT. POSS. return-CI. go-PERF.
**Later** she returned to her home.

**Accusative of unspecified nouns**
When a noun in the accusative is not specified, it usually has a zero form. This usage is also typical of colloquial Mongolian.

Ex.:  *əm ju orozə-i čoaχ ta šu **gida jav-maq** gidaɹ-m ji-ɣʲi.*
Lit. One two Russian-GEN. soldier ACT. ultimately **spear-0ACC. hold-CP**. Thrust CI. come-PERF.
Some Russian soldiers were approaching him, **bearing spears** and threatening to attack him.

## 2.2.1 Nominative

The Sibe nominative is a case with no grammatical affixes. Its main function in a sentence is to express the subject or the nominal predicate. It is also likely that separate clauses inserted into a sentence and introduced by the verb *zə-* 'to say' (Ex. 4, 5) should be classified as nominative clauses. The most frequent questions that receive a nominative reply are: *ai* 'what?', *və* 'who?', *ai jaq* 'what thing = what?'

Ex. 1:  *dəɣəmə śieⁿ yila-ʁə na?*
Lit.: **Aunt** well stay-NOM. PERF. QUEST.
How are you, **Aunt**?
Note: A honorific address using the 3ʳᵈ person.

Ex. 2:  *ər gəɹ śi-ⁿ **jaq** o-ʁů na?*
Lit.: This too 2sg.-GEN. **thing** become-NP. QUEST.
This is also **yours**?
Note: Mild scolding of a child for taking someone else's things.

Ex. 3:   *ərə-f gəɹ **saf** zə-m ut-kʲi!*
         Lit.: This too **shoe** say-CONV.PRES. wear-PERF.
         She wears this as **shoes**!
         Note: Displeasure about strangely looking fashionable shoes.

Ex. 4:   *śivə naⁿ suyeⁿ nanə-f suyeⁿ **moň** zə-m.*
         Lit.: Sibe person yellow person-ACC. yellow **monkey** say-IMP.
         Sibe people call a blonde person 'yellow **monkey**'.

Ex. 5:   *śivə nan-ᵃi juhtə-rəŋə **dʲøf**.*
         Lit.: Sibe person-GEN. worship-NI.II. **fox**.
         The Sibe people worship (mainly) the **fox**.

### Adding the particle 'əi' to nominative

The particle *əi*, which has probably developed from the interrogative pronoun *ai* (what), can be defined as slightly generalizing or derogating the noun to which it is attached. In some cases it can be translated as 'some'.[8]

Ex. 1:   *wuniŋ **uj-əi** gum ambu.*
         Lit.: Wuning **head-what** all big.
         Wuning has **a** big **head**. **Even** Wuning's **head** is big.

Ex. 2:   *diørgu-t **jaq-əi** bi na?*
         Lit.: Inside **thing-what** is QUEST.
         Is there **anything** inside?

Ex. 3:   *yiqaⁿ **saʁənj-ei** bi na?*
         Lit.: Chinese **girl-what** is QUEST.
         Is **(any)** Chinese girl there?

Ex. 4:   *ajiguruⁿ baʁənə-r **jaq-əi** vaq.*
         Lit.: Children can-NI. **thing-what** not.
         This is not **something** children could do.

Ex. 5:   *taqůru-r **jiʁ-ai** bi na?*
         Lit.: Use-NI. **money-what** is QUEST
         Do you have **enough money** (to live on?)

### The emphasizing vowels -a/-ə/-o

The emphasizing vowels *-a/-ə/-o* (variants of one vowel which changes according to vowel harmony) seem to fall somewhere between suprasegmental and morphological usage. They often occur in various positions as mere emphasis. Attached to the nominative, however, they

---

[8]   A similar shift in the direction of generalization may be seen in the use of the interrogative expression *shenme-de*, lit. 'what-GEN.', attached to the noun in Mandarin Chinese.

51

can sometimes function almost as a copula. The shorter the sentence, the more it seems to require this emphasizing vowel (Ex. 1, 2).

Ex. 1: *ər ai **nan-ə**?*
> Lit.: This what **person-EMP**.
> What **kind of person** is this? Who is this? (also used as a rhetoric question)

Ex. 2: *ai bait-ə?*
> Lit.: What **matter-EMP**.
> What is the **matter**?

Ex. 3: *ər ai jaq **saʁənj-e**?*
> Lit.:This what thing **girl-EMP**.
> What kind of a **girl** is this?
> Note: This sentence may express either a slight displeasure or a hidden admiration.

Ex. 4: *tər sorq śiňi **sorq-o**!*
> Lit.: That awl only **awl-EMP**.
> Only that awl was **an awl**. (= That was a really good awl).

## 2.2.2 Genitive

The genitive is an adnominal case in Sibe. Usually a noun to which something is attributed is in the genitive case. Most postpositions are construed with nouns in the genitive . The most frequent questions answered by the genitive are: *ai* 'what, which, of what'; *ai jaqə-i* 'of what thing, what kind of' ; and *və-(i)* 'whose'.

### *Forms of the genitive*

In the spoken language, the genitive has a single suffix *-i*. This suffix often has a zero form and sometimes it merely causes the (otherwise unpronounced) vowel at the end of the word to be pronounced.

If a word in the genitive case occurs separately (without its determinatum) the suffix *-niŋ(ə)* is used, which is formed by joining another genitive suffix *-ni* (found in written Manchu and in Sibe possessive pronouns) and a substantivizing formant *-ŋ(ə)*. This form of double attribution is often used in possessive constructions when something is attributed to a person or object which is then itself attributed to the subject or main agent of the sentence, which cannot be in the first or second person.

#### a) The suffix *-i*

The full form of the suffix

Ex.: ***nan-ᵊi** bo-t gənə-m čaʁa-qŭ-ʁⁿi.*
> Lit.: **Person-GEN**. house-DL. go-IMP. like-(NI.)-NEG.+(become)-NP.-NEG.
> I don't like visiting (**people**) any more.

The shortened form (pronouncing the final vowel)

Ex.:  *śi **louz-ə fəjərgi-t** ɛli-mə yila!*
Lit.: 2sg.(GEN.) **building below-DL.** wait-CI. stand-IMP.
Wait for me **downstairs**.

The zero form

Ex.:  *ər əmbič **jalən** na$^n$, əmbič abbanš-k guru$^n$ bi-y$^ə$ye.*
Lit.: This maybe **world (0GEN.)** person, maybe how-born folk is-PERF.
Are those people **from this world**, or are they some other beings?

### b) The suffixes *-niŋ/-yiŋ/-ŋə*

Ex. 1:  *śi və **boo-ňiŋə?***
Lit.: You who(0GEN.) **house-S.G.**
Whose child are you? To whose **family** do you belong?

Ex. 2:  *əraɴ bodo-mə yila-ʁə-də **əňi-ŋə** buh finyə ňi ɢůňin-t døš-k$^ə$i.*
Lit: Like this think-CI. stand-NP.+DL. **mother-GEN.II** give
NP. hair POSS. mind-DL. enter-PERF.
While she was thinking (about what to do), she remembered the (magic) hair which her **mother** gave her.

### *Use of the genitive*

Nouns in the genitive are mostly used as attributes, or they are followed by various postpositions. In literary Manchu, the suffix *-i* is also used for the instrumental case (*roditel'no-tvoritel'nyj padež*; Zaharov 1879, p. 125). Spoken Sibe has an instrumental suffix *-maq*. People of the older generation, however, sometimes use *-i*, which is perceived as a more formal style. On the contrary I have never witnessed the use of *-i* as an instrumental among bilingual young people with a limited knowledge of the Sibe language.

### a) The genitive form as an attribute

Ex. 1:  *əmkə$^n$ ňi **gury-u-i** duru$^n$, əmkə$^n$ ňi **nan-$^ə$i** duru$^n$.*
Lit.: One-POSS. **animal-GEN.** form, one-POSS. **person-GEN.** form.
One of them has an **animal** form, the other has a **human** form.

Ex. 2:  *ɢaʐn guru$^n$ **nan-$^ə$i** bov li fətərə-m.*
Lit.: **Village (0GEN.)** folk **person-GEN.** house-ACC. LIM. dig-IMP.
**People in Chabchal** spend all their time sticking their noses in other peoples' businesses.
Note: One of the frequent negative statements about the relations inside the Sibe community.

Ex. 3: **nan-ᵊi** [9] *saʁǝnji-maq amʁǝ-m vajǝ-maq...*
Lit.: **Person-GEN.** daughter-SOC. sleep-CI. finish-CP.
Having already slept with an**other's daughter** ...

Ex. 4: *ɢazn **sǝr-ǝ** muku ňi hǝⁿ amtiŋǝ.*
Lit.: Village **spring** water F. very tasty.
The water **from the spring** in Chabchal is very tasty.

Ex. 5: *ǝr ǝm jaqǝ **dǝr-ᵊi** soqŭ ňi jiram.*
Lit.: This one thing **face-GEN.** skin POSS. thick.
His skin on **the face** is thick (= he is assertive).

Ex. 6: **hut-u-i** *dǝvǝryǝⁿ jaqǝ!*
Lit.: **Ghost-GEN.** whelp thing!
Rascal!

Ex. 7: *saʁǝnjie, **nan-ᵊi** ǝryǝn-maq ǝm ivǝr-ǝ.*
Lit.: Daughter, **person-GEN.** life-IS. PROH. play-NI.
Daughter, do not play with **other people's** lives.

Ex. 8: *ǝr χaʁǝč, bi ta-yǝŋ, **jalǝⁿ-0 nan-ᵊi** arvǝⁿ bi.*
Lit.: This boy, Isg. see-NP.II. **world-0GEN. person-GEN.** appearance is.
It seems to me that this boy comes **from the human world**.

Ex. 9: *śiaŋgaŋ-f amnǝ-m śaqśaq azǝɹ-m **nan-ᵊi** duruⁿ vaq.*
Lit.: Hongkong imitate-CI. coquettish behave-CI. **person GEN. shape** not.
She behaves coquettishly (she has seen it) in the Hongkong films, horrible to see.

### b) The genitive forms used with postpositions

The genitive is used with postpositions expressing the basic spatial relationships, like *nuŋut* above; *fǝjǝrgit* 'below'; *tiuɹyut* 'outside'; *diørgit* 'inside'; *daɹvǝt* 'next to'; *jaqǝt* 'besides'; *dat* 'next to', 'close to' and some others.

Ex. 1: **nan-ᵊi** *ɢal-ǝ **fǝjǝryǝ-t** vǝilǝ-m o-m.*
Lit.: person-GEN. **hand-(GEN.) below** work-CI. become-IMP.
He can only work **under** others' **hand** (=leadership).

Ex. 2: *nan-ᵊi ǝryǝⁿ vajǝ-maq, χaʁǝjuzǝ ňi nanǝ-f χŭlǝ-mǝ **bo-i tiuɹyut** yaqŭru-m.*
Lit.: Person-GEN. life finish-CP. son-PART.N. POSS. person-ACC. call-CI. **house-GEN. outside** bow-IMP.

---

[9] As in Mongolian (and in spoken Chinese) one of the frequent figurative meanings of the expression for 'person, man' is 'other people', and the genitive form of the word for 'person' is the most common expression for 'strange, extraneous, alien'. *nan-ᵊi saʁǝnč* – Lit.: A daughter of other people – shows concern about the girl's parents – probably the sentence would be finished with the phrase 'he did not marry her'.

When somebody dies, his male children go to other peoples' homes and bow **outside their houses**.

Note: The fact that people announcing their parent's death remain outside is emphasized, because by entering the house they may cause misfortune to the family.

Ex. 3: *χam-ᵊi diørɣ-u-t moqsan tandə-r əm duruⁿ banjə-m.*
Lit.: **Dung-GEN. inside** stick beat NI. beat one form live-IMP.
They live like beating **dung** with a stick.
Note: A proverb about disorderly life.

Ex. 4: *χal-ᵊi diørɣ-u-t sadulə-vu-qᵘ̊.*
Lit.: **Clan-GEN. inside** make kinship-CAUS.-(NI.)-NEG.
It is not allowed to marry **inside the clan**.

Ex. 5: *śieⁿ naⁿ jaq-ᵊi nuŋu-t ji-m, ɢaɹvaɴ naⁿ gizuⁿ-0 nuŋu-t ji-m.*
Lit.: Good person thing-GEN. above come-IMP., bad person **word-0GEN. above** come-IMP.
A good man comes **at mealtime**, a bad man comes **when people talk about him**.
Note: A proverb used to make a guest who enters at mealtime feel at ease.[10]

**c) The genitive form used as a predicate (suffix '-niŋ (ə)')**

Ex. 1: *ər so-ⁿ tašqů-niŋ na?*
Lit.: This 2pl.-GEN. **school-GEN.II QUEST**
Does this **belong to your school**?

Ex. 2: *śi yavaniŋə? bi ɢůlja-niŋə.*
Lit: 2sg. **where-GEN.II?** I Ghulja-G-II.
**Where** are you **from**? I am **from Ghulja**.

## 2.2.3 Dative-locative

The dative-locative expresses both static location (answering the question 'where') and dynamic location (answering the question 'where to'). The questions answered by the dative-locative case may be:

*yava-t* 'where/to where'; *ye-t* 'where/to where'; *ye-či* 'where to'; *ɛvi-t* 'where'; *və-t* 'to whom, by whom, in whom'; *ai-t* 'in what'; *aitiŋ* 'when'; *an* 'why' and others.

### The forms of the dative-locative

The suffix of the dative-locative has two allomorphs *-t* and *-də*. The second, less frequent variety is used when the word in DL. occurs at the end of a sentence or of a prosodic unit (Ex. 1), or, sometimes, before a suffix or a particle beginning with a consonant (Ex. 2).

---

[10] According to Kicengge, the usage of the word *nunŋud* in such phrase sounds incorrect and may possibly be a calque from Mongolian. Personal communication, October 2011.

55

Ex. 1:  *śoro χali$^n$ fəjilə, yiʁa$^n$ χorʁoň-i χozə-də…*
        Lit.: Jojoba tree below, cattle pen-GEN. **corner-.DL**.
        Under the jojoba tree, **in the corner** of the cattle pen …
        Note: From a popular song.

Ex. 2:  *əm **qarun-də** ňi əm maŋi$^n$ bi.*
        Lit.: One **fortress-DL. F**. one *maŋin* is.
        In every **fortress** there is one *maŋin*.[11]

### *The use of the dative-locative*

It seems that the dative-locative has a relatively compact semantic field, in the centre of which we find the meaning of location in space. In attempting to describe the usage of this case, the examples may be divided into several groups according to range of meaning and function:[12]

a) 'static location' (occurrence at a place) and that of a 'dynamic location' (mainly arrival at a certain place; direction of motion). As in Mongolian, these semantic designations seem to be perceived as identical in spoken Sibe.
b) adding, assignment, competency, owing, possession
c) the 'dative' meaning – to whom, for whom, referring, applying to someone or something
d) various constructions with the meaning of reason, cause, and so on
e) temporal meaning

An important syntactical function of the dative-locative is that of the agent in passive constructions, including phrases with verbs of perception (f).

### a) The meaning of location – occurrence at a certain place or arrival at a certain place

Ex. 1:  *mi-$^n$ **jaq-ə-t** banč!*
        Lit.: **My place-DL**. live-IMP.
        Stay **at my place**.

Ex. 2:  *fodə-f **duqa-t** liekə-m.*
        Lit.: Fod-ACC. **gate-DL**. hang-IMP.
        The fod is being hung on **the gate**.
        Note: From an account about funeral rites. The *fod* is a stripe of red silk with a piece of black cloth which is hung at the gate of the house where somebody has died.

Ex. 3:  *šuda **fərə-d** ňi izanč mamə χûarə$^n$ bi.*
        Lit.: Completely **bottom-DL. POSS**. Izanj grandmother court is.
        **At the very end** there is the palace of the goddess *Izanj mame*.

---

[11] *Maŋins* are lower deities of the Sibe shamanistic pantheon. In the traditions of the Jungarian Sibes they are associated with the eighteen fortresses through which the shaman has to pass on his way to the highest deity.

[12] Here I list the meanings which would be perceived as different by a speaker of a European language. The goal of this description is to specify the range of meanings as narrowly as possible. It is my conjecture that the speakers of Sibe do not perceive the above listed meanings as different.

Ex. 4:   *loʁǔ-i **jǝyin-dǝ ňi** suyeⁿ χoźiⁿ sǝktǝ-m.*
Lit.: Sword-GEN. **edge-DL. POSS.** yellow paper spread-IMP.
They cover the **edges** of the swords with the yellow paper.

Ex. 5:   ***if χůarǝn-t** bǝnǝ-rǝŋǝ-f giraⁿ čiči-v-m zǝ-m.*
Lit.: **Grave court-DL.** take-NI.II-ACC. corpse go out-CAUS.-IMP. say- IMP.
Taking the dead body **to the graveyard** is called 'taking the corpse out'.

Ex. 6:   *vajǝ-mǝ tǝva-dǝri **na-t** maχtǝ-m.*
Lit.: Finish-CI. there-ABL. **ground-DL.** throw-IMP.
Finally they throw him from there down **to the earth**.

Ex. 7:   *gulgul **bo-t** ji-m.*
Lit.: Often **house-DL.** come-IMP.
He often comes to **see us**.

Ex. 8:   *gizuⁿ ňi **saⁿ sǝskǝ-t** latǝ-qů.*
Lit.: Word POSS. **ear chin-DL.** stick-(NI.)-NEG.
His speech is not pleasant to listen to.

Ex. 9:   *ǝr ňuŋk **nanǝ-t** latǝ-m.*
Lit.: This disease **person-DL.** stick-IMP.
This disease is infectious.

Ex. 10: *yiqaⁿ saʁǝnč ǝr **χaʁǝji-t** luk lat-kǝi.*
Lit.: Chinese girl this **boy-DL.** firmly stick-PERF.
That Chinese girl got really hung up **on that boy**.

Ex. 11: *maɴ bait biš ta **uju-t** tuza-mǝ śiňi taqǝ-m.*
Lit.: Difficult matter be-CC. ACT. **head-DL. fall-CI** only know IMP.
One learns about troubles only when he **himself** gets into them.

**b) The meaning of assignment: belonging, ownership, being a part of something.**

Ex. 1:   *γaγa **baitǝ-t** gum dor bi.*
Lit.: Any **matter-DL.** all rule is.
**Everything** (that has to be done) has its rules.
Note: From an account of funeral rites.

Ex. 2:   ***ǝndüri-d ňi** gǝɹ ǝjǝⁿ čiš-kǝi.*
Lit.: Deity-DL. F. also ruler come out-PERF.
Among the deities, there also appeared a ruler.

Ex. 3:   *muduri **śivǝ-t** aqů.*
Lit.: Dragon Sibe-DL. not.
The **Sibe** do not **have** a dragon (in their culture).

Ex. 4:   *śivə-t laft tuta-ʁᵊye.*
        Lit.: **Sibe-DL**. much stay-PERF.
        There is much (of the traditions) left **among the Sibes**.

Ex. 5:   *asqəⁿ ərin-t čoaʁə-t yav-ʁᵊi.*
        Lit.: Young time-DL. **army-DL**. go-PERF.
        In his youth he was in **the army**.

Ex. 6:   *śivə-t da əza naⁿ bi.*
        Lit.: **Sibe-DL**. ACT. quite person is.
        There are quite many (gifted) people **among the Sibe**.

Ex. 7:   *saman-də ňi bəy-i vəč-k əndür bi.*
        Lit.: **Shaman-DL**. F. body-GEN. worship-NOM.PERF deity is.
        **Shamans have** their own (protecting) deity which they worship.

### c) Relation to somebody, an action directed towards somebody

Ex. 1:   *čiškə fietə-mə-š gəɹ udun-t tuza.*
        Lit.: Sparrow fart-CI.-COND. still **wind-DL**. help.
        Even a sparrow's fart can **help the wind**.
        Note: A proverb meaning that any effort can give some results.

Ex. 2:   *ərə-f bi miⁿ əňi-t gia-m-bu-yᵊi.*
        Lit.: This I my **mother-DL**. take-CI.-give-PERF.
        I bought this **for** my **mother**.

Ex. 3:   *antqələ-r nanə-t arχ bi.*
        Lit.: Bashful **person-DL**. ruse is.
        There are ways to **make** a bashful **guest** eat.

Ex. 4:   *taqə-qᵘ nanə-t fien-š da, muduri bi zə-m.*
        Know-(NI.)-NEG. **person-DL**. ask-CI. ACT. dragon is say-IMP.
        If you ask **somebody** who does not understand it, he would say that we have dragons
        (= that there are dragons in the traditional Sibe mythology).

Ex. 5:   *śivə naⁿ dievə-t χaɹdə-qᵘ.*
        Lit.: Sibe person **fox-DL**. offend –(NI.)-NEG.
        The Sibe people do not harm **foxes**.

### d) The meaning of 'reason, goal, sake'

Ex. 1:   *ai baitə-t əksə-mie?*
        Lit.: **What matter-DL**. hurry-IMP.
        **What** are you doing now? **What** are you busy **with**?

Ex. 2:  *bi ňi ərang baitə-t fančə-r nan vaq.*
Lit.: I F. **like this matter-DL**. be angry-NI. person not.
I am not the kind of person who gets angry **about such things**.

#### e) Temporal use

Ex. 1:  *ai ərin-t ačə-m-ů-ʁ<sup>ů</sup>o?*
Lit.: **What time-DL**. meet-CI.+become-PERF.
**At what time** shall we meet?

Ex. 2:  *ajig ərin-t gum təvat iv-m gənə-m.*
Lit.: **Small time-DL**. all there play-CI. go-IMP.
**In our childhood** we all were going there to play.

#### f) Agent of passive constructions

Ex. 1:  *gəɹ yiqan-t χoɹtu-v-ʁ<sup>ə</sup>i barə.*
Lit.: Still **Chinese-DL**. cheet-CAUS.-PERF. PROB.
It seems that you were cheated again **by the Chinese**.

Ex. 2:  *nanə-t sərə-vů-qů-mə da o-ʁ<sup>ů</sup>i.*
Lit.: **Person-DL**. notice-CAUS.-(NI.)-NEG.+(become)-CP. ACT. become-PERF.
Just do not let **other people** know.

Ex. 3:  *čəksə huizə-t tandə-v-ɣ<sup>ə</sup>i.*
Lit.: Yesterday **Uighur-DL**. beat-CAUS.-PERF.
Yesterday he was beaten **by the Uighurs**.

Ex. 4:  *śin-t gəɹ təraɴ sərə-v-mɛi na?*
Lit.: **You-DL**. still like that feel-CAUS.PRES.CONT. QUEST.
**Do you** also **have** that feeling?

Ex. 5:  *aʁa-t uš-k na<sup>n</sup> śiliŋ-deri gələ-q<sup>ů</sup>.*
Lit.: **Rain-DL**. get wet-NP. person dew-ABL. be afraid-(NI.)-NEG.
Somebody who got drenched **in rain** would **not be** scared by dew.

Ex. 6:  *tər χaʁəč gulɣun ňinəŋ **udun-t** diy-ɣə, **aʁa-t** fičav-ʁə ...*
Lit.: That boy whole day **wind-DL**. fly, rain-DL. zip-CAUS.-PERF.
The whole day the boy had been **swept up by the wind** and lashed by the rain ...

### Examples of more frequent constructions of verbs with the dative-locative:

1. **adanə-** *to participate*

Ex.:  *tərə-i śidən-t nan-<sup>ə</sup>i **śierin-t** adanə-m ojů-q<sup>ů</sup>.*
Lit.: That-GEN. between person-GEN. **wedding-DL**. participate become-(NI.)- NEG.
During that time one is not allowed to take part in other people's **weddings**.

59

2. **fienji-** *to ask*

Ex.:     *gəɣə gugu śie$^n$ dienjie, dønš-ka-qǔ-či* **min-t** *fienjie.*
Lit.: Elder sister, Aunt well listen-IMP., hear-(NP.)-NEG.-CC. **me-DL.** ask-IMP.
Sister, aunt, listen carefully; if you have not understood, tell **me**.
Note: From a contemporary song.

## 2.2.4 Accusative

The accusative in Sibe is mainly an object case. In addition to denoting the object, it is sometimes used with a spatial meaning to answer the question 'which way'. This usage comes from literary Manchu, where the accusative suffix -**be** fills part of the 'gap' caused by the lack of an instrumental case suffix. Spoken Sibe prefers using the instrumental or ablative case to convey the meaning 'which way'. However, among the older generation, the accusative is used as well.

The most frequent questions answered by the accusative are: *ai-f/ai* 'what'; *ai jaqə-f* 'what'; *və-f* 'whom' and *yava-f/ɛvi-f* 'which way'.

### *Forms of accusative*

The accusative suffix has the sandhi variants -*f/-v/-və* (Lit. Ma. -*be*). -*f* is the most frequent form. -*v/-və* are pronounced mostly before the particle -*ňi*.[13] After -*m* and -*n* sometimes -*b* is pronounced.A final -*n* is assimilated into -*m* before the suffix. In the modern spoken language, however, the suffix -*b* is often weakened or dropped, so that the sound of the resulting form is -*m*. The final -*b* is always preserved when the emphatic vowel is added (e.g. *qarə$^n$* 'fortress' – *qarə-m(b)/ qarə-mb-ə* 'fortress-ACC'.

When in the oral pronunciation a noun finishes in a consonant (usually with the exception of -*n/-m*), a prothetic vowel is inserted before the accusative suffix (e.g. *ɢaχ* 'crow' *ɢaʁ-ə-f* 'crow-ACC'.

The accusative often has a zero suffix. As in Mongolian, the use of the suffix depends on the categories of **definite** and **indefinite** together with **rational** and **irrational**. The accusative suffix is obligatory with concrete rational beings and virtually obligatory with specified irrational beings and objects. It is less frequently used with unspecified rational beings; most unspecified objects or irrational beings occurring as grammatical objects do not use the suffix.

### *Use of the accusative suffix*

#### 1. The meaning of object

Ex. 1:     *aʌə-v ňi yaqsə-v-ʁ$^ə$i.*
Lit.: **Mouth**-ACC. POSS. close-CAUS.-PERF.
He shut **his mouth**.

---

[13] The distribution of allomorphs in the examples above also depends on the actual manner of speech of the utterance. For example, in the case of slow and distinct speech a pause occuring after the grammatical object often conditioned the voiceless allomorph -*f* to occur even if the following word began with a vowel.

Ex. 2:  **laoha-m-f** *əmda^n yavə-f-χ bi-ɣ^əi.*
Lit.: **Laohan-ACC.** once go-CAUS.-NP. be-PERF.
Once he made a fool of **the laohan**.
Note: *Laohan* – Chin. *laohan* 'old man, taoist deity' – is a reference to an older man, mostly with a touch of respect. *yavəf-*, a causative form of *yaf-* 'to go', is used figuratively as 'to make a fool of sb.'. The verbal form *biɣi* at the end of the sentence refers to a previously known fact.

Ex. 3:  **miʁa^n-0** *gia-m-o-či* **məɣəjə-mf** *ta,* **sarʁa^n-0** *giam-o-či* **əňi-v ňi** *ta.*
Lit.: **Piglet-0ACC.** take-CONV.IMP –become-CC. **sow-ACC.** look-IMPER., **wife-0ACC.** take-CONV.IMP –become-CC. **mother-ACC.** POSS. look-IMPER.
When buying a piglet, look at the sow; when taking a wife look at her mother. (Proverb)

Ex. 4:  **antq-ə-f** *učulum,* **saʁanj-i-f** *učulum, ai-f saf-š-ta ai-f učulu-m.*
Lit.: **Guest-ACC.** sing-IMP. **girl-ACC.** sing-IMP., what-ACC. see-CC.-ACT.what-ACC. sing-IMP.
They sing about the guest, about the girl, they sing about whatever they happen to see.
Note: From the explanation of the 'Field Song', which is mostly an improvisation within the framework of the fixed structure of the verses.

Ex. 5:  **gizu^n-ai-f** *laft gizərə-m.*
Lit.: **Word-what-ACC.** much talk-IMP.
He talks a lot (he is chatty).

Ex. 6:  **huzu-mb ňi** *baitəɹ-m vaju-qǔ əm duru^n azəɹ-m.*
Lit.: **Strength-ACC.** his use – COVN.IMP. finish –(NI.)-NEG. one form behave-IMP.
He acts as if his **strength** was inexhaustible.

Ex. 7:  *śivə dor o-či, jus dazə ňi* **am guru-mb ňi** *bierɣə-m.*
Lit.: Sibe custom become-CC. children base-F. **big folk-ACC.** F collect-IMP.
It is a Sibe tradition that children take care of their **parents**.
Note: *bierɣə* – 'to collect' means taking the parents to their own house.

Ex. 8:  **jiʁa fonq-ǔ-f** *śorʁǔ-m.*
Lit.: **Money hole-ACC.** poke-IMP.
He pokes into the **money-hole**.
Note: This saying, implying poking into the hole in the middle of Chinese copper coins, refers to a greedy person.

Ex. 9:  *χači^n ba-t gənə-m* **aN-ə-f** *unča-m.*
Lit.: Kind place-DL. go-CONV.PRES. **mouth-ACC.** sell-IMP.
He talks everywhere about everything he knows.
Note: 'Selling the mouth' is a translation from a colloquial Chinese idiom meaning 'to spill the beans'.

Ex. 10: *śivə na<sup>n</sup> jiʁa-f oyuɴ ta-q<sup>ŭ</sup>, guanśi-v ňi oyuɴ ta-m.*
> Lit.: Sibe person **money-ACC**. important look-(NOM.IMP).-NEG. **relationship-ACC.F.** important look-IMP.
> The Sibe people do not consider **money** important; the (family) **relationship** is important for them.

Ex. 11: *tər jaq šuda śi<sup>n</sup> **fašq-ə-f** da-ʁ<sup>ə</sup>i!*
> Lit.: That thing absolutely your **rear-ACC**. folow-PERF.
> He has been following you closely! He is so fond of being with you!

Ex. 12: *ɢaɹ-f ɢaš!*
> Lit.: **Hand-ACC**. bring-IMPER.
> Give me your **hand** (give me your **paw**)!

Ex. 13: *ər maf **ud-u-v** ňi taqəm, **ji-v** ňi taqəq<sup>ŭ</sup>.*
> Lit.: The forebear **'how many'-ACC. F.** know-IMP., **'child'-ACC. F.**, know (NI.)-NEG.
> The oaf did know the word 'how many', but he did not know the word 'child'.
> Note: From an anecdote about a young Sibe man who did not understand his grandmother's asking about his children, mistaking the word *ji* 'child' for the Chinese word for a hen.

Ex. 14: *tər **ju nan-ə-i bait-ə-f** bi təňi ta-χ<sup>ə</sup>i.*
> Lit.: That **two person-GEN. matter-ACC.** I just know-PERF.
> I have just learned what happened to **those two people**.

Ex. 15: ***nan-ə-f** yazə-t qafči-q<sup>ŭ</sup>.*
> Lit.: **Person-ACC**. eye-DL. coop in-(NI.)-NEG.
> He is puffed up, arrogant, scornful to people.

Ex. 16: ***nan-ə-f** jav-m iv-m čaʁa-ɴ.*
> Lit.: **Person-ACC**. cath-CP. play-CONV. IMP. likes.
> She likes to catch people and play (to joke **with people**, to play tricks).

Ex. 17: *gənkəndi əm na<sup>n</sup> **uči-0** fierə-m.*
> Lit.: Suddenly one person **door-0ACC**. beat-IMP.
> Suddenly somebody is beating **on the door**.

## 2. Spatial use of the accusative

Ex. 1: ***əva-f** yaf!*
> Lit.: **Here(this place)-ACC**. go-IMPER.
> Go **this way**!

Ex. 2: *tər **joʁŭ-mb** yaf!*
> Lit.: That **way-ACC**. do-IMPER.
> Take that **way**.

## Examples of constructions with the accusative

### 1. The vicarious verb *ainə-* 'to do what'

Ex.: *məzə-i **ňimʁa-f** ainə-mie?*
Lit.: 1pl.incl.-GEN. **fish-ACC.** do what-IMP.
**What shall we do** with this **fish**?

### 2. The verb *azəl-* to behave, act, arrange, settle, fix…

Ex.: *ər **bait-ə-f** məz afš azəɹ-mie?*
Lit.: **This matter-ACC.** 1pl.incl. how settle-IMP.
What shall we do **about it**?

### 3. The verb *zə-* 'to say'

a) *zə-* 'to call, say about sth./sb.'

Ex.: *śivə naⁿ **śigua-f** duNa zə-m…*
Lit.: Sibe person **watermelon-ACC.** (=Chin. western pumpkin) *duNa* **call-IMP.**
The Sibe people call 'eastern pumpkin' what should be the 'western pumpkin'.
Note: An allusion intended as a joke saying that the Sibe do everything the other way round. In Sibe 'watermelon' (Chin. 'western pumpkin') is called by a Chinese word homophonic with 'eastern pumpkin'.

b) *zə-* 'to order sb. to do sth.'

Ex.: *afanti **lüz-ə-f** əči yaf sə-či tə-či yav-m.*
Lit.: Effendi **donkey-ACC.** here go-IMPER. **say-CC.** there go-IMP.
When Effendi's **donkey is ordered** to go here, he goes the other way.
Note: Effendi is the character of a wag from Middle-Eastern folklore, who became popular in the Muslim parts of China. Effendi's donkey is a personification of stubbornness.

### 4. The verb *gizər-* 'to talk'

Ex.: *tər 'hairačuqa min-i bo ɢašan'zə-r gizun-t **yiqam-f** gizər-ɣᵊi.*
Lit.: That pitiable my house village say-NI. word-DL. **Chinese-ACC.** talk-PERF.
By the words 'My pitiable homeland' he **spoke about the Chinese**.

### 5. The verb *učul-* 'to sing'

Ex.: *ər babəli učun-t **düri-f** učuɹ-ɣᵊi, tukumə **ňuňu dɵži-r jaq-ə-f** učuɹ-ɣᵊi.*
Lit.: This lullaby song-DL. **craddle-ACC.** sing-PERF., then **baby enter NI. thing-ACC.** sing-PERF.

63

In that lullaby, they **sing** first **about** the **cradle**, then about the **things the baby is swaddled in**.

**6. The verb *danə-* 'to take care about sb., sth., to care about'**

Ex.:   *tər set mamə-f və hɛmi-mie, nan-ᵊi hamtə-m śitə-r **bait-ə-f** gum danə-m.*
Lit.: That old grandmother-ACC. who bear-IMP., person-GEN. defecate-CI. urinate-NI. **matter-ACC.** all take care-IMP.
Who can bear that old woman, she pokes her nose into everyone's **business**.

**7. The verb *ačə-* 'to meet'**

Ex.:   *čaksə əm **nan-ə-f aš-qᵊi**.*
Lit.: Yesterday one **person-ACC.** meet-PERF.
Yesterday I met one **person**.

## 2.2.5 Ablative

The ablative in Sibe is a directional case with the meaning 'from something/somebody'. In addition to its fundamental spatial use, it often expresses a temporal relationship. The main questions answered by the ablative are *yava-dəri/ɛvi-dəri* 'where from'; *və-dəri* 'from whom'; *aitiŋ-dəri* 'from what time' etc.

### Form of the ablative

In the colloquial language, the suffix/particle *-dəri* is used as an ablative marker. It is etymologically connected with the verb *dərif-* 'to begin'. In literary Manchu the suffix *-či* is used, which in spoken Sibe functions as the lative case. In the speech of elderly people with a knowledge of literary Manchu, the suffix *-či* sometimes occurs with the ablative meaning.

### Use of the ablative

The basic meanings of the ablative are
a) spatial meaning 'from where', 'from what' etc.
b) temporal meaning 'since when'
c) ablative is also used for comparison
d) In the Sibe settlement of *Ičə ɕazn* (Huocheng) and perhaps in other Sibe enclaves outside Chabchal, the suffix *-dəri* is sometimes used as the instrumental.

**a) The meaning of direction – from where, from what, from whom**

Ex. 1:   *təsk ɕor ba-dəri ji-ɣᵊi.*
Lit.: Thus **distant place-ABL.** come-PERF.
Why, you came from such **a faraway place**.
Note: This phrase is often used to appease a shy guest, as a reply to an apology etc.

64

Ex. 2:  *mi-ⁿ amə **jalən-dəri** aɹč-qᵊi.*
Lit.: 1sg.-GEN. father **world-ABL**. leave-PERF.
My father has deceased (has **left this world**).

Ex. 3:  ***neimoɴ-dəri** beijiŋ śidəⁿ ňonǔⁿ dəyi-m zə-r.*
Lit.: **Inner.Mongolia(Chin.)-ABL**. Peking-between sand fly-IMP. say-NI.
It is said that the sand **from Inner Mongolia** flies down to Peking.

Ex. 4:  ***biɹʁa-dəri** ɢaɹ čiči-m.*
Lit.: **Throat-ABL**. hand come.out IMP.
A hand is reaching out **from my throat**.
Note: A funny description of an eager expectation of coming food.

Ex. 5:  ***san-dəri** yaɴk čiš-čiňi gizərə-m.*
Lit.: **Ear-ABL**. wax come.out-CT. talk-IMP.
He talks so much that the ear-wax leaks from the listeners' **ears**.

Ex. 6:  *śi-ⁿ əňi **uva taʁaɹ-dəri** čiš-kᵉi.*
Lit.: 2sg.-GEN, mother flour **sack-ABL**. come out-PERF.
Your mother has just crawled **out of a flour sack**.
Note: From the account of a friend relating her father's joking about her mother who was trying to lighten her dark skin by using white powder.

Ex. 7:  *ər saʁanj-ᵉi ujufunku-ňi ɢor **mamə-dəri** ulav-ᵉm ji-ɣᵊi..*
Lit.: This girl-GEN. scarf-POSS. **far grandmother-ABL**. inherit-CI come-PERF..
This girl has inherited her **grandmother's** scarf.

Ex. 8:  *bi **əňi amə-dəri** jiʁa ɢaš zə-m duɹʁa-qᵘi.*
Lit.: 1sg. **Mother Father-ABL**. money bring-IMPER. say-CI. pass-NP.-NEG.
I have never asked for money **from my parents**.

Ex. 9:  ***irgən-dəri** gəɹ jiʁa gia-m.*
Lit.: **Citizen-ABL**. still money take-IMP.
They were collecting money even **among the common people**.

Ex. 10: *ər učum-b bi oros **mamə-dəri** taš-qᵊi.*
Lit.: This song-ACC. 1sg. **Russian grandmother-ABL**. learn-PERF.
I learned this song **from the old Russian woman**.

### b) Temporal meaning: From when

Ex. 1:  ***ajig ərin-dəri** dønš-kə dønš-kə ɢaɹ o-ɣᵘi.*
Lit.: **Little time-ABL**. hear-PERF.(-IS.) hear-PERF.(-IS.) 'ɢaɹ' become-PERF.
**From my childhood** I heard that so often that I got fed up with it.
Note: ɢaɹ is an onomatopoetic word which implies a feeling of being annoyed or fed up with something that has been repeated too long and too often. The reduplicated

verbal form as '*dønške dønške*' is rendered as NP.+INSTR. (*-ha+-i*) – literally translatable as 'by having been doing' in the Manchu writing system and is used for a prolonged action leading to a certain result. In the spoken language, however, the instrumental *-i* is usually unrecognizable.

Ex. 2: *moɴ-maq banš-k ərin-dəri moɴ gəf laft.*
Lit.: Mongol-INSTR. live-NP. **time-ABL.** Mongol name many.
**From the time** when (we) lived with the Mongols we have many Mongol names.

### c) Comparative use

Ex. 1: ***yoq-dəri** yaqši.*
Lit.: **NEG.(Uig.)-ABL.** good(Uig.).
Better than **nothing**.
Note: A pun based on the parallel structure of this phrase in Sibe and Uighur (Sibe *aqᵘ-dəri śieⁿ*, Uighur *yoq-tin yakši*, meaning literally 'Better than non-being/non-having'). Its humor for the Sibe listener consists mainly in the use of the two most commonly known Uighur words in one Sibe sentence.

Ex. 2: *śiⁿ amə **miⁿ amə-dəri** sə ambu.*
Lit.: Your father **my father-ABL.** age big.
Your father is older **than my father**.

## *Examples of common constructions with the ablative*

### 1. With the verbs *baχ-* 'to find, to get' and *biɛ* 'to look for'

Ex. 1: ***bait-aqᵘ baitə-dəri** bait biɛ-m.*
Lit.: Matter-NEG. **matter-ABL.** matter search-IMP.
He can make a big issue **of nothing**, he finds a problem in anything.
Note: The phrase *baitaqᵘ bait*, lit.: 'a matter without matter', is often used to express the meaning of an 'unimportant thing'.

Ex. 2: *ər bitkə-f bi **ɢuɹja-dəri** ba-χʲi.*
Lit.: This book-ACC. 1sg. **Ghulja-ABL.** get-PERF.
I found/got this book **in Ghulja**.

### 2. With the verb *gəl-* 'to be afraid'

Ex.: *naᶜ **gurh ɢasqə-dəri** gələ-m banš-kʲi.*
Lit.: Man wild **animal bird-ABL. fear-COMV.IMP.** live-PERF.
The people were living in fear of **wild animals and birds**.

**3. Constructions with the words *unčᵘ* 'different (by quality)' and *cᵘa* 'other, the other, another'**

Ex. 1:  *iškʲa-r baitə ňi gum **nanə-dəri unčᵘ**.*
Lit.: Arrange-NI. matter POSS. all **man-ABL. different.**
He does everything in a different way **than (normal) people.**

Ex. 2:  *miⁿ **amə-dəri cᵘa naⁿ** ər baitə-f sa-qᵘ.*
Lit.: 1sg.-GEN. **father-ABL. other person** this matter know-(NI.)-NEG.
**No one but my father** knows about it.

**4. With the postposition *tiuɹgut* (lit., 'outside') – but for, except for**

I was informed about this postposition during my studies and encountered it in real speech, but it is mainly a literary phrase corresponding to the Chinese and the Mongolian parallel forms. I have not encountered it in the material which I used for this work.

## 2.2.6 Lative

The directional case – lative or prolative (Ramstedt 1957, p. 44) refers to a direction from one point to another.
The questions answered by the lative are: *ye-či* 'to where', 'to what'; *yava-či* 'to which place'; *və-či* 'to whom', and others.

### *Form of the lative*

The directional case in Sibe has a single suffix *-či*. It has a single allomorph with most nouns.[14] It is interesting to note the semantic shift with respect to literary Manchu, which uses this suffix for the ablative.

### *Use of the lative*

The lative case in Sibe, as in Mongolian, most often expresses direction of movement, but does not automatically imply reaching the destination. In this it differs from the directional meaning of the dative-locative, which includes the implication of attainment of the goal of the movement: *bo-t gənyᵊi* 'he went home' (and presumably arrived); *bo-či yavyᵊi* 'he set out on his way home'. In Sibe the dative-locative cannot be used to indicate direction (to look at something, to talk to somebody etc).
In literary Manchu, the suffix *-či* functions as the ablative and the semantic field of the lative is divided between the dative-locative and the complex postposition *ba-ru*.[15]

---

[14] A related suffix *-š* (*-si* in written Manchu) is part of the half-petrified directional spatials, e.g. *vie-š* (Lit. Ma. *wa-si*) 'to the west', *di-š* (Lit. Ma. *de-si*) 'to the east', *am-š* (lit. ma. *ama-si*) 'to the north', *ju-š* (Lit. Ma. *jule-si*) 'to the south'. This suffix is apparently also related to the Mongolian directional suffix *-š*, which is used as well only with spatials (*baruun-š* 'to the west', *züün-š* 'to the east' etc.).

[15] This postposition, composed probably from the word **ba-** 'place' and a directional suffix *-ru*, known from Mongolian as *-ruu/-luu*, does not occur in the spoken language. However, a connection with the modal particle *ere/uru* cannot be ruled out.

The lative has, on certain occasions, the meaning of a direction:

a) a concrete direction in space or
b) a focus of sight, speech etc.
c) more abstractly the meaning of a focus, trend, sight (of development, evolution, thinking etc.).

The primary accent is always on the direction at some target, but the reaching of the target, even if it is sometimes clear from context, is secondary.

### a) Signifying a concrete direction in space

Ex. 1: *śivə-f nənəm **girin-či** guri-v-yᵊi.*
   Lit.: The Sibe-ACC. first **Girin-LAT**. move-CAUS.-PERF.
   The Sibes were first moved **to Girin**.

Ex. 2: *tər ərin-t oros **ba-či** vəɹgieⁿ dulu-v-m.*
   Lit.: That time-DL. Russian **place-LAT**. pig pass-CAUS-IMP.
   At that time they were selling pigs to Russia.
   Note: From a tale about a period at the beginning of the 20th century, when the Sibes were the only nation in Xinjiang to breed pigs and became rich by exporting them to present-day Khazakhstan.

Ex. 3: *nan-ᵊi uju ňi **ištə ərgi-či** yila-m.*
   Lit.: Man-GEN. head F. **right side-LAT**. stay-IMP.
   The dead man is laid so that his head points **to the right**.
   Note: From a tale about funeral rites.

Ex. 4: ***bo-či** yaf!*
   Lit.: **House-LAT**. go-IMPER.
   Go **home**!

Ex. 5: *tər **bo-či** yaf!*
   Lit.: That **house-LAT**. go-IMPER.
   Let us go **to** that **room**.

Ex. 6: *əvat naⁿ aqᵘ̊, gum **alin-či** yav-ʁᵊi.*
   Lit.: Here man NEG.EX., all **mountain-LAT** go-PERF.
   There is nobody here, all went **to the mountains**.

Ex. 7: ***bo-či** dianχ̊ua tant.*
   Lit.: **House-LAT**. telephone (Chin.) hit-IMPER.
   Call your **home**.

**b) Signifying focus, way, trend and other figurative meanings**

Ex. 1:  *ər gizuⁿ ju χačin-či bodə-m o-m.*
Lit.: This word **two kind-LAT** think can-IMP.
This word can be understood in **two ways**.

Ex. 2:  *ajigurun-t gia-m zə-r jaqə-f bu-m ojŭ-qᵘ, əɣə-či tači-m.*
Lit.: Children-DL. take-IMP. say-NI. thing-ACC. give-CI. can (NI.)-NEG, bad-LAT.
**wrong-LAT learn-IMP**.
It is not possible to give the children everything they want, because **they will get spoiled**.
Note: The word *əh* is a qualitative noun meaning bad, wicked, wrong etc., but it is often used as a substantive meaning 'wickedness, evil' etc. The phrase *eɣe-či tačim* is an idiom: 'spoiling somebody by wrong education'.

Ex. 3:  *əm χačin-či azələ-qᵘ-či ojŭ-qᵘ.*
Lit.: **One kind-LAT**. arrange-(NI.)-NEG.-CONV-COND. can-(NI.)-NEG.
We have to do something about it (to solve it in **some way**).

Ex. 4:  *saʁənji ñi yiqan-či yav-ʁᵊi.*
Lit.: His daughter POSS **Chinese-LAT**. go-PERF.
His daughter became **close with the Chinese**.
Note: Although the word-for-word translation of the sentence would imply that the girl has gone to one particular Chinese, the speaker meant that she went 'to the Chinese side'; became like the Chinese.

## 2.2.7 Instrumental-sociative

This case, which is used in spoken Sibe, has an instrumental meaning (answering the questions 'by what, through what, by means of what' etc.) but is also used as sociative (commitative) (answering questions 'with what, with whom'). In this, Sibe differs from Mongolian and other Altaic languages, which possess a special sociative case suffix.

### Form of the instrumental-sociative

This case, which has only one form, the suffix *-maq(a)*, has no equivalent in literary Manchu, where its grammatical meaning is divided between accusative and genitive.[16]

### Use of the instrumental-sociative

The case is used in two basic meanings, which may be defined as instrumental (1) and sociative (2). The latter meaning was probably originally used only with the grammatical word

---

[16] In literary Manchu we encounter a particle *aimaqa* meaning 'like' (only in the construction *aimaqa … adali*, lit. 'like … the same', etymologically comprised of *ai* 'what' + *maka*). The lexical meaning of *maka* (expressing doubt, ignorance – *maka ainaha niyalma,* lit. DOUBT what-done person – Who knows what sort of a man he is) does not suggest a relationship to the instrumental suffix.

*əmbat* 'at one place', i.e. 'together', which is no longer obligatory in the spoken language. Questions answered by this case are *ai-maq* 'by what, with what, by means of what' etc., *və-maq* 'with whom' *afš* 'how' and others.

### a) Meaning of the instrumental

Ex. 1:  *manju-i əjə$^n$ čᵒaʁə-v ňi **favən-maq** jav-m.*
Lit.: Manchu-GEN. Emperor soldier-ACC. F. **law-IS**. hold-IMP.
The Imperial soldiers were **subject to** the Manchu Emperor's **laws**.

Ex. 2:  *ajig ərin-t ňimʁa-f **ɢaɹ-maq** jav-m.*
Lit.: Little time-DL. fish-ACC. **hand-IS**. catch-IMP.
In our childhood we used to catch fish **with (our) hands**.

Ex. 3:  ***gənčeɹ-maq** jəm na?*
Lit.: **Spoon-IS**. eat-IMP.QUEST.
Will you eat **with a spoon**?

Ex. 4:  *χazəq guru$^n$ erki-f **čavaɹ-maq** ɛm-mie.*
Lit.: Kazakh people liquor-ACC. **tea-glass-IS**. drink-IMP.
The Kazakhs drink liquor **with tea-glasses**.

### b) The sociative meaning

Ex. 1:  ***moɴ-maq** banš-q ərin-dəri moɴ gəf laft.*
Lit.: **Mongol-IS**. live-NP. time-ABL. Mongol name many.
From the time when we lived **together with the Mongols**, there are many Mongolian names (among us).

Ex. 2:  *ər baitə-f **nan-maq** əm gizərə-r.*
Lit.: This matter-ACC. **person-IS**. PROH. speak-NI.
Do not talk about this **with other people**.

Ex. 3:  *bo gum oros **ajigurun-maq** χ$^ü$as-k$^ə$i.*
Lit.: 1pl.excl. all Russian **children-IS**. grow-PERF.
We all grew up together **with** Russian **children**.

Ex. 4:  *bo-t gənə-mə mi$^n$ **əňi-maq** paraɴ sənda!*
Lit.: House-DL. go-CI. 1sg.-GEN. **mother-IS**. talk (Uig.) put-IMPER.
You can go to our home and chat **with my mother**.

Ex. 5:  ***nan-maq** γav-m čaʁa-q$^ü$.*
Lit.: **person-IS**. go-CI. like-(NI.)-NEG.
She is not too sociable.

Ex. 6:  ***mo-maq*** *kimiⁿ bi na?*
> Lit.: **Wood-IS**. vengeance is QUEST.
> Do you have any unsettled accounts **with wood**?
> Note: A humorous admonition of an older person to a boy who was cutting wood too
> fiercely.

## Phrases with sociative

Phrases with the verb *adašə-* 'to resemble'

Ex.:  ***əyi-maq-ə ňi*** *adašə-m banš-kᵊi.*
> Lit.: **Grandfather-IS. POSS**. resemble-CI. be born-PERF.
> He resembles **his grandfahter**.

# 3 QUALITATIVE NOUNS

Qualitative nouns are those nouns which have been conventionally labelled as 'adjectives.' The qualitative nouns of spoken Sibe, as with pronouns and numerals, form a part of the broader class of nouns, and in their inflection they display no differences from the latter. The main reason for dedicating a separate chapter to them is to provide a more plastic description of the living language by showing their functional and formal characteristics stemming from their semantic features. The term 'qualitative nouns' reflects the fact that these nouns in their basic forms are used as an abstract term for a quality (e.g. 'goodness'), for the designation of a property (e.g. 'good'), as well as the designation of the bearer of the quality (e.g. 'the good one'). While the basic questions of the definition and classification of nouns and verbs of the Altaic languages have been explored in depth, the question of category as concerns adjectival and adverbial expressions inthese languages remains unresolved.

According to G. J. Ramstedt, the 'adjectives' of the Altaic languages do not differ in their morphology from the 'substantives' and together with them form a single category of nouns (Ramstedt 1952, pp. 22–23). A similar view for Manchu is expressed by Zaharov (1879, p. 78), in that he regards Manchu 'adjectives' as nouns.

Other scholars (e.g. Baskakov in: Ramstedt 1952, p. 226, note 1; Sunik 1982, p. 3; Sechenbaatar 2003, p. 55) point out the semantic difference of the adjectives from the substantives (Sechenbaatar 2003, p. 55), as well as their syntactical peculiarities (Poppe 1951, pp. 32–39). They tend to classify adjectives as a distinct word class or subclass of nouns. In many Altaic languages some specific formants, usually recently evolved in relation to a qualitative signification, can be found.

O. P. Sunik, basing his conclusions on his own study of the morphologically rich Tungusic languages, maintains that Manchu-Tungus 'adjectives' and 'adverbs' essentially differ both from the 'substantives' and from each other. He considers as well that the frequent cases of homophony are no more than an external coincidence or a result of conversion which is a common word-forming mechanism in the Altaic languages.

It would, however, be hard to believe that a speaker of the relatively gramatically uncomplicated Sibe language would consider the expressions *qᵘariaɴ saʁənč* 'a beautiful girl', *qᵘariaɴ učulu-m* 'he sings beautifully', and *qᵘariaɴ(f) čaʁaɴ* 'he likes beauty' to be three different categories. If this would indeed be true, it would certainly be mainly due to the influence of the Chinese grammar schoolbooks which are based on Western linguistic approaches.

Thus the Manchu and Sibe qualitative nouns can, to express it simply, be classified as a particular subgroup of nouns, which agree with other nouns in the category of case as well as number,[1] but are marked by several peculiarities on the semantic and syntactic levels (qualitative signification, constructions with a particle expressing a certain degree of quality.) The qualitative nouns occur particularly often in the function of verb-determinants, a function which is not contradicted for other nouns, but is rare with them, and which in addition to their general nominal morphological characteristics (the category of case and number[2]) have some special properties, namely a set of typical derivational suffixes. Qualitative signification is related to the category of comparison, most notably on the syntactical level, but also by the use of special suffix *-qan*[4] (which is, however, used with numerals as well).

### Types of qualitative nouns

Zaharov (1879, p. 77) classifies the 'adjectives' in literary Manchu as 'root' and 'derived' adjectives. He then divides the latter into primary (derived from words of other word classes) and secondary (derived from other adjectives).

The division into root and derived adjectives reflects the fact that two types of nouns of slightly differing nature have been placed into one sub-class of words. While the 'root qualitative nouns' (in Sibe e.g. *am(bu)* 'big, great, much etc.'; *cor* 'far, distant'; *ja* 'easy/ easily, cheap'; *fə* 'old') have virtually no properties except for their signification to distinguish them from other nouns, some of the suffixes, by which 'derived qualitative nouns' are formed, are connected to qualitative signification. Another feature that distinguishes the two types of qualitative nouns is that verbs are often formed from the roots of the derived qualitative nouns, whereas root qualitative nouns never function as verbal roots.

## 3.1 Qualitative nouns formed by derivational suffixes

In his Manchu Grammar Zaharov mentions various suffixes used for forming the attributive forms of nouns, including genitive forms and participles, among the 'adjectival' suffixes.

Besides the formants, which are clearly genitive suffixes (*-i, -ni, -ningge*) he lists:
1) the suffix *-ngga*[3] (which he claims to be composed of a genitive suffix and a component -**ga**[3] and thereforeassigning it to the genitive forms)
2) suffixes of verbal nouns or participles
3) the suffix *-ba*[3], which he assumes to be derived from the noun *ba* 'place'
4) the suffix *-čuka/-čuke*
5) the suffix *-su*.

The suffixes *-ngga*[3], *-ba*[3], *-čuka/-čuke* and *-su*, are related to a qualitative signification. However, the nouns formed by them, like all the qualitative nouns, bear no formal distinctions from nouns in general and can be used as subject, object, attribute and verbal determinants, as is the case with all other nouns.

---

[1]  In Sibe the suffix of number may be used with qualitative nouns in fixed forms taken from the literary language as *sakda-sa* 'the old (people)'.

[2]  The category of number is attested with the qualitative nouns of literary Manchu (e.g. *saisa* 'the good ones', *sakdasa* 'the old people'). In spoken Sibe, due to the generally limited use of the forms with the number marker, the existence of the category of number within the qualitative nouns cannot really be confirmed or denied.

Furthermore he notes suffixes of degree, among which he lists:

1) *-kan*[3]
2) *-lian/-lien*
3) *-linggu/-linggū*
4) *-saka*
5) *-hun/-hūn, -shun/-shūn* (Zaharov 1879, pp. 77–84).

These suffixes are, through their prevailing signification of degree of quality, closely connected to the concept of qualitative nouns. However, most of them form nouns with no morphological distinction from other nouns, and some, especially the suffix *-shun/-shūn*, is used to form nouns like *yamjishūn* 'evening' from *yamji* 'night'.

As concerns qualitative nouns, the fact that literary Manchu probably conserved or even resuscitated some non-productive or dying grammatical forms for the purposes of linguistic enrichment is especially significant. This may explain the major shift from the situation described by Zaharov to that of the contemporary spoken Sibe language.

If we exclude the genitive and participle suffixes, there is only one productive derivational suffix *-N(a)/-ŋ(ə)*, which corresponds to the *-ngga*[3] of literary Manchu, one productive suffix of degree *-qan*[3] and a partly productive suffix of degree *-liaɴ* (< *-linggū/-linggu*). Forms with the other suffixes listed above either do not occur at all, or occur as indivisible roots. In both the literary and spoken languages, however, other petrified expressions, formed by other suffixes than those listed by Zaharov (in particular the suffix *-min*, mentioned by Haenisch 1986, p. 37), are used.

In the contemporary spoken language, we encounter, from the synchronic point of view, several unproductive historic suffixes, most of which had been retained as means of word-formation in literary Manchu. Interestingly, the tradition of using long-lost suffixes to form new words has not been forgotten. Even today the members of the Committee of Language in Urumchi research these historical suffixes to order to explore their use in the formation of neologisms to describe modern phenomena).

Examples of these suffixes are:

1) *-n, -(y)en,*
2) *-lan/-lən/-lun/-lun, -run/-rūn,*
3) *-min,*
4) *-ɣun/-kun/-ʁūn/-qūn,*
5) *-škun/-šqūn.*

All these suffixes except *-n* are complex, their second component being the nominalizing *-n*, which falls away when other grammatical formants follow.

In addition there are two productive suffixes in the spoken language:

6) *-šk* and
7) *-ŋ/-N.*

## Non-productive suffixes

1) the suffix *-n*
Most of the adjectival suffixes are compounds, whose second part is formed by the multifunctional suffix *-n*.

One group of qualitative nouns derived by means of this suffix is formed by attaching it directly to the root. The suffix -$^n$ is dropped when the adjectival suffix of degree -*qan*[3] is attached (*uya-*$^n$ 'liquid' > *uya-qan* 'slightly liquid'). Some of the roots of this group of qualitative nouns are also employed as verbal roots (*ujə-*$^n$ 'heavy' > *ujə-lə-* 'show respect'). Other roots occur in other word classes (*də-*$^n$ 'high', *də-lə* 'above', *də-r-gi* 'upper, eastern'). As is often the case with Manchu and Mongolian, many of these Manchu adjectival roots occur in Mongolian in various word classes: Si. *uya-*$^n$ 'liquid, non-solid', Mo. *uya-ra-* 'mellow'; *uda-n*$^n$ 'slow', Mo. *uda-* 'to last' etc.).

Examples:
*uya-*$^n$ 'liquid, non-solid'
*də-*$^n$ 'high'
*ujə-*$^n$ 'heavy'
*χůdu-*$^n$ 'quick, quickly'
*uda-*$^n$ 'slow, slowly'
*ərsu-*$^n$ 'bad, ill-tempered, terrible, terribly' etc.

In observing the expressions for colours, it can be noted that most of the Manchu terms for colours are formed by the complex suffix -*(i)yan*, pronounced as -*(i)en* in the spoken language. Some of the colour names are, however, formed by the suffix -*n*.

|        | literary Manchu | spoken Sibe |
|--------|-----------------|-------------|
| white  | *ša-yan*        | *śiaŋə-*$^n$ |
| black  | *sahal-iyan*    | *yeči-*$^n$ |
| red    | *fulg-iyan*     | *fəɹg-ie*$^n$ |
| green  | *niowangni-yan* | *ňuŋň-e*$^n$ |
| yellow | *suwa-yan*      | *su-ye*$^n$ |
| blue   | *lamu-n*        | *giŋ-(ň)i*$^n$ |

2) The suffixes -*la-n*/-*le-n*/-*lu-n*/-*lu-n*, -*ru-n*/-*rů-n*
These suffixes are attached to many complex stems of qualitative nouns. The final -$^n$ is dropped when other formants follow.

Examples:
*fiaN(-)qa-lə-*$^n$ 'low'
*fio(-)ʙů-lů-*$^n$ 'short, shortly' (> *fioʙů-lů-qů*$^n$ 'slightly short, shorter')
*sa(-)ʙů-rů-*$^n$ 'cold, coldly' (> *saʙů-r aqů* 'not cold')

3) the suffix -*mi-*$^n$
The affixation of this suffix forms a group of several frequently used qualitative nouns which mostly designate properties connected with appearance, space or consistence. In both spoken and literary languages it is an unproductive suffix and has probably not even been

exploited in the word formation apparatus of literary Manchu. The final -$^n$ is dropped when other formants follow.

Examples:
ɢoɹ-mi-$^n$ 'long' (>ɢoɹ-mi-sχůn elongated, oblong)
śu-mi-$^n$ 'deep'
tø-mi-$^n$ 'thick'

### 4) The suffix -ɣu-$^n$/-ku-$^n$/-ʁů-$^n$/-qů-$^n$

This suffix, which in literary Manchu usually has the form -**hun**/-**hūn** and may be composed from the derivational suffix -**hu**/-**hū** and a nominal suffix -**n**), can generally form nominal expressions, but is most frequently used to form qualitative nouns. In literary Manchu it is a partially productive suffix; during the entire period when Manchu was in active usage, it was employed to form new expressions.

Many basic qualitative nouns in the sphere denoting sensory perception (taste, smell, temperature, etc.), and in literary Manchu, a whole parallel spectre of the 'weak' colours, is formed by this suffix (*fulgiyan* 'red' – *fula-hū-n* 'pink', 'reddish', *suyan* 'yellow' – *so-hū-n* 'yellowish' *niowangniyan* 'green' *nio-hū-n* 'light green, greenish'). In the literary language these parallel colours are used in the calendar. Some of these expressions also exist in the spoken language, but it is possible that the entire scale was artificially created.

Most roots of the qualitative nouns formed by this suffix serve also as roots for other expressions. Some of them are also found in Mongolian. Sometimes (for example in the words *tar-ʁů-$^n$* 'fat' or *oɹ-ʁů-$^n$* 'dry') a verbal stem is formed by cutting off the final -**n** – *tarʁů-* 'to grow fat', or, *oɹʁů-* 'to dry').

Examples:
ɢos-qů-$^n$ 'bitter, spicy', ɢoźi- 'to be spicy'
χat-qů-$^n$ 'salted', χaten 'sharp, burning'
tar-ʁů-$^n$ 'fat, fleshy', tarʁů- 'to grow fat'
far-ʁů-$^n$ 'dark, dusky'
χaɹ-ʁů-$^n$ 'warm, hot' (Mo. *hala-*' to burn, to feel hot, to be hot')
vei-ɣu-$^n$ 'living'
oɹ-ʁů-$^n$ 'dry', oɹʁů- 'to dry'
nar-ʁů-$^n$ 'narrow, fine' (Mo. *nariin* – 'narrow, fine')

### 5) The suffix -š-ku-n/-š-qů-n

This suffix, whose written form is -**ču-hū-n**/-**ču-hu-n**, is, like the preceding one, partially productive in the literary language. This appears to be a composed suffix, whose second part may be identical with the previous suffix -ɣu-$^n$/-ku-$^n$/-ʁů-$^n$/-qů-$^n$. In the spoken language it occurs in several expressions.

Examples:
ma-š-qů-$^n$ 'slim, skinny' (Lit. Ma. *ma-ču-hů-n*)
nien-š-ku-$^n$ 'to stink' – e.g. of fish (Lit. Ma. *niyen-ču-hu-n*)

### *The productive suffixes*

1) Suffix *-šk*
This complex suffix (Lit. Ma. *-ču-ke*, *-ču-ka*) is mainly used to create deverbal qualitative nouns, most often to express the meaning 'proper to something'.

Examples:
*gir-šk*     'shameful' < *gir(i)-* 'to be shy, ashamed'
*fərɢo-šq*  'amazing, outstanding' <*fərg(ə)-* 'to praise'
*gaɹ-šk*   'awful, awesome' < *gəl(ə)-* 'to fear, to be afraid'

2) Suffix *-ŋ(ə)/-N(a/ə)*
This suffix is one of the most universally used suffixes in both Manchu and Sibe. Its basic function is most likely the formation of adjectival and adverbial expressions. In spoken Sibe many qualitative nouns and adverbs are derived, mostly from nominal stems, by this suffix. While most of thus derived forms occur in both Sibe and Manchu (e.g. Lit. Ma. *baitangga* Si. *baitiŋ* 'needed, necessary, useful' < Ma. *baita* Si. *bait* 'matter, thing, need'), some of them are not attested in written Manchu. Some of the examples, moreover, from my materials, may be idiolectic forms or forms created ad hoc (as in the expression *sərəŋ muku* 'spring water', which I recorded only once: the usual expression in literary Manchu is *šeri muke* and in spoken Sibe *səri muku*).

Examples:
*baiti-ŋ*    'needed, necessary, useful' < *bait* matter, thing, need
*mori-ŋ*    'mounted, equestrian' < *morin* 'horse'
*yafhə-N*  'pedestrian, on foot' (cf. Mo. *yavgan* 'pedestrian, on foot')
*yuɹdu-ŋ*  'convenient, advantageous' < *yuɹduⁿ* 'chance'
*amti-ŋ*    'sweet, tasty' (cf. Mo. *amt* 'taste')

Many of the qualitative nouns of the spoken language are derived by this suffix from a stem whose meaning is traceable neither in Sibe, nor in Manchu. Some expressions, like *ɢaɹvaN* 'bad' and *qᵘariaN* 'beautiful' are known only from spoken Sibe and do not have written forms.

Examples:
*ɢaɹvaN*   'bad'
*iča-N*      'proper, agreeable'
*oyu-N*     'important'
*qᵘariaN*   'beautiful'[3]

Examples of some frequently used qualitative nouns:
*śieⁿ* 'good, well', *χoš* 'good,well' – *ɢaɹvaN* 'bad, badly'
*am(bu)* 'big, great' – *ajik* 'small, little'
*ičə* 'new, newly' – *fə* 'old' (for inanimate objects)

---

[3]   This expression, known only in the spoken language, is reminiscent of the Monglian root *go-a* beautiful.

77

*set* 'old' (for animate beings) – *asqə$^n$* 'young'
*ɢor* 'far, distant' – *χanč* 'close'
*ma$^n$* 'difficult' – *ja* 'easy, easily'
*χŭdu$^n$* 'quick, quickly' – *uda$^n$* 'slow, slowly'
*də$^n$* 'high' – *fiaɴqalə$^n$* 'low'
*ɢoɹmi$^n$* 'long' – *fioʁŭlŭ$^n$* 'short, shortly'
*onč$^u$* 'wide, widely' – *narʁŭ$^n$* 'narrow, narrowly'
*q$^u$ariaɴ* 'beautiful(ly)' – *ərsu$^n$/ursu$^n$* 'bad, wicked (ly)'
*χaɹʁŭ$^n$* 'hot, warm(ly)' – *saʁŭru$^n$* 'cold(ly)'
*ujə$^n$* 'heavy' – *vuyuk* 'light', *doɴdoɴ* 'hard' – *uluk* 'soft', *oɹʁŭ$^n$* 'dry' – *ušku$^n$* 'wet'
*uya$^n$* 'liquid, not solid', *yoloq* 'soft, smooth' *fiźi$^n$* 'dense'

colours: *śiaŋə$^n$* 'white', *yeči$^n$* 'black', *fəɹgie$^n$* 'red', *suye$^n$* 'yellow', *niungnie$^n$* 'green', *gingi$^n$* 'light blue', *jam* 'violet, orange', *suɣe$^n$* 'whitish' *fulaʁŭ$^n$* 'reddish, pink', *soʁŭ$^n$* 'yellowish', *ňoʁŭ$^n$* 'greenish'.

### The use of qualitative nouns

It may be assumed that the basic role of qualitative nouns in spoken Sibe is to fulfill the function of a noun-attribute (1). Otherwise, they are used as adverbials (2) and nominal predicates (3).

In addition, most of the qualitative nouns may function as a subject, an object or another nominal part of speech (4). The degree of the potential to do so varies among particular qualitative nouns. The meaning of a qualitative noun used as a noun proper then becomes an abstract term for that particular quality (e.g. *χaj* 'loving, beloved, love' *saʁŭrŭ$^n$* 'cold, chill', *boɹʁŭ$^n$* 'clean, cleanliness').

## 3.1.2 Qualitative nouns in the function of an attribute

Ex. 1: *əm na$^n$ **ɢor** ba-dəri ji-y$^ə$i, vajə-maq gəɹ **ɢor** joʁŭ$^n$ yav-m zə-mə if χ$^u$arən-t bənə-m vajə-maq ta śinaq utu-vu-q$^ŭ$.*
Lit: One person **distant** place-ABL. come-PERF., finish-CP. still **distant** way go say-CI. grave yard-DL. escort- CONV.IMP finish-CONV.PERF-ACT. weeds put on-CAUS.-(NI.)+NEG.
When somebody comes from a **distant** place and has still to go a **long** way back, he need not wear the weeds after the burial.

Ex. 2: *baňiχa, təsk **ɢor** ji-y$^ə$i.*
Thank you, so.much **far** come-PERF.
Thank you for coming such a **long way**.

Ex. 3: *erk dolo-m-bu-mə nənəm **da** mavə-d ňi dolo-m-bu-m.*
Lit.: Liquor pour-CI.-give- CONV.IMP first **original** forefather-DL. POSS. pour-CI.-give-IMP.
When liquor is offered, they first offer it to the **Great** forefather (of the clan).

Note: The word *da*, which is very frequent in spoken Sibe, contains the primarily substantive meaning of 'base, root, essence, chief' etc. Here it clearly conveys an adjective meaning :'original' (*da maf* is the expression for the mythical ancestor of the clan).[4]

Ex. 4: *śie$^n$ ñinəŋ śønji-mə da śeri$^n$ ara-m.*
Lit.: **Good** day choose-CI. ACT wedding make-IMP.
They chose an **auspicious** day and celebrated the marriage.

Ex. 5: *min-t əm **giršk** bait bi.*
Lit.: 1sg.-DL. one **shameful** matter is.
There is something I **feel ashamed of**.

Ex. 6: *jinčüe$^n$ guru$^n$ **sərə** muku ɛm-maq gizu$^n$ ñi əyir muku əm duru$^n$ čiči-m.*
Lit.: Jinquan(Chin) folk **spring(ADJ.)** water drink-CP. speech POSS. flow-NI. water one form come out-IMP.
The people from Jinquan drink **spring** water and so their speech is fluent like running water.
Note: This sentence mirrors the self-consciousness of the internal language diversity among the Chabchal villages. The idiom of the First and Third Banners, known as the Golden Spring[5] (Ma. *Aisin seri*, Mo. *Altanbulag*, Chin. *Jinquan*) is commonly considered to be the most pure and the most correct of all three.

## 3.1.3 Qualitative nouns determining verbs

Many of Manchu and Sibe qualitative nouns are used as well as verb-determinants. In literary Manchu, most of the qualitative nouns in this function take the instrumental suffix *-i*. In spoken Sibe, however, most of the qualitative nouns are used in their unmarked form and the suffix occurs only with some fixed expressions.

### *Qualitative nouns determining verbs in unmarked form*

Ex. 1: *na$^n$ **ambu** cůňi-mə śiňi am bait išk$^j$a-m mutə-m.*
Lit.: Man **great** think-CI. only great matter arrange-CI. can-IMP.
Only with **great** (and courageous) thoughts can one do great things.
Note: The expression 'to think greatly' is connected with the idioms *cůňi$^n$ ambu* 'great thought' (courage, broadmindedness, generosity) and *cůňi$^n$ ajik* 'little mind' (narrow-mindedness, cautiousness).
The expression for 'big, great' – lit. Ma. *amba* – has two variants in the spoken language: The shorter form *am* is mostly used as an attribute, while the longer form *ambu* is used in the function of an adverbial, a nominal predicate or a substantive.

---

[4]  For a more detailed analysis of the word *da*, see Zikmundová 2005.
[5]  The Mongolian variant seems to be the earliest attested version. After settling in this region, the Sibes translated the name into Sibe as *Aisin seri/ aiźi$^n$ sər*. This name is still broadly used, but is gradually being replaced by the Chinese translation *Jinquan*.

Ex. 2:   *ůNaⁿ da-f śieⁿ giŋul.*
Lit.: Elder root-ACC. **well** respect-IMPER.
Show respect to elders (your parents-in-law).

Ex. 3:   *yiɣiⁿ həh śieⁿ **χaj** χⁱᵘaliazůⁿ banč.*
Lit.: Husband woman well **love** peace live-IMPER.
Live in peace and **love** (with your husband).

Ex. 4:   *ər aji maf ičə oruⁿ **χoš** banš-kə-v ňi gəɹ ta-ɣə...*
Lit.: This little forefather new daughter-in-law **well** be born-NP.-ACC. POSS. still
look-PERF ...
The little guy was looking at the **beauty** of the new-married woman ...

Ex. 5:   *ər ašta-f **χoš** sav-ɣə na?*
Lit.: This youngster **well** see-NP. QUEST.
Did you take **a fancy** in that young man?
Note: The expression *χoš sav-*, lit. 'to look well', means 'to take a fancy to something,
to start liking something or somebody'.

Ex. 6:   *gəɹ **əmɣuⁿ** yav-mɛi na?*
Still **lonely** go-PROG. QUEST
Are you still **alone**?

Ex. 7:   *čoqo χůla-χ aməɹ gəɹ emfaləⁿ afqa gərə-qů, tər ərin-t naⁿ usuⁿ **amtiŋ** amʙə-m.*
Lit.: Hen call-NP. after still a while sky dawn-NI.-NEG., that time-DL. person very
**sweet** sleep-IMP.
After the rooster crows, there is still a while before dawn, when everybody enjoys
very **sweet** sleep.

### Qualitative nouns in adverbial function with the instrumental suffix -yi/-ye

Ex. 1:   *χojə-ye ərɣə-m gia-s.*
Lit.: **Well-IS**. rest-CI. take-IMPER.
Have a **good** rest.

Ex. 2:   *ɛmil čoqo bi-či ňilmaʙůⁿ-t **ja-yi** døźi-m mutə-m.*
Lit.: Male hen be-CC. *ňilmaʙůⁿ*-DL. **easy-IS**. enter-CI. can-IMP.
When (the dead) has a rooster with him, he can **easily** enter the *ňilmaʙůⁿ*[6].
Note: The expression *ɛmil* for 'male' (and its opposite *əmil* for 'female') is used
almost exclusively for 'rooster' or 'hen'. The Manchu expressions *amila čoko* and
*emile čoko* are one of the well known examples of how the Manchu language uses
vowel qualities.

---

[6]   The expression *ňilmaʙůⁿ*, designating the 'Realm of the Dead,' is not widely used. Most speakers use the
expression '*yin jaleⁿ*', in which *jalaⁿ* means 'world' and *yin* is the Chinese expression for 'shade, female principle'
(the opposite of *yang*). The word *ňilmaʙůⁿ* may be etymologically connected with the Manchu name *Ilmun han*
(the ruler of the Realm of the Dead), mentioned among others in the Tale of Nišan Saman.

Ex. 3:   *lalə-m bəčə-maq gəɹ **ma-yi** χamtə-m.*
Lit.: Starve-CI. die-CP. still **thick-IS**. defecate-IMP.
After having died of hunger he still defecates **thickly**.
Note: A humorous saying about a 'strong man'.

### Qualitative nouns as nominal predicates

   The use of qualitative nouns as nominal predicates is extremely common in the spoken language. While in literary Manchu such nominal sentences are usually terminated by a particle, in the spoken language the noun is sufficient to form a predicate. The exceptions are the cases when the adjective forms part of a complex predicate with an auxiliary verb *bi-* 'to be', *o-* 'to be, to become' or *zə-* 'say'.

Ex. 1:   *śivə naⁿ ribən gizuⁿ tači-mə həⁿ **ja** zə-r.*
Lit.: Sibe person Japan language learn-CI. very **easy** say-NI.
It is said that Japanese is very **easy** for the Sibe people.

Ex. 2:   *gučᵘ ɢarʁəⁿ ačə-m ji-ɣə-də erkʰi va ñi gəɹ ai **χojo**.*
Lit.: Friend branch meet-CI. come-NP.-DL. liquor-GEN. taste POSS. still what **nice**.
Liquor tastes **fine** when friends meet.
Note: From a popular song sung mostly at feasts.

Ex. 3:   *ər urumči ñi naⁿ banjə-r ba vaqa, tə gəɹ tutduruⁿ **saʁůrůⁿ**, ɢůlja-t tə afqa əza χaɹʁůⁿ o-ʁᵘi.*
This Urumči F. person live-NI. place not, now still that-form **cold**, Ghulja-DL. now sky quite **warm** become-PERF.
This Urumči is not a place for people to live, now it is still so **cold**, in Ghulja the weather has already become quite **warm**.

Ex. 4:   *ai yono, ərai **fərgoško**, śi əmdaⁿ ta-m ta.*
Lit.: What **funny**, how **amazing**, 2sg., once look-CI. look-IMPER.
How **interesting**, how **strange**, have a look.

Ex. 5:   *saʁənjⁱe, śi-ⁿ ər uča aⁿ jazm əm duruⁿ **tarʁůⁿ**?*
Lit.: Daughter, 2sg.-GEN. this waist why pumpkin one form **fat**?
Daughter, how come, your waist is **fat** like a pumpkin?

Ex. 6:   *yamsqůⁿ naⁿ yav-m vajə-maq-ta afqa **farʁůⁿ** o-maq jus daz ñi if χᵘarəⁿ-t gənə-maq duŋlo tiɛv-m.*
Lit.: Evening person go-CI. finish-CP. ACT. **sky dark** become- CP. child-PART. base-PART.-POSS. grave yard-DL. go-CI. lantern light-IMP.
In the evening after everybody leaves, when **darkness comes**, his children go to the graveyard and light a lantern.

Ex. 7:   *śivə naⁿ guanśi-f **oyůɴ ta-m**.*
Lit.: Sibe person relationship(Chin.)-ACC. **important look-IMP**.
Family relationships **are important** for the Sibe people.

81

Phrases like *oyǔn ta-* lit. 'important(ly) look', meaning 'take, consider as important' are formed by a contraction, a process which is typical for spoken Sibe. According to the grammatical 'logic' of an Altaic language the full expression should be *oyǔn zə-m ta-* lit. 'important say-CI. look'. Such elision of grammatical markers under the influence of Chinese grammatical thinking takes place in both written Manchu and spoken Sibe, but is far more frequent in the latter.

### Qualitative nouns in the function of an object[7]

Most of Manchu and Sibe qualitative nouns may be used as nouns expressing either the abstract designation of a certain quality (a), or the bearer of a particular property (b).

#### The abstract designation of a quality

Ex. 1:  *śivə na$^n$ **boлʙǔm-f** oyǔn ta-m.*
Lit.: Sibe person **clean-ACC.** important look-IMP.
**Cleanliness** is important for the Sibe people.

Ex. 2:  *śalaq zə-yəŋ da, **q$^u$ariaɴə-f** čaʙaɴ[8].*
Lit.: Futile say-NP.II. ACT., **beautiful-ACC.** likes.
The expression 'śalaq' (futile) means, that he likes **beauty**.

#### Designation of the bearer of a property

When an adjective refers to the bearer of a quality, it is often marked by the suffix *-niŋ* (Lit. Ma. *-ningge*). This suffix has probably been formed with the genitive suffix *-ni*, and the substantivizer *-ŋ*, which, as the suffix *-h* in Mongolian, is used with an independent attributive expression. This suffix is far more frequent in the literary language than in the spoken language.

Ex. 1:  ***ambu-niŋə-v ňi** gia-q$^u$ na?*
Lit. Big- G.II-ACC. POSS. take-NI.-NEG. QUEST.
Why don't you take the big one?

Ex. 2:  *yiqam-f giaš ta šuda **q$^u$ariaɴ-v ňi** gia-s.*
Lit. Chinese-ACC. take-CC. ACT. completely **beautiful-ACC POSS.** take-IMPER.
If you marry a Chinese (girl), take the most **beautiful** one.
Note: This statement shows a very pragmatic way of thinking. A Chinese daughter-in-law is mostly unwelcome by the elders. Due to cultural differences she usually cannot perform the numerous and difficult duties expected of Sibe women. Here a father

---

7    The qualitative nouns can also function as the subject or other nominal sentence members.
8    Spoken Sibe has two ways to express the meaning 'to like': the use of the regular form of the verb *čaʙaɪ-* (Lit. Ma. *cihala-*) 'to like' is the main method in the literary language. Otherwise the qualitative noun *čaʙaɒ* is used: it is been derived from the Manchu nominal stem *ciha* 'will, liking' by the use of the adjectivizing suffix *-ɒ*, and corresponds closely to the Khalkha Mongolian expression *durtai < dur* 'will, liking' + SOC.

tells his son that external beauty is the only means by which a Chinese woman can contribute to the family.

### 3.1.4 Specific grammatical categories of qualitative nouns

Manchu and Sibe do not manifest the category of comparison in a similar form as is found in the Indo-European languages. They do, however, possess several morphological and lexical means by which the degree of quality of the qualitative noun in question is expressed.

Spoken Sibe has two suffixes, which are used for the most part with qualitative nouns:

1. The suffix -*qan³*, which is both morphologically and semantically identical to the Mongolian suffix -*han⁴*, and to which the particle -*di* may be added.
2. The suffix/particle -*li(aN)*, possessing basic meanings of both comparison and emphasis.
3. Furthermore, spoken Sibe (as in other Altaic languages) contains the means of intensifying quality through reduplication of the first syllable of the root.

For the purpose of comparison of the degree of quality ascribed to two nouns the ablative case is used (see ablative).

#### The suffix -qan(di)/-kən(di)/-qon(di)

The suffix -*qaⁿ*/-*kəⁿ*/-*qoⁿ* (just as in the use of -*han⁴* in Mongolian) is employed in the spoken language for a moderate emphasis of quality (*laf(t)-qaⁿ gias* 'take a little more'). In some contexts, however, it serves to soften an expression or to make it more agreeable (the expression ***yono-qoⁿ*** *sərəvm* 'it appears **funny**, **awkward** to me' sounds gentler as compared to the basic form *yono* 'funny, strange'). Most often, however, this suffix expresses a personal engagement or emotion towards the object of the speech and often it is the only function of this suffix. Its meaning is therefore sometimes stylistically close to the Slavic diminutives. The ending -*di*, according to some informants, comes from the Chinese adverbial particle *de*, which is alternatively pronounced as [di] and is above all a matter of prosody – it practically does not change the meaning of the suffix, except for adding length and emphasis to it.

Ex. 1:  *əraN gizərə-mə bi əm χačiⁿ* **yono-qon-di** *sərə-v-m*.
Lit.: Thus talk-CI. 1sg. one kind **funny-MOD**. feel-CAUS.-IMP.
When people talk like this, I feel **somehow strange** about it.

Ex. 2:  *əm saʁənč fəkśi-maq ji-ɣʲi,* **aji-kən-di** *saʁənč*.
Lit.: One girl run-CP. come-PERF, **little-MOD**. girl.
A girl came running, a **little** girl.

Ex. 3:  ***ful-qůn-di utᵘ!***
Lit.: **More-MOD**. put on-IMPER.
Put on **more** clothes.

Ex. 4: *ənəŋ **ərt-kən-di** bədər-kie, fonqoɴ savəf χůlias-kie...*
Lit.: Today **early-MOD.** come back-VOL., holey shoe-ACC. change-VOL. …
Today I will come home **early** and change my torn shoes…
Note: Text of a contemporary song.

Ex. 5: *doufu o-mə da **yolo-qon-di** jaq, ajiguruⁿ yeɹ əm duruⁿ.*
Lit.: Doufu be-CI. ACT. **tender-MOD.** thing, children-0G. flesh one form.
Tofu is such a **tender** thing, like baby skin.

### Intensifying quality by reduplication of the first syllable of the root

A maximum degree of quality may be expressed by reduplication of the first syllable of
a qualitative noun. As in Mongolian, this method is not commonly used with all qualitative
nouns, but is rather conventional. This echo-syllable is most often closed by the consonant
'v', but other consonants occur as well. The meaning of this reduplication may be rendered
as 'completely,' 'absolutely,' etc.

Ex. 1: *jaqůnč sə o-maq gəɹ **təf təkšiⁿ** yav-mɛye.*
Lit.: Eighty years become-CP. still **completely straight** go-PROG.
Being already eighty years old he still walks **absolutely straight**.

Ex. 2: *əm yavə-r, joʁůn ňi **fak farʁůⁿ**, əm jaq əɹdəⁿ aqů.*
Lit.: PROH. go-NI., way F. **completely dark**, one thing light (is) NEG.
Don't leave now, the way is **completely dark**, there is not a single lamp.

Ex. 3: *čira ňi **yev yečin** tia-ʁəi.*
Lit.: Face POSS. **completely black** burn-PERF.
His face was sunburnt **totally black**.

Ex. 4: *tər jaq **pak paka** o-mə gəɹ **taf tarʁůⁿ**...*
Lit.: That thing **completely low** become-CI. still **completely fat**…
He is **very short** and **very fat**.
Note: Using the intensified expressions makes this statement derisive and scornful.

A high intensity of colour, with the exception of black (Ex. 3), is usually expressed with
the help of the parallel set of 'pale' or 'weak' colours (cf. 3.1.2.3) This way is commonly
used with four colours: *suɣəⁿ śiaɴəⁿ* 'very white, snow-white' (implies purity contrary to *biak
śiaɴəⁿ* 'pale, colourless'), *soʁůⁿ suɣeⁿ* 'bright yellow', *fulaʁůⁿ fəɹgieⁿ* 'scarlet, deep red' (often
used for human face), *ňoʁůⁿ ňuŋňeⁿ* 'deep green' (often used for green vegetation).

Ex. 1: *tər saʁənč hən qůariaɴ, **suɣeⁿ śiaɴəⁿ**.*
Lit.: That girl very beautiful, **whitish white**.
The girl is beautiful, she has **snow-white** skin.

Ex. 2:  *giri-maq čira ňi **fulaʙů$^n$ fəɹgie$^n$** o-ʙů$^i$i.*
Lit.: Shame-CP. face POSS. **reddish red** become-PERF.
He **blushed** from shame.

## 3.1.5 Other ways of expressing quality, appearance, etc.

Certain lexical means closely connected with the meaning of quality or appearance form an important part of the descriptive system in Manchu and Sibe. Of these, the most frequent are phrases with the noun *duru$^n$* 'appearance, form' and with the verb *banjə-* 'to be born'.

### *Description by means of comparison using the noun 'duru$^n$' form, appearance*

Phrases with this word are often close to constructions with postpositions. They are used either for the description of an appearance by means of equation to a particular object, or for the expression of similarity between two or more objects. They are also used figuratively to refer to properties pertaining to the intangible or non-visible, such as qualities and states.

The word *duru$^n$* is used either alone, following the word it determines, or in a phrase *əm duru$^n$* 'one form' (eventually emphasized as *əməli duru$^n$* 'a single form'). When following a verbal noun it has the meaning of a mode of action expressed by the verbal noun (e.g. *si$^n$ yavər duru$^n$* lit. '2sg.-GEN. walk-NI. form' – 'the way you walk').

A common idiom is formed by the noun *duru$^n$* (or a phrase including it) with the verb *banjə-* 'to be born, to grow', which may be translated as 'to look like'.

### The word '*duru$^n$*' used alone

When the word *duru$^n$* comes after a word which it determines, it should in the main be translated as 'as', 'like,' etc. The determinatum takes genitive case.

Ex. 1:  *əmkən ňi **nan$^ə$-i duru$^n$**, əmkən ňi **guryů-i duru$^n$**.*
Lit.: One-POSS **animal-GEN. form**, one-POSS **person-GEN. form**.
One of them has an **animal form**, the other has a **human form**.

### The word '*duru$^n$*' with the numeral *əm* 'one'

The postposition *əm duru$^n$* 'one form' or *əmə li duru$^n$* 'only one form, a single form', has the meaning of 'the same', 'similar'. This expression, analogous to the Chinese postponed phrase *yi yang* 'one form' = 'similar', has fully replaced the postposition *adali* 'similar' hailing from literary Manchu.[9] The postposition is used either with the genitive or with the sociative, often, however, with a zero suffix.

---

[9]  While it is unlikely as to whether this literary Manchu expression, which seems to be a Mongolian loan, has ever been used in the spoken language, the postposition *gese*, probably a Tungusic word with a very similar meaning ('like something') is marginally used in spoken Sibe. Concerning the word *adali*, the influence of Chinese phraseology can be seen in the written Manchu expression *emu adali* 'one similar'–'all the same', as well as in the Inner Mongolian dialects in the phrase *negen adil* 'one similar' conveying the same meaning.

Ex. 1:  *χaʁəji ňi amə-maqe ňi əmə li duruⁿ, qoɹ-maq gia-ʁᵊi.*
Lit.: Son-POSS. father-IS. POSS. **one LIM**. form, peel-CP. take-PERF.
Their son looks **exactly like** his father, as if they had peeled him [off from themselves].

Ex. 2:  *tər naⁿ laft śieⁿ, ai-f gəɹ dane-qᵘ̊, šuda **lam əm duruⁿ**.*
Lit.: That person very good, what-ACC. still care-NI.-NEG., ultimately **monk one form**.
He is a very kind person and does not get upset about anything, just **like a Buddhist monk**.

Ex. 3:  *mo-ⁿ bo-t dači təraɴ **fišk əm duruⁿ** jaq bi.*
Lit.: 1pl.-GEN. house-DL. before such **Buddha one form** thing is.
A long time ago we had something **like a Buddha-image** at home.

Ex. 4:  *əm aqə-r, śiⁿ baitə-f **śiⁿ ɢuňiⁿ əm duruⁿ** iškⁱa-m bu-m.*
Lit.: PROH.-worry-NI., 2sg.-GEN. matter-ACC. 2sg.-GEN. **thought one form** arrange-CI. give-IMP.
Do not worry, I will arrange it precisely **according to** your **wishes**.

### The word '*duruⁿ*' in phrases with verbal nouns

Following verbal nouns the word *duruⁿ* forms a phrase meaning 'the mode, the way' of the action expressed by the verbal noun.

Ex. 1:  *śi-ⁿ tər **yalə-r durum-b ňi** bi ta-mə gəɹ-yᵊi.*
Lit.: 2sg.-GEN. that **ride-NI. form-ACC. F.** watch-CI. 1sg. fear-PERF.
When I saw the **way** you **rode** I became frightened.

Ex. 2:  *ju naⁿ ɢuňiⁿ ňi əm duruⁿ, **iškⁱa-r duruⁿ** ňi adašə-qᵘ̊.*
Lit.: Two person thought POSS. one form, **arrange-NI. form** resemble-(NI.)-NEG.
Both have the same idea, but they do it **in a** different **way**.

### *Description by means of the verb* 'banjə-' *'to be born, to grow up'*

The verb *banjə-* 'to be born' (for people and animals), 'to grow' (for plants), or 'to live' (for all rational beings) is widely used for description of external form, appearance and quality, but also to describe the essence or reasons or course of actions. The most suitable general translation is 'to look (like)'.[10]

Ex. 1:  *go səf həyə ňi **yono banš-kᵊi** ba?*
Lit.: Go teacher woman POSS. **funny be born-PERF.** PROB.
The wife of Professor Go **looks funny** (= **ugly**), doesn't she?

---

[10] This idiom is analogous to the Chinese expression *zhang* 'to grow' and the expression *tör-* 'to be born' of the Inner Mongolian dialects, e.g. Chin. *zhang de piaoliang,* lit. '(her) having grown is beautiful', Mo, *saiḫan törson,* lit. '(she) was born beautiful', both conveying the meaning of '(she) is beautiful'.

Note: The expression *yono* 'funny, interesting' is often used as a euphemism for a negative judgement.

Ex. 2:   *ai ursuⁿ **banš-kᵊye** śi?*
         Lit.: What **ugly be born-PERF**. 2sg.?
         Oh, how **ugly you look**!
         Note: Teasing a grimacing child.

## 3.1.6 Vicarious qualitative nouns and other anaphoric expressions

Various anaphoric expressions form an important part of the qualitative noun system in spoken Sibe. I propose to divide these expressions of various types and origins into three groups:

1) Regular or 'system-forming' vicarious qualitative nouns
2) Expressions with the meaning of 'other, different'
3) Phrases with the expression *χačiⁿ* 'kind, way to do'

### The 'system-forming' vicarious qualitative nouns

The qualitative pronouns may be divided into two groups – those pointing to the essence or internal qualities of an object or an action, and those referring to its external qualities.

*Adjectival pronouns referring to the essence of an object or action*

The most frequent vicaria, which refer to the quality or way of doing something, are expressions derived from the regular demonstrative stems *ə-, tə- mə-* and the interrogative stem *a-* by the suffix *-aɴ*, which is probably itself a variation of the general adjectival and adverbial suffix *-ɴ: əraɴ* 'such, like this' and *təraɴ*' like that', *məraɴ*' just like this' and *mətəraɴ* 'just like that'. These pronouns are usually employed to point to the main, essential qualities of an object, matter or action, and are thus more often used to determine verbs or qualitative nouns. The interrogative equivalent of these pronouns is *afś(e)* 'how'.

If these pronouns are used together with the verb *banjə-* 'to grow, to be born', then they usually refer to the origin of an object or the reason or cause of a matter or action.

Ex. 1:   *oi, **təraɴ** gizərə-m o-jŭ-qᵘ!*
         Lit.: Oh, **thus** speak-CI. become-(NI.)-NEG.
         Oh, you cannot say **such** things!
         Note: Most often a polite reaction to somebody's apology, or thanks.

Ex. 2:   *əraɴ śønš-kᵊi, əraɴ taš-kᵊi, əraɴ saməⁿ o-ʁᵘi, əva-t ji-yᵊi.*
         Lit.: **Thus** choose-PERF., **thus** study-PERF., thus shaman become-PERF., here come-PERF.
         He was chosen **like this**, studied **like this**, **in this way** he became a shaman and came here.
         Note: From an account about the shaman initiation – the lower deities inform the highest deity about the new shaman adept.

87

Ex. 3:  *bəš-k jalən-t əmkə<sup>n</sup> tuɴaɹə-m ba-χən gəɹ əm **araɴ** jaqə-t tuɴaɹ-ɣ<sup>ə</sup>ye.*
Lit.: Die-NP. world-DL. one encounter-CI. get-NP.II. still one **such** thing-DL. encounter-PERF.
After my death, when at last I met one (man), it is again **the same** case as before.
Note: From a folktale – a soul of a woman complains that in her human life she had a husband without a penis, and once again she has encountered the same dilemma.

Ex. 4:  *mi-<sup>n</sup> uf da **məraɴə**.*
Lit.: 1sg.-GEN. fate ACT. **just.such.**
My fate is **just like this.**

Ex. 5:  *mətəraɴ da o-ʁ<sup>ů</sup>i.*
Lit.: **Just.like that ACT.** become-PERF.
It is all right **like this** (this is sufficient).

Ex. 6:  *śi-<sup>n</sup> yavə-r baitə ňi **afš** o-ʁ<sup>ů</sup>ie?*
Lit.: 1sg.-GEN go-NI. matter-POSS. **how become-PERF.**
**What (is new)** about your departure?

Ex. 7:  *tər nan **afše?***
Lit.: That person **how-is?**
**What** is he **like**? (**How** do you feel about him?)

Ex. 8:  ***afš** śie<sup>n</sup>? vəɹgie<sup>n</sup> əm duru<sup>n</sup> śie<sup>n</sup> na?*
**How** good? Pig one form good QUEST.
**How** good is it? Good as a pig?
Note: A humorous reply to somebody's positive judgement about anything. It refers to the fact that the traditional Sibe food used to be pork meat.

Ex. 9:  *tər na<sup>n</sup> ɢaɹvaɴ. – **afše?***
Lit.: That person bad. – **How?**
He is a bad person. **How [is that]** so?

Ex. 10: *məs yav-m na, **afše?***
Lit.: 1pl.incl. go QUEST, **how?**
So **what if** we go?

Phrases with the verb *banjə-* 'to be born, to look like' are often used when speaking about the causes leading up to a specific event or the essence of something.

Ex. 1:  *o, saʁənč, **təraɴ banš-k bait!***
Lit.: Oh, daughter, **thus be born-NI. matter!**
I see, daughter, **this is how it is!**

Ex. 2: *ab-banš-k* bait?
**How-born (how+be born-NI.) matter?**
**What's the matter? What's going on?**

*Vicarious expressions referring to the external appearance of an object*

The second group includes pronouns formed by a demonstrative or interrogative pronominal root with the suffix *-li(aŋ)/-liŋ*, whose main function is the description of a form or appearance by means of comparison. These constructions usually describe objects or characterize actions or matters through comparison. Although the ranges of use of this form and the previous one (the suffix *-aN*) in the spoken language at times overlap, the meaning of forms with suffix *-liaN* always remains more descriptive and points to the external aspect of the phenomena being described. The demonstrative forms are *əraliaN/əraliŋ* 'like this' and *təraliaN/təraliŋ* 'like that'; the interrogative form is *ailiaN* 'like what'.

Ex. 1: *tukumaq ta śi-ⁿ həɣə-f ɢa-m gənə, zə-maq ta **əraliaN** avəv-ʁᵊi.*
Lit.: After.that-ACT. 2sg.-GEN. wife-ACC. take-CI. go-IMPER. say-CP.-ACT. **like.**
**this** order-PERF.
She ordered him **like this**: 'After that take your wife and go.'

Ex. 2: *tə ñi təraN vaq o-ʁᵘ̊ie, dači **təraliŋ**.*
Lit.: Now F. thus not become-PERF, formerly **like.that**.
Now it is not that way any more, earlier it used to be **like that**.

Ex. 3: *śivə naⁿ **ailiaN** naⁿ zə-či, jaləⁿ jəčən-t bəy-i gizuⁿ viri-maq ji-h əm uksur.*
Lit.: Sibe person **like.what** person say-CC., generation frontier-DL. body-GEN. language retain-CP. come-NP. one nation.
**How would I characterize** the Sibe people – they are a nation which have preserved their own language in the world.

### The expressions ɢᵘ̊a and unčᵘ meaning 'other, the other, different'

A special group of reference expressions are the terms for 'different (than), other (than), the other one' – *cᵘ̊a* a ***unčᵘ***. While *cᵘ̊a* other refers to the identity of the objects, persons or matters (a), ***unčᵘ*** (*different*) refers to their qualities (b).

*The expression ɢᵘ̊a 'other, the other'*

The word *cᵘ̊a* refers to the identity of a noun. It functions as an attribute, a subject, or an object and it cannot determine a verb. It can,in the phrase with the determined noun, convey the meaning of 'other', 'the other', 'another' etc., or function as a relative determination, when a distinction is expressed between the determined noun and a whole ('other(s) than…'). The expression *cᵘ̊a*, unlike the expression *unčᵘ*, rarely occurs independently without the determined noun and is not reduplicated.

Ex. 1:   *ər baitə-f cᵘa nanᵊ-maq əm gizərə-r.*
      Lit.: This matter-ACC. **other person-IS**. PROH. speak-NI.
      Do not tell **others** about it.

Ex. 2:   *o-ʁᵘi, cᵘa baitə-v ňi śiram gizər-kie.*
      Lit.: Become-PERF., **other matter-ACC. POSS.** later speak-VOL.
      All right, let us talk **about the rest** later.

Ex. 3:   *miⁿ boiguruⁿ-dəri cᵘa naⁿ ər baitə-f sa-qᵘ.*
      Lit.: My **house.folk-ABL. other person** this matter-ACC. know-(NI.)-NEG.
      No one **except my wife** knows about it.

*The word* unčᵘ *'different, in a different way'*

The expression *unčᵘ* is mainly used in the context of characteristics and properties ascribed to nouns and verbs. In addition to determining nouns and verbs it can stand independently, most often as a predicate. It is often used reduplicated with a distributive meaning 'various', each in its own way' etc.

Ex. 1:   *cᵘa uksur ňi unčᵘ unčᵘ gizərə-m.*
      Lit.: Other nation F. **different different** speak-IMP.
      The other nationalities have **different** words for them.

Ex. 2:   *ter haʁəč gizərərəŋ ňi nanᵊ-dəri unčᵘ.*
      Lit.: The boy speak-NI II. matter POSS. **person-ABL. different**.
      That boy talks in a different way than **other ('normal') people**.

**The word** χačiⁿ **'kind'**

The word *χačiⁿ* 'kind, type' etc. often creates a reference descriptive expression. It is a partly grammaticalized word which occurs in several functions:
1. Used with numerals, it functions similarly as a numerative.
2. In some cases it serves to emphasize the fact that a quality of something is concerned.
3. When reduplicated, or used in phrases *gərəⁿ χačiⁿ* 'all kinds' or *χala χačiⁿ* (a pair of homonyms), it acquires the meaning of 'various', 'varied'. In these two phrases the first member is often elided.

*The numerative function*

The word *χačiⁿ* is used to count mostly abstract entities or objects of one category.[11] Its use implies a qualitative difference of the counted objects, e.g. *ju χačiⁿ bitkə* – 'two different books'.

---

[11] In Mongolian the expressions *züil* 'kind', *yanz* and certain other expressions are used in a similar way.

Ex. 1:  *dači ɢuɹja guruⁿ laft-ton ňi duyiⁿ* **sunja χačiⁿ gizuⁿ** *baʁənə-m.*
Lit.: Originally Ghulja folk many-number POSS. four **five type language** know-IMP.
The people in Ghulja (often) used to know **four or five languages**.

Ex. 2:  *ərᵊ diørgut* **ju χačiⁿ bait** *bi.*
Lit.: This inside two kind **matter is**.
**There are two** (interesting; important) **matters** here.

### Emphasizing the meaning of a quality

Phrases with the word *χačiⁿ* in this function are often used as a determinant for verbs or qualitative nouns. The most frequent phrases are *əm χačiⁿ*, lit. 'one kind' which carries the signification of 'of some kind, certain, in a certain way' etc., and *unčᵘ χačiⁿ*, lit. 'different type', conveying the meaning 'of some other type, in another way' etc.

Ex. 1:  *mo-ⁿ əvat* **unčᵘ χačiⁿ** *gizərə-m.*
Lit.: 1pl.excl. here **other kind** speak-IMP.
Here at our place we say it **differently**.

Ex. 2:  *təraɴ gizərə-me bi* **əm χačiⁿ** *ičaqᵘ sərəv-yᵊi.*
Lit.: Thus talk-NI. 1sg. **one kind** improper feel-PERF.
When he talked like this, I felt it as **somehow** improper.

Ex. 3:  *gul gizərə-qů-mə oɴů-r gəɹ oɴů-qᵘ, gizər-mači-mə əm* **χačiⁿ** *ačəna-m na, ačəna-qᵘ na zəm ɢůňi-mači-m.*
Lit.: Often speak-(NI.) -NEG.-CI. forget- NI. still forget- (NI.)-NEG., speak-INC.-CI. **one kind** agree-IMP. QUEST, agree-NI.-NEG. QUEST say-CONV.IMP think-INC.-IMP.
When I do not speak (Sibe) often, although I do not forget it, but I have **a kind of** feeling, that I do not know whether I am speaking correctly or not.

Ex. 4:  *əňi jai əm śiŋči ji-r śidəⁿ da* **yaya χačiⁿ baitə-f** *əm čiči-və-r.*
Lit.: Mother next one week come-NI. between ACT. **what-what kind matter-ACC**. PROH.-go out-CAUS.-NI.
Don't get into **any** mischief, before I (your mother) come back next week!

### Reduplication and idioms with semantically close words

Reduplication of the word *χačiⁿ* has a distributive meaning of variety, diversity and plurality. It resembles the equivalent expressions in Mongolian (*yanz yanziin*, lit. 'kind kind-GEN.' - various) and Northern Chinese (*yang yang*, lit. 'kind kind', *ge zhong*, lit. piece type', both meaning 'various'). In some idiomatic expressions (e.g. with the word *ba* 'place' or *bait* 'matter') the reduplicated expression is often reduced to one word (*χačiⁿ χačiⁿ bait* 'kind kind matter'> *χačiⁿ bait* 'kind matter') and the meaning of 'diversity' is understood from the context (Ex. 2–4).

Ex. 1:   * əndüri-d ňi ai əndür$^i$ bie, **χači$^n$ χači$^n$** əndur$^i$ bie.*
         Lit.: Deity-DL. F. what deity is, **kind kind** deity is.
         What kinds of deities do we have – there are **various** deities.

Ex. 2:   *yila$^n$ aň-i aməɹ ər saʁənč jalə$^n$ jəčə$^n$ **χačin ba-t** dəyi-mie.*
         Three year-GEN. after this girl world frontier **kind place-DL**. fly-IMP.
         In three years, this girl will fly **all over** the world.

Ex. 3:   *suda **χači$^n$ bait** gizərə-m, soɴů-m.*
         Lit.: Completely **kind matter** talk-IMP., cry-IMP.
         She speaks **nonsense** and cries.

Ex. 4:   *gum **χači$^n$ ba-t** yiqa$^n$ ji-maq **χači$^n$ ba-v** ňi əjəɹ-maq diškə ňi yed$^i$e.*
         Lit.: All kind place-DL. Chinese come-CP. **kind place-ACC. POSS**. occupy-CP. fuel
         F. where-is.
         The Chinese have come and encroached upon **various places (in Chabchal)** and
         where is the grass for fuel (=it has disappeared).
         Note: The word *dišk*, Lit. Ma. *deijikū*, is an appellation for a special kind of grass
         which used to grow mostly at the foot of Usun alin mountain. It was cut down by the
         Sibes in large quantities and used for fuel.

Ex. 5:   *jiʁa bi o-maq **χala χači$^n$** jaq giɛ-m.*
         Lit.: Money is become-CP. **clan kind** thing buy-IMP.
         Only she gets money, she wastes it on **useless** things.

# 4 PRONOUNS

Pronouns in Manchu and Sibe belong to the parts of the lexicon which are particularly close to Mongolian, both from a formal standpoint and by their function. Most of the Manchu pronominal roots can be traced to Mongolian. Similarly, the functional peculiarities of pronouns in the two languages are virtually identical: The inclusive and exclusive forms of the 1st person plural, the absence of the 3rd person pronoun in the modern language and its substitution by a demonstrative pronoun, usually amended by the word 'person' or 'thing', the existence of the 'reminding' pronouns for an object known to both speakers from a previous context, and others.

A peculiarity of spoken Sibe, which developed in close contact with the Khorchin dialect of Mongol, is the pronominal root *mə-*, expressing foregrounding ('precisely this' etc.).

For the purposes of description, the pronouns in spoken Sibe may be divided into three basic groups according to their roots: **personal**, **demonstrative** and **interrogative**.

## 4.1 Personal pronouns

The personal forms of pronouns are:

| | |
|---|---|
| 1. sg.  *bi* 'I' | 1. pl.  *bo/məs* 'we' |
| 2. sg.  *śi* 'you' | 2. pl.  *so* 'you' |
| 3. sg.  (*ər*) 'he/she/it' | 3. pl.  *əs/təs* 'they' |

The pronouns are inflected regularly, similar to other nouns, with the exception of 1sg *bi*, the case endings of which, with the exception of the nominative, are derived from the root *mi-n-*, and 1pl. excl. *bo*, the case endings of which are derived from the root *mo-n-*.

| | **1. sg.** | **2. sg.** | **(3. sg.)** |
|---|---|---|---|
| genitive: | *mi-ⁿ* 'my' | *śi-ⁿ* 'your' | (*ər-ə-i*) 'his' |
| dative: | *mi-n-t* 'to me' | *śi-n-t* 'to you' | (*ər-ə-t*) 'to him' |
| accusative: | *mi-m(bə)* 'me' | *śi-m(bə)* 'you' | (*ər-ə-f*) 'him' |

93

| ablative: | *mi-n-dəri* 'from me' | *śi-n-dəri* 'from you' | (*ə-dəri/ər-ə-dəri*) 'from him' |
|---|---|---|---|
| lative: | *mi-n-či* 'in my direction' | *śi-n-či* 'in your directon' | (*ər-či*) 'in his direction' |
| instrumental – sociative: | *mi-maq* 'with me' | *śi-maq* 'with you' | (*ər-maq*) 'with him' |

|  | **1. pl.** | **2. pl.** | **3. pl.** |
|---|---|---|---|
| genitive: | *mo-ⁿ* 'our'(e.)/*məz-ə-i* 'our (i.)' | *so-ⁿ* 'your' | *əz-ə-i/tə-zə-i* 'their' |
| dative: | *mo-n-t* 'to us' (e.)/*məz-ə-t* 'to us' (i.) | *so-n-t* 'to you' | *əz-ə-t/təz-ə-t* 'to them' |
| accusative: | *mo-m(b)* 'us '(e.)/*məz-ə-f* 'us' (i.) | *so-m(bə)* 'you' | *əz-ə-f/təz-ə-f* 'them' |
| ablative: | *mo-n-dəri* 'from us' (e.)/ *məz-ə-dəri* 'from us' (i.) | *so-n-dəri* 'from you' | *ə-zə-dəri/tə-zə-dəri* |
| lative: | *mo-n-či* 'in our direction' (e.)/*məz-ə-či* 'in our direction' (i.) | *so-n-či* 'in your direction' | *əz-ə-či/təz-ə-či* 'to them' |
| instrumental – sociative: | *mo-maq* 'with us' | *so-maq* 'with you' | *əz-maq/təz-maq* 'with them' |

In the **genitive**, certain speakers, for the most part older people, use the longer forms, which correspond to the pronunciation of the literary language – for example *soňi* 'your' instead of *soⁿ*.

In the **accusative**, the final *-f* is often elided in the spoken language – for example *mim/mim(bə)*.

## 4.1.1 Personal pronouns in nominative

Ex. 1: *bi śi-maq əm baitə-f gizər-š ta **śi** fančə-m ba?*
Lit.: **1sg**. 2sg.-SOC. one matter-ACC. talk-CC. ACT. you be.angry-IMP. PROB.
Would **you** get angry if I tell you something?
Note: A common introduction to a discussion which might be disagreeable for the interlocutor.

## 4.1.2 Personal pronouns in genitive

Ex. 1:  ***mi-ⁿ*** *bait laft[1]*.
Lit.: **1sg.-GEN.** matter many.
**I** am causing trouble.

Ex. 2:  *ərə-i baitə-f bi gum śieⁿ taqə-m.*
Lit.: **This-GEN.** matter-ACC. 1sg. all well know-IMP.
I know **him** well, I know all about him.

Ex. 3:  *ər **mi-ⁿ** jaq na, **śi-ⁿ** jaq na?*
Lit.: This **1sg.-GEN. thing** QUEST., **2sg.-GEN. thing** QUEST.
Is this **mine** or **yours**?
Note: The word *jaq* (thing) is here in its common auxiliary function – to form an independent pronoun.

## 4.1.3 Personal pronouns in dative

Ex. 1:  *śi **mi-n-t** χaj o-š, bi **śi-n-t** χaj o-š, ju naⁿ ojŭ-qŭ na?*
Lit.: 2sg. **1sg.-DL.** loving become-CC. 1sg. **2sg.-DL.** become-CC. two person become-(NI.)-NEG. QUEST.
If you love **me** and I love **you**, is it not enough?
Note: From a contemporary song.

Ex. 2:  *huis guruⁿ **śi-n-t** χaɹdə-maʁa-qŭ na?*
Lit.: Uighur people **2sg.-DL.** offend-NPROG.-NEG. QUEST.
Do the Uighurs not offend **you**?

Ex. 3:  *tər jaq **śi-n-t** maχtə-v-mie.*
Lit.: That thing **2sg.-DL.** throw-CAUS.-IMP.
He does not measure up **to you** (he is not as good as **you**).
Note: The expression *maχtəf-* (a causative/passive form of *maχtə-* 'to throw' - lit. 'to let oneself be thrown back') is often used when comparing abilities, skills, knowledge, and so on, when the speaker wishes to convey the meaning of 'not as good as…'

## 4.1.4 Personal pronouns in accusative

Ex. 1:  ***təʑ-ə-f*** *bi biɛ-m čaʁa-qŭ.*
Lit.: **3pl.-ACC.** 1sg. look.for-CI. like-(NI.)-NEG.
I don't like to ask **them** a favour.

---

[1]  The phrase *bait laft* – 'having many matters' corresponds to its Chinese equivalent (*shir duo*), from which it probably originated. It designates (for the most part, in relation to females) a way of behaviour or a personal characteristic which focusses on too many useless things and futile, trifling details. It is a very common admonition in bringing up children. In this case it was used by a young woman to excuse herself for being slow.

Ex. 2:  *tər naⁿ **mi-m-f** əmdaⁿ jaf-š ta sənda-qᵘ̊.*
      Lit.: That person **1sg.-ACC**. once catch-CC ACT. release-(NI.)-NEG.
      When he runs **into me**, he never lets me go (i.e., hekeeps on talking to me).

Ex. 3:  *ər χaʙəj-ᵊi əňi ňi **śi-m-b** usuⁿ śieⁿ azəɹ-m bi-ɣᵊye.*
      Lit.: This boy-GEN. mother POSS. **2sg.-ACC**. very well handle-CI. be-PERF.
      The mother of this boy is being very nice **to you**.

## 4.1.5 Personal pronouns in ablative

Ex. 1:  ***və-dəri** banš-k jaq gəɹ sa-qᵘ̊.*
      Lit.: **Who-ABL**. give.birth-NP. thing still know-(NI.)-NEG.
      It is even not clear **whose** bastard this is.
      Note: A humorous taunt expressed by my friend's mother, who used to call her little
      dog her 'daughter'.

Ex. 2:  *śi **mi-n-dəri** laft jaq baʙə-m mutə-mie.*
      Lit.: 2sg. **1sg.-ABL**. many thing acquire-CI. can-IMP.
      You can learn many things **from me**.

Ex. 3:  ***śi-n-dəri** χûzuⁿ gia-mɛye...*
      Lit.: **2sg.-ABL**. strength take-PRES.CONT.
      I am using **your** strength (I am tiring you out).
      Note: The expression *χûzuⁿ gia-* "to take strength" comes from the frequent use of the
      word *χûzuⁿ* (strength), which refers to manual labour. This phrase is generally used as
      a courteous expression when asking someone for help.

## 4.1.6 Personal pronouns in lative

Ex. 1:  ***śi-n-či** qᵘariɴ ta-mɛye!*
      Lit.: **2sg.-LAT**. beautiful look-PRES.CONT.
      Look how nicely she is looking **at you**!

Ex. 2:  *fanš-k χoron-t fienš-kəŋə, **mi-n-či** kira-mə gizər-ɣə...*
      Lit.: Be.angry-NP. awe-DL. ask-NP.II. **1sg.-LAT**. squint-CI. say-PERF.
      I asked her angrily, but she squinted **at me** saying ...
      Note: From the lyrics of a contemporary song.

## 4.1.7 Personal pronouns in instrumental-sociative

Ex. 1:  ***śi-maq** həⁿ paraɴ sənda-mɛye!*
      Lit.: **2sg.-IS**. very talk(Uig.) release-PRES.CONT.
      He is talking **to you** eagerly.

Ex. 2:   *tər əyi* **mi-maq** *hə$^n$ śie$^n$*.
          Lit.: That grandfather **1sg.-IS**. very good.
          That old man likes **me** very much.


## 4.2 Remarks on the personal pronouns

### 1) The pronouns bo 'we' (excl.) and məs 'we' (incl.)

The 1st person plural has both the inclusive and exclusive forms: the exclusive form is
*bo* (written form *be*) (a) and the inclusive is *məs* (written *muse*) (b). In view of the fact that
whenever the meaning is clear from context the use of personal pronouns is not compulsory,
the use of the inclusive pronoun *məs* always adds a shade of closeness or familiarity. In
particular, the genitive form *məzəi* is often used as a means to achieve a more agreeable,
sometimes humorous tone.


a)
Ex. 1:   *śim-b baʁə-m savǔ-qǔ-mə afš azəɹ-m-ǔ-ʁǔ* **bo**?
          Lit.: You-ACC. find-CI. see-(NI.)-NEG.(become)-CI. how solve-CI.-become-PERF.
          **1pl.(excl.)**?
          How shall **we** live without seeing you?


Ex. 2:   **mo-$^n$** *saʁənč davɹ ɢošk azəɹ-maš-k$^ə$i*.
          Lit.: **1pl.(excl.)** daughter too awful behave-INC.PERF.
          **Our** daughter became too naughty.


b)
Ex. 1:   **məs** *tə jaq jə-kie*.
          Lit.: **1pl.(incl.)** now thing eat-VOL.
          Let **us** eat something.
          Note: The personal pronoun is not obligatory here, but it stresses the cordiality of the
          invitation to a meal.


Ex. 2:   *tə yet gənə-mie* **məz-ə**?
          Lit.: Now where go-IMP. **1pl.(incl.)**.
          Where shall **we** go now?
          Note: As in the previous example the use of the personal pronoun is not obligatory,
          it only stresses the fact that the hearer is included and thus a more amiable tone is
          achieved.


Ex. 3:   **məz-ə-i** *ər guŋčaŋdaŋə ji-h ərin-də ňi samə$^n$ qoms o-ʁ$^ǔ$i*.
          Lit.: **1pl.(incl.)-GEN**. this Communist.party come-NP. time-DL.-POSS. shaman few
          become-PERF.
          When **the** Communist party came, the number of shamans decreased.

Note: Using the pronoun *məzəi* in this way is a frequent pattern which implies that an object marked by it is familiar to all participants of the conversation. The familiar tone, however, does not apply so much to the object itself as to the shared knowledge about it.

Ex. 4:   **məz-ə-i** *ñimʁa-ʃ gəɹ gia-kie.*
Lit.: **1pl.(incl.)** fish-ACC. still take-VOL.
Let **us** take the (our) fish too.
Note: From a conversation that occurred among several elderly women at the end of a funeral banquet, wondering whether they should take the leftover food home. The utterance was strongly humorous, because the participants in the conversation were aware of a certain inadequacy of what they were about to do, and the use of the pronoun *mezei* stressed the conspiratorial slant of the sentence.

Ex. 5:   *ər bait* **məz-ə-t** *daɹj-aqⁱ̆.*
Lit.: This matter **1pl.(incl.)**-DL. relation-NEG.
This does not concern **us**.

### 2) The 3ʳᵈ person singular pronoun

Whereas in written Manchu the third person pronouns *i* 'he, she' and *ce* 'they' are present, colloquial Sibe has apparently lost these pronouns and in the paradigm they are replaced by the demonstrative pronouns. This resembles the situation in Mongolian, including the fact that the demonstrative pronouns in this function, especially the singular forms *ər* 'this' and *tər* 'that', are rarely used alone. In most cases they are combined with the word *naⁿ* 'person', which makes the expression more polite. In colloquial Sibe another expression, the addition of the word *jaq* 'thing', has became so widespread, that it has nearly lost its somewhat derogatory tone,[2] and is used almost as a regular 3ʳᵈ person singular pronoun. The constricted forms, *əjaq* < *ər jaq* 'this thing' and *təjaq* < *tər jaq* 'that thing', are used in common speech instead of the personal pronouns 'he' and 'she' for people of the same age or younger. However, when talking about elder people, as well as in any situation that requires a certain degree of politeness, the forms *ər/tər naⁿ* 'this/that person' are used.

Ex. 1:   **ər nan-ᵊi** *sə ñi mi-maq əm duruⁿ.*
Lit.: **This person-GEN.** age POSS. 1sg.-IS. one from.
**He** is as old as me.

Ex. 2:   **tər naⁿ** *śieⁿ ba ñi gəɹ bi.*
Lit.: **That person** good place POSS. still is.
**He** has strong points too.

Ex. 3:   **əjaq** *gizuⁿ ñi həⁿ laft.*
Lit.: **This thing** word POSS. very much.
**She** is too talkative.

---

[2]   In Mongolian an analogical expression *ene/ter yum* 'this/that thing', as generally using the word *yum* 'thing' for people, has a pronounced derogatory connotation and is most often used to express slight displeasure.

Ex. 4:  *təjaq hə$^n$ yono gizu$^n$ gizərə-mə čira ňi injə-q$^{\mathring{u}}$.*
Lit.: **That thing** very funny word speak-CI. face POSS. laugh-(NI.)-NEG.
**He** says very funny things without smiling.

### 3) The use of the genitive with certain forms of personal pronouns

Certain complex expressions using personal pronouns are formed by using the genitive case. These are most often forms expressing number, e.g. 'the two of us' in the first- and second-person (a) or in periphrastic expressions which are most often used when characterizing a person or when describing the abilities of a person (b).

a) 1. pl.
Ex. 1:  ***mo-$^n$ ju na$^n$** gizər-ɣə gizər-ɣə-də əri$^n$ oɴ$^{\mathring{u}}$-maq sənda-ʁ$^ə$i.*
Lit.: **1pl.-GEN. two person** speak-NP. speak-NP.-DL. time forget-CC. put-PERF.
**We (the two of us)** were talking and talking and forgot about the time.

Ex. 2:  ***mo-$^n$ yila$^n$ jaq** dači gum əmbat iv-m.*
Lit.: **1pl.-GEN. three thing** originally all together play-IMP.
Formerly the **three of us** used to play together all the time.

b) 2. pl.
Ex.:  ***so-$^n$ ju na$^n$** a$^n$ inji-maq dut-k$^ə$ye?*
Lit.: **2pl.-GEN. two person** why laugh-CP. lie down-PERF?
Why are **you two** laughing all the time?

c) 1. sg.
Ex. 1:  ***mi-$^n$ ər na$^n$** gizu$^n$ tači-m mutə-q$^{\mathring{u}}$ ba ...*
Lit.: **1sg.-GEN. this person** word learn-CI. be able-NI.- NEG. PROB.
I am afraid that **I** am not able to learn foreign languages …
Note: The use of the periphrastic expression implies an external viewpoint, looking "from outside" onto oneself.

Ex. 2:  *mi-$^n$ **ər ašta** paqa zə-či davɹ tarʁ$^{\mathring{u}}$$^n$ vaq…*
Lit.: **1sg.-GEN. this youngster** short say-CC. too fat not …
**I** am short but not so fat …
Note: From a contemporary song.

Ex. 3:  ***mi-$^n$ bey** da morin yaɹ-m mutə-kŭ*
**1sg.-GEN. body** ACT. horse ride-CI. can-(NI.)-NEG.
**I** cannot ride horses.

### 4) The enclitic forms of personal pronouns

Spoken Sibe employs enclitic forms of the possessive pronouns. However, with the exception of the widely used third-person enclitic pronoun *ňi* they are rarely used in the Chabchal subdialect. The higher frequency of their use in the communities outside Chabchal is probably due to the influence of the neighbouring Turkic and Western Mongolian languages, and, in the case of Tarbagatai, the influence of Evenki as well. As well as the extremely frequent third-person singular and plural pronoun *ñi* and the somewhat less frequent second-person singular form *śiñi*, I have also encountered a second-person plural form *soñi*. I have not to date encountered any enclitic forms of the first-person pronouns.

a) The third-person enclitic pronoun *ñi* is an important means in formation of possessive constructions. Apart from that, however, it functions as a particle, which highlights a noun, or separates the subject part of a sentence form the predicate.

b) The second-person singular pronoun *śiñi* is less frequently used. I have noted a high frequency of its use in a family whose members speak the Tarbagatai subdialect.

c) The use of the second-person plural form *soñi* is relatively rare. I have encountered it several times in the conversations of the family mentioned above.

### a) The third-person pronoun *ñi*

1) possessive constructions

Ex. 1:  *χaʁəji-d **ñi** əm jaq bənšə<sup>n</sup> aqᵘ̊.*
Lit.: **Son-DL. POSS**. one thing ability NEG.
**His son** has absolutely no abilities.
Note: Here the enclitic pronoun is used in its original meaning of a third-person possessive pronoun.

Ex. 2:  *təvat əm **bəy ñi** də<sup>n</sup>, **uju ñi** χot na<sup>n</sup> yila-ʁ<sup>ə</sup>ye.*
Lit.: There one **body POSS**. high, **head POSS. bald** person stand-PERF.
A t**all bald man** is standing there.

Ex. 3:  *śi-<sup>n</sup> foɹʙů **ñi** mo-<sup>n</sup> bo-t bi.*
Lit.: **2sg.-GEN. bag POSS**. 1pl.-GEN. house-DL. is.
**Your bag** is at our place.
Note: In this case the enclitic pronoun is only a supplement or completion of the possessive phrase with the second-person pronoun.

Ex. 4:  *ji-v **ñi** həɣə-d **ñi** bu-ɣə, ər maf morin-dəri uvə-rəŋ da **fayiŋə-v ñi** ɢam-maq yav-ʁ<sup>ə</sup>i.*
Lit.: **Child-ACC. POSS. woman-DL. POSS**. give-PERF., this forefather horse-ABL. alight-NP.II ACT. **soul-ACC. POSS**. take-PERF.
He gave **his child to his wife**, and as he was alighting from the horse, (the ghost woman) took away **his soul**.
Note: From a folktale about a young man who conceived a child with a dead woman. Later he stole the child from her and brought it to his wife. The ghost, however, took revenge by stealing his soul.

2) The pronoun 'ñi' functioning as a particle

The third-person enclitic pronoun 'ñi' also functions as a particle which stresses a noun or topicalizes a subject. It is used as well in a distributive sense (Ex. 1). This particle corresponds, both formally and functionally, to the Mongolian particle *n'* and has a similar etymology.

Ex. 1:   *əmkə<sup>n</sup> ňi gəvə-v ňi baijihua, əmkə<sup>n</sup> ňi gəvə-v ňi baiyüśiaŋ zə-r.*
Lit.: **One F.** name-ACC. C Baijihua, **one C** name-ACC. C Baiyuxiang say- NI.
**One of them** was called Baijihua, **the other** was called Baiyuxiang.

Ex. 2:   *gəyə ər bo-d ňi dutə, bi na-t dut-ki.*
Lit.: Elder sister this **house-DL F.** lay-IMPER. 1sg. ground-DL. lay-VOL.
Elder sister, you sleep in **the room**, I will sleep on the ground.

### b) The 2nd person singular enclitic possessive pronoun

Ex. 1:   *baitə-f śiňi iškⁱa-m vaš-kə na?*
Lit.: **Matter-ACC. POSS.2sg.** arrange-CI. finish-PERF. QUEST.
Have you done everything you **needed to do**?

Ex. 2:   *jaqə-f śiňi bierh!*
Lit.: **Thing-ACC. POSS.2sg.** collect-IMPER.
Pack **your belongings**!

### 6) The expression bey 'body' in the function of a reflexive pronoun

The pronoun *bəy* (lit. 'body'), part.n. *bəy-zə* is a frequently used pronoun with a reflexive meaning. It can be translated either as 'oneself' or 'personally'; in this meaning it is often followed by an enclitic possessive pronoun (a). When it is repeated, it may mean 'mutually'(b). It is also used as a polite address in the second person singular (*bəy*) or plural (*bəy-zə*) (c).

### a) The meaning of 'self, personally'

Ex. 1:   *šuda nuŋu-d ňi, isanjᵘ mamə bəy ňi.*
Lit.: Absolutely up-DL. POSS. Isanj grandmother **body POSS.**
On the top there is the grandmother (= goddess) Isanj **herself.**

Ex. 2:   *bəy śiňi ta, jim mutə-mə-š da ju.*
Lit.: **Body POSS.2sg.** look-IMPER. come be able-CI. (become)-CC.=ACT. come-IMPER.
Decide for **yourself** if you can come, then do so.

Ex. 3:   *bəy gizər-maq bəy ňi injə-maš-kⁱi.*
Lit.: **Body** speak-CP. **body POSS.** laugh-INC.-PERF.
**He** talked about it and then he **himself** started laughing.

Ex. 4:   *bəyə-f bəy ňi jav-m mutə-qᵘ.*
Lit.: **body-ACC. body POSS.** hold-CI. be able-(NI.)-NEG.
**He** can not control **himself.**

101

Ex. 5:  **bəyi-də ñi** *da mutə-qᵘ ba.*
Lit.: **Body-DL. POSS.** ACT. be able-(NI.)-NEG. PROB.
It seems to be **due to his character** that he is not able to do it.

**b) The meaning of 'mutually'**

Ex. 1:  *tər ərin-t samᵊⁿ taškieⁿ ye fiškə-i taškieⁿ* **bəy bəyə-f** *coško li va-m.*
Lit.: That time-DL. shaman religion and Buddha-GEN. religion **body body-ACC.**
fiercely LIM. kill-IMP.
In that time the followers of the shamans and the Buddhists were exterminating **each other**.

Ex. 2:  *ər ju naⁿ* **bəy bəy-maq** *hᵊⁿ śieⁿ.*
Lit.: The two person **body body-IS.** very good.
These two people like **each other**.

**c) Honorific address**

Ex.:  *aitiŋ ji-y°ye? –və? –* **bəye.**
When come-PERF. – Who? – **Body.**
When did (you) come? – Who? – **You.**
Note: A common model of conversation, when, for the sake of being polite, the first speaker does not address his collocutor directly, and consequently the latter has to make sure whether it was he who was being asked the question.

## 4.3 Demonstrative pronouns

In Sibe the following pronouns can be classified as demonstrative: *ər* 'this', *tər* 'that', *mər* 'exactly this' a *mətər* 'exactly that', and the interrogative pronouns *ai* 'what', 'which' a *ya* 'which'. These pronouns occur either independently – as substitutes for nouns – or as attributes of nouns. The latter differ from the adjectival pronouns in that they do not stand in for a quality or property but instead for the identity of their determinatum.

### 4.3.1 The demonstrative pronouns ər and tər

The basic pair of demonstrative pronouns is *er* 'this' and *tər* 'that'.

As in Mongolian, these pronouns are regularly declined:

| Case | proximate demonstrative pronoun | distal demonstrative pronoun |
|------|-------------------------------|------------------------------|
| genitive | *ər-ə-i* | *tər-ə-i* |
| dative-locative | *ər-ə-t* | *tər-ə-t* |
| accusative | *ər-ə-f* | *tər-ə-f* |

| ablative | *ə-dəri* | *tə-dəri* |
| lative | *ər-či* | *tər-či* |
| instrumental-sociative | *ər-maq* | *tər-maq* |

The pronouns *ər – tər* are used either independently as noun-substitutes (a), or as attributes of other sentence elements (b). In the latter instances they do not take case suffixes.

*The demonstrative pronouns* ər – tər *as noun-substitutes*

1) the pronouns *ər – tər* in the nominative

Ex. 1:  *ər aie?*
Lit.: **This** what?
What is **this**?

Ex. 2:  *tər ňi o-mə mi-ⁿ ambamə.*
Lit.: **This F.** become-CI. 1sg.-GEN. uncle.
**This** is my uncle.

2) The pronouns *ər – tər* in dative-locative

Ex.:  *ərə-d ňi ju bait bi.*
Lit.: **This-DL. F.** two matter is.
There are two important matters **in this** (= in what has just been said)

3) The pronouns *ər – tər* in genitive

Ex.:  *tərə-i śidəⁿ da əňi ňi iźinə-maq ji-ɣᵊi.*
Lit.: **This-GEN. between** ACT. mother POSS. reach-CP. come-PERF.
**In the meantime** her mother arrived.

4) The pronouns *ər – tər* in the accusative

Ex.:  *ərə-f gəɹ ai zə-m čiči-v-ɣᵊye?*
Lit.: **This-ACC. still** what say-CI. come out-CAUS.-PERF.
Why did you take **this** out?
Note: Scolding a child.

5) The pronouns *ər – tər* in ablative

Ex. 1:  *ə-dəri češ təraɴ gizərə-qᵘ̯ ta o-ʁᵘ̯i.*
Lit.: **This-ABL.** further like.this speak-(NI.)-NEG. ACT. become-PERF.
**From now on** it is not necessary to speak like this (i.e., do not say this).

Ex. 2: *śi-maq χᵘaliazuⁿ banjə-mɛye, ə-dəri čeś afš banjə-mie?*
Lit.: 2sg.-IS. peace live-PRES.CONT., **this-ABL**. further how live-IMP.
I live in peace with you, how should I do better **than this**?

6) The pronouns *ər – tər* in lative

Ex.: **ər-či tər-či** *amčə-m zə-ɣəŋ doʁûr-maq ta ulan-či tu-hᵊi.*
Lit.: **This-LAT. that-LAT**. hunt-IMP. say-NP.II. roll-CP. ACT. pit-LAT. fall-PERF.
While she was running **here and there** after (the hen), she (stumbled) and rolled into a pit.
Note: From the lyrics of a humorous song.

7) The pronouns *ər – tər* in instrumental-sociative

Ex.: *oi **ər-maq** afš mo sačə-mie?*
Lit.: Oh **this-IS**. how wood cut-IMP.?
How should I cut wood **with this**?

*The pronouns ər – tər in the attributive position*

Ex. 1: **ər ju naⁿ** *ai śieⁿ set-kᵊye!*
Lit.: **This two person** what good age-PERF.
How fine did **this couple** become old!
Note: From an account about a ninety-year-old couple who retained their mental vivacity.

Ex. 2: **tər ərin-t** *junguo-i jəčəⁿ balhašnorə-t bi, təva-i jəčəm-f χaskə-t danə-v-ʁᵊi...*
Lit.: **That time-DL**. China border Balkhash-lake-DL. is, there border-ACC. Kazakh-DL. care-CAUS.-PERF.
**At that time** the border of China extended around Lake Balkhash, and the border was entrusted to the Khazakhs.

## 4.3.2 The pronouns *mər* and *mətər*

The pronouns *mər* and *mətər* are composites of the demonstrative pronouns *ər* 'this' and *tər* 'that', and the Mongolian pronominal expression *mön* 'indeed, the same, also'[3]: *mər* ('precisely this, just this' – for objects, persons or events in an immediate spatial or temporal proximity and *mətər* ('exactly that, that same' – for more distant objects, persons or events). Both pronouns are used only in the attributive function.

Ex. 1: **mər** *jaqə,* **mər** *jaq!*
Lit.: **Just this** thing, **just this** thing!
That is him, that is **exactly** him!

---

[3] Sechenbaatar classifies the expression *mön* in Chahar as a copular particle which developed from an older pronominal root. The same seems to apply to modern Khalkha, whereas in the Khorchin dialect the word *mön* seems to have retained part of its pronominal characteristics (*mön hün* 'precisely this person' etc.) and the doubled expressions *mön ene* 'exactly this' and *mön ter* 'exactly that' are particularly frequent. It seems that these expressions were adopted by the Sibe during the time of their vassalage to the Khorchins.

Note: From an account about a woman who in the bazaar suddenly noticed a man who had nearly caused the death of her son.

Ex. 2:  ***mər*** *jiɹʁaⁿ,* ***mər*** *jiɹʁaⁿ mi-m əm diovr amʁə-v-ʁa-q$^{\tilde{u}}$!*
Lit.: **Exactly/just this** sound, **Exactly/just this** sound 1sg.-ACC. one night sleep-CAUS.-NP.-NEG.
**That noise** did not let me sleep the whole night!

Ex. 3:  ***mətər*** *ba-t ačə-m na?*
Lit.: **Exactly/just that** place-DL. meet-IMP. QUEST.
Shall we meet **at the same** place (as last time)?

Ex. 4:  ***mətər*** *ňinəŋ śi-ⁿ amə ji-ɣⁱi.*
Lit.: **Just that** day 2sg.-GEN. father come-PERF.
Your father arrived on **the same** day.
Note: The pronoun *mətər* here refers to a day on which another event occurred that was mentioned in the preceding conversation.

Ex. 5:  *gəɹ* ***mətər*** *ba-t šaŋbaɹ-m na?*
Lit.: Still **just/exactly/right at that** place-DL. work-IMP. QUEST.
Do you still work **at the same** place (as before)?

## 4.3.3 The pronouns *ək* and *səkəi/skəi*

The expressions *ək* and *sk$^{ə}$i* belong to the colloquial language, and should be placed within the context of the demonstrative pronouns. *ək* 'the one', 'that thing' usually represents a subject or an object, while *sk$^{ə}$i/səkəi* 'that', 'such' usually refers to an attribute. The etymology of both is unclear. The form *sk$^{ə}$i* occurs in rapid speech and is more frequent than the (most likely original) form *səkəi*, which is used for the most part by older speakers.

The basic function of these pronouns is to refer to objects known both to speaker and interlocutor (it is therefore a similar type of anaphora as the Mongolian pronouns *nögöö* and *önöö*). In speech, however, these pronouns are often used as interjections or as a means of slowing down the flow of speech. In particular, the pronoun *ək* is often used by speakers when they cannot call to mind a certain expression or alternatively wish to feign doing so.

The pronoun *ək* is used mostly for inanimate objects (a), or as an interjection used in connection with persons and events (b). The pronoun *səkəi/sk$^{ə}$i* is used as an attribute to any noun (c).

### 1) The pronoun *ek* representing a nominal sentence element

Ex. 1:  ***əkə-v*** *ňi ɢaš-kə na?*
Lit.: **That one-ACC. POSS.** bring-PERF. QUEST.
Did you bring **that one of it**?
Note: The speaker meant a microphone belonging to a recorder.

Ex. 2:   *məzə-i **ək** ji-ɣⁱi.*
Lit.: 2pl.(incl.)-GEN. **that** come-PERF.
Our **that one** came.
Note: Unlike the Mongolian expression *nögöö*, the Sibe pronouns *ək* and *skⁱi* are usually not intended to conceal the referent of the enonciation from other listeners. Sometimes, however, this can occur involuntarily. In one incident, a humorous situation evolved because the speaker, trying to recall the name of an American, used the pronoun *ək* as a time-gaining device. It seemed, though, as if the pronoun was used instead of the person's name, which would be highly unsuitable. Later on this joke was repeated many times deliberately.

## 2) The pronoun ek in the function of an interjection

Ex. 1:   *dučiurə-t **skⁱi** tər **ək**, miao bi vaq na?*
Lit.: Fourth.banner-DL. **that.kind.of** that **that one**, temple is not QUEST.
In the Fourth Banner there is (**that one, you know what**) temple.
Note: Here both pronouns are used mainly for the purpose of slowing down the flow of speech to introduce the important word 'temple'.

Ex. 2:   ***ək**... śin-t čimar solo bi na?*
Lit.: **That one**. you-DL. tomorrow free.time is QUEST
(**Hey**) … Are you free tomorrow?
Note: Here the word *ək* is used merely as an interjection to attract the attention of the listener.

## 3) The pronoun skⁱi

Ex. 1:   *ju naⁿ vešhuⁿ fosχǔⁿ ta-m yila-ʁə-də **skⁱi** χaʁəji-f sav-maq gia-ʁə.*
Lit.: Two person upwards downwards look-CI. stand-NP.-DL. **that** boy-ACC. see-CI. take-PERF.
Both of them were looking up and down, and suddenly they noticed **the** boy.
Note: Here the pronoun *skⁱi* refers to a person mentioned previously.

Ex. 2:   *tuku-maq da **skⁱi** fa-i fonqo-dəri əmdaⁿ gul-ɣuŋ da ju jaq da inji-m iv-m.*
Lit.: After that ACT. **that** window-GEN. hole-ABL. once peer-NP.II. ACT. two thing ACT. laugh-IMP. play-IMP.
Then she looked in through **the** window opening and saw the two (children) laughing and playing.
Note: Here the pronoun *skⁱi* does nor refer to any concrete fact mentioned in the previous text, but recalls the commonly known form of the old type of windows in ancient dwellings.

Ex. 3:   *ər χaʁəč da naⁿ-i favən-t døš-kəŋ, arʁ-aqǔ da **skⁱi** χovəi diørgit qotoɴ zə-m da døš-kⁱi.*
Lit.: This boy ACT. person-GEN. law-DL. enter-PERF, method-NEG. ACT. **that** coffin-GEN. inside qotoɴ(ONOM.) say-CI. ACT enter-PERF.

The boy had no other choice but to follow the (other person's) order, and so he entered **that** coffin with a thud.

Note: Here *skᵊi* does not refer to anything that was known previously. It only expresses the speaker's reluctance before uttering the rather disturbing word, 'coffin'.

## 4.4 Interrogative pronouns

The pronouns *ai, ya, yam, yamkᵊⁿ* are the interrogative equivalents of the demonstrative pronouns.

The pronoun *ai* ('what', 'which', 'what kind of') asks, for the most part, either about the identity of a nominal part of thesentence (subject, object, nominal predicate), or about its properties (as an attribute).

The pronoun *ya* ('what, which') rarely occurs in its basic form. It is mainly used as a way of signifying 'which one, which of them'. It usually occurs in expressions formed by adding the numeral *ᵊm* ('one' – before a noun) – resulting in *yam* 'which' or *ya ᵊmkᵊⁿ* ('one' – standing for a countable noun) resulting in *yamkᵊⁿ* 'which one'. While the pronouns *ya* and *yam* are always attributes bound to another noun, *yamkᵊⁿ* is an independent part of the sentence. Consequently *ya* and *yam* are not subject to declension, while *ai* and *yamkᵊⁿ* are declined regularly.

The pronoun *vᵊ* 'who' is the interrogative equivalent of the personal pronouns and it is declined in the same way as the personal pronouns.

### 4.4.1 The pronoun 'ai'

#### 1) The pronoun ai in the meaning of 'what' – as an independent sentence element

Ex. 1:  *aie?*
  Lit.: **What?**
  **What?** What happened?
  Note: Usually used as a response when being called by name or addressed by someone.

Ex. 2:  *ňinᵊŋ **ai** jᵊkᵊ-ŋᵊ?*
  Lit.: Day **what** eat-NP.II.
  **What** did you have for lunch?
  Note: Questions about meal-time form a part of a usual polite conversation along with questions such as 'What are you doing' and 'Where are you going'.

Ex. 3:  *ᵊr **aiɛ**?*
  Lit.: This **what**?
  **What** is this?

Ex. 4: *ər naⁿ tont⁴, **ai** zə-š ta **ai**.*
    Lit.: This person straight, **what** say-CC. ACT. **what**.
    He is very straightforward, when he says **something**, he really means it.

Ex. 5: *čaʁa-qᵘ̊ **vaq aiɛ**.*
    Lit.: Like-NEG. **not what**.
    **Of course** I do not like it.
    Note: The expression *vaq aie*, which may be rendered as 'what, if not so', is a very frequent expression of approval in the spoken language.

### 2) The pronoun ai as an attribute

Ex. 1: ***ai** baitə?*
    Lit.: **What** matter?
    **What** is the matter?

Ex. 2: *ər gəɹ **ai zə-m** ji-yᵖye?*
    Lit.: This still **what say-CI**. come-PERF.
    **What** is he doing here again?
    Note: The phrase *ai zəm* lit. 'saying what' is, as in Mongolian, a common question concerning aim or purpose. Used in a rhetorical question it usually expresses displeasure with somebody's activity and is often used for scolding children.

Ex. 3: ***ai** yiʁam-f ačə-rə-ŋə-f sa-qᵘ̊.*
    Lit.: **What** cow load-NP.II.-ACC. know-(NI.)-NEG.
    He did not know **which** bull he should load.

## 4.4.2 The pronoun ya – 'which' as an attribute

Ex. 1: ***ya** ərin-t ačə-m-ů̊-ʁᵘ̊o?*
    Lit.: **Which** hour-DL. meet-CI.-become-PERF.
    **At what time** shall we meet?

## 4.4.3 The pronoun yam (< ya əm –'which one')

Ex. 1: *śi ərə-f **yam** nanə-t bu-yᵖi?*
    Lit.: You this-ACC. **which.one** person-DL. give-PERF.
    **To whom (of them)** did you give it?

Ex. 2: ***yam** bo-t døźi-m-ů̊-ʁᵘ̊o?*
    Lit.: **Which.one** house-DL. enter-CI.-become-PERF.
    To **which** room should we go?

---

[4] The expression *tont* – 'straightforward, sincere' conveys an important ethical category concerning sincerity, straightforwardness, and simplicity of behaviour and thinking. These characteristics are viewed as positive and as typical of the Sibe people in contrast to cunningness and artfulness, which are ascribed mainly to the Chinese and Uighurs.

## 4.4.4 The pronoun *yamkən* ('which one' – an independent part of speech)

Ex. 1: ***yamkə$^n$?*** *ər əmkə$^n$ na, tər əmkə$^n$ na?*
Lit.: **Which one**? This one QUEST, that one QUEST.
**Which one**? This one or that one?

Ex. 2: *dietti śidə$^n$* ***yamkəm-b ňi*** *tiorʁǔ-v-maq gəɹ daʁə-v-ʁə?*
Lit.: While between **which one-ACC. POSS**. turn round-CAUS.-CP. still follow-CAUS.-PERF.
Note: **Which (boy)**'s head did she again turn during the little while?
From the text of a contemporary song.

## 4.4.5 The pronoun *və* ('who')

Ex. 1: ***və-dəri*** *banš-k jaq gəɹ sa-q$^ǔ$.*
**Who-ABL**. give birth-NI. thing still know-(NI).-NEG.
It is even not clear **whose** bastard this is.
Note: A humorous taunt expressed by my friend's mother, who used to call her little dog her 'daughter'.

# 4.5 Notes on demonstrative and interrogative pronouns

### *1) The demonstrative and interrogative pronouns determining verbs and qualitative nouns*

The pronouns *ər, tər, ya, ai, mər* and others are often employed as verb-determinants qualitative nouns in terms of their position, which in Indo-European linguistics would be labelled as adverbial. Most frequently they specify degree, but other functions are also encountered.

Ex. 1: *o-ʁ$^ǔ$ye,* ***ər*** *məji baitə-də...*
Lit.: Become-PERF., **this** little matter-DL. ...
Do not be silly (and do not thank me) for **such** little thing ...

Ex. 2: *ainə-mie,* ***tər*** *laft jiʁa-v ňi?*
Lit.: Do.what-IMP., **that** much money-ACC. POSS.
What would I do with **so** much money?

Ex. 3: ***tər*** *məji li!?*
Lit.: **That** little LIM.
Only **that** little!?

Ex. 4: *śoro tərə χalin-də ňi śoro yiɭʙa ňi ai lavdo.*
   Lit.: Jujube that tree-DL. F. jujube flower POSS. **what** many.
   Oh, **how** many flowers are there on that jujube tree.
   Note: A verse from the folk song known as *taləi učuⁿ* – 'the field (or grassland) song', a popular song with verses composed in a regular parallel structure. The singer improvises within several simple patterns, one of which is the ending *ai lavdo* 'how much/many'.

Ex. 5: *ənəŋ afqa ai śieⁿ.*
   Lit.: Today sky **what** good.
   Oh, **what** a nice weather is it today!

Ex. 6: ***mər fəkśi-m li!***
   Lit.: **Just this** run-IMP LIM.!
   And **at once** he runs!!
   Note: From a story about a boy who was chasing a bull that had ran away.

### 2) The interrogative pronouns in rhetorical questions

The interrogative pronouns often occur in rhetorical questions used in the sense of a negative or disapproving response.

Ex. 1: ***ai-v ňi*** *ɢajə-mie, ji-ɣəŋ da o-ʁᵘ̈i.*
   Lit.: **What-ACC. POSS**. bring-IMP., come-NP. ACT. become-PERF.
   **What** should you bring, it is enough when you come yourself.

Ex. 2: ***ai*** *gizuⁿ ...*
   Lit.: **What** word …
   **What** are you saying?
   Note: Mainly used to politely decline an apology.

Ex. 3: *o-ʁᵘ̈ye,* ***ai-v ňi*** *gizər-m-ů-ʁᵘ̈o.*
   Lit.: Become-PERF., **what-ACC. POSS**. say-CI.-become-PERF.
   Let me alone, **what** should I speak about.
   Note: In this case the speaker politely refused to be interviewed.

Ex. 4: ***ai ňi*** *set-kᵊye, set-qa-qᵘ̈ye ...*
   Lit.: **What F.** get.old-PERF., get.old-NP.-NEG.
   **What** (are you saying about) aging, you have not become old.

### 3) Interrogative pronouns with the noun jaq thing

The interrogative pronouns in their various meanings are often used with the proper noun *jaq* 'thing'. The meaning of the interrogative pronoun does not change, but the entire expression becomes more emphasized.

Ex. 1: ***ai jaqə?***
Lit.: **What thing**?
**What**?
Note: This question may be used when the speaker does not understand what the collocutor said.

Ex. 2: *ɢazn-t **ai jaq** bie? – moriⁿ jaq bie, yiʁaⁿ jaq bie ...*
Village-DL. **what thing** is? – Horse thing is, cow thing is …
**What** is there in Chabchal? – There are horses, cows …
Note: A question asked of a child who had returned from her grandparents' house. She replied with a list of animals.

Ex. 3: ***yam jaqə-v ňi** gia-ʁʰi, am jaqə-f na, aji jaqə-f na?*
Lit.: **Which thing-ACC. F.** take-PERF, big thing-ACC. QUEST. little thing-ACC. QUEST.
**Which one** did you take, the big one or the small one?

### *4) A specific use of the interrogative pronoun və 'who'*

The interrogative pronoun *və* 'who' is often used in place of a concrete proper name or the specific designation of a person. It occurs when the speaker does not wish to pronounce a name or specific information, or tries to delay its conveyance. Very often this form of expression is used when the speaker has forgotten a name or does not know it, but at times also when hesitating to pronounce a name directly out of politeness. Often a sentence is pronounced first with the interrogative pronoun in order to alert the speaker before imparting the whole of the information. I have noted the use of this expression as well with foreign names, which are difficult to pronounce for Sibe speakers.

Ex. 1: ***məzə-i və** ... arien əm jašqaⁿ ji-ɣʰi.*
Lit.: **1pl.(incl.)GEN. who** … Arienne one letter come-PERF.
Arienne wrote me a letter.
Note: Here the speaker is afraid of pronouncing the foreign name incorrectly. The phrase *məzəi və* ('our who') is often used to imply a close relationship of the speaker and listener to the mentioned person.

Ex. 2: *tuku-maq ta **ər və** døźi-m ji-ɣʰi – anməi mamə døźi-m ji-ɣʰi.*
Lit.: Do.so-CP. ACT. **this who** enter-CI. come-PERF. – Anmei grandmother enter-CI. come-PERF.
Then Grandmother Anmei came in.
Note: In this case it is possible that the speaker could not recall the name, but in any case he draws the listener's attention to the new participant of the story being related by describing the new situation before pronouncing the name.

# 5 NUMERALS

The system of numerals in spoken Sibe is relatively simple as compared to both literary Manchu and Mongolian. While literary Manchu has four kinds of suffixes to form numeral classes (Haenisch 1986, pp. 45–46) and the Chahar dialect of Mongolian, according to Sechenbaatar, has three suffixed and two lexically marked classes (Sechenbaatar 2003, p. 70), in spoken Sibe there is, besides the basic – cardinal numerals, a single suffix -*či*, which forms ordinal numerals.

The manner of using numerals in spoken Sibe calls for a short commentary. In many ways it resembles the situation of most of the non-Chinese ethnicities in China, and in particular the speakers of the Altaic languages. It is probably due to the extreme simplicity, both phonetic and morphological, of the Chinese numeric system that leads most speakers of these languages to use Chinese expressions in everyday speech to form constructions more complex than a single word.[1] Most speakers, therefore, including the younger generation, have a passive knowledge of the single digits up to 9, and at times culturally important numerals such as 15 (the full moon). Generally speaking, people who grew up before the Cultural Revolution, except for the oldest speakers with literary education, use Sibe words for single numerals but Chinese words for more complex constructions (dates, numbers over 10, and counting operations, for example) and in the numbering of almost anything. Speakers who grew up during the Cultural Revolution and later usually know only the first two Sibe numerals *əm* 'one' and *ju* 'two'. Only older, educated and "self-conscious" speakers use Sibe numerals in complex forms such as dates and in arithmetic operations.

Some younger speakers are familiar with some numerals used in proverbs and sayings (e.g. **nadəⁿ** *saʁənč əm čiškə bətkəf jəm vajəqᵘ*. '**Seven** girls would not finish eating one chicken leg.')

---

[1] To give an example, the year 1968, in Chinese pronounced as '*yi jiu liu ba*', in spoken Sibe sounds '*əm miI)an uyin taI) injə jaqǔⁿ*', and the date of the Sibe transmigration to Xinjiang, the 18th day of the 4th lunar month, in Chinese '*si yao ba*' is called '*duyiⁿ biya jǔan jaqǔⁿ*'.

# 5.1 The cardinal numerals

Table of the literary Manchu and Sibe cardinal numerals:

| Lit. Ma. | Sibe | | Lit. Ma. | Sibe | | Lit. Ma. | Sibe | |
|---|---|---|---|---|---|---|---|---|
| *emu* | *əm(kə$^n$)* | 1 | *orin* | *ori$^n$* | 20 | *mingga$^n$* | *miNan* | 1,000 |
| *juwe* | *ju* | 2 | *gūsin* | *ɢoẑi$^n$* | 30 | *tumen* | *tumən* | 10,000 |
| *ilan* | *yila$^n$* | 3 | *dehi* | *dih* | 40 | | | |
| *duin* | *duyi$^n$* | 4 | *susai* | *suzai* | 50 | | | |
| *sunja* | *sunja* | 5 | *ninju* | *inč* | 60 | | | |
| *ninggun* | *ňiŋu$^n$* | 6 | *nadanju* | *nadənč* | 70 | | | |
| *nadan* | *nadə$^n$* | 7 | *jaqūnju* | *jaqůnč* | 80 | | | |
| *jaqūn* | *jaqů$^n$* | 8 | *uyinju* | *uyinč* | 90 | | | |
| *uyin* | *uyi$^n$* | 9 | *tanggū* | *taN* | 100 | | | |
| *juan* | *j$^u$a$^n$* | 10 | | | | | | |

The only peculiarity of the colloquial language as compared to the literary language is the use of the form *əmkə$^n$* (< *əm* 'one' + *-qan⁴* – the suffix of degree). This form is used when the numeral stands independently. When a noun follows, the original form *əm* is used.

Manchu and Sibe numerals over 10 are formed regularly by adding the single numerals to the decimal numerals. When the numeral 'one' is attached to a decimal numeral, it has an irregular form *emu: jůa$^n$ əmu* 11, *ori$^n$ əmu* 21.

In both literary Manchu and spoken Sibe an irregular form for 15, borrowed probably from Khitan, is used: Si. *tofχo$^n$* (Lit. Ma. *tofohon*).

# 5.2 The ordinal numerals

The ordinal numbers are derived by attaching the suffix -*č*, a colloquial form of the literary suffix -*či*. When the numeral ends in -*$^n$* this final -*$^n$* falls off before the suffix -*či/č*.

| | | | |
|---|---|---|---|
| *ujui* | first | *ňiŋuč$^i$* | sixth |
| *jai/jač$^i$* | second | *nadəč$^i$* | seventh |
| *yilač$^i$* | third | *jaqč$^i$* | eighth |
| *duyič$^i$* | fourth | *uyič$^i$* | ninth |
| *sunjač$^i$* | fifth | *j$^u$ač$^i$* | tenth |

The forms of the first two numerals are irregular– the numeral *ujui* 'first' is a genitive form of the noun *uj* 'head (beginning)' and the numerals *jač$^i$/jai* 'second' correspond to the irregular literary forms *jači/jai*.

## 5.3 The idiomatic use of numerals

Due to their specific meaning and symbolism, numerals are, in many languages, present in various idioms. The situation in spoken Sibe has changed somewhat as Chinese numerals are frequently used instead of the Sibe numerals. There still exist, however, some idioms using Sibe numerals.

When meanings such as 'both of us' or 'the three of us' are conveyed, the possessive (genitive) forms of personal pronouns are used, e.g. *mo$^n$ ju na$^n$*, lit. 'our two people', 'both of us'; *so$^n$ yila$^n$ na$^n$*, lit. 'the three of us'.

In the linguistic milieu of Northern China the figurative use of the numeral 2, meaning 'a few', is common: *ju ňinəŋ*, lit. 'two days' – 'a couple of days'.

In addition, a term for the most important national festival – 'The Day of Arrival', has retained its original form *duyi$^n$ bia j$^u$anjaqŭ$^n$*, lit. 'four month eighteen' – 'the eighteenth day of the fourth lunar month'.

In everyday speech, however, Chinese numerals are used to express dates.

A literary form of the numeral 7 (*nadan* instead of the colloquial form *nadə$^n$*) is used to designate the seven-day period after the death of a person, a period important for funeral rituals.

# 6 SPATIALS

Spatials are a group of nominal expressions through which speakers orient themselves in space. Spatials, as a part of overall systems of spatial orientation among the peoples of Inner Asia, have been subject to several recent studies.[1]

In written Manchu and spoken Sibe, as in Mongolian, this nominal subclass is characterized by a limited number of roots and a special set of suffixes is used specifically for the expression of spatial relationships. Some of the spatials are also used figuratively to express time relationships.

As a result of their linguistic development one group of the originally inflected suffixes tends to behave as derivational suffixes, often forming stems to which common nominal case suffixes are added. These features, together with the defectivity of the paradigm, present a picture of an archaic, now only partially productive system.

Spatials occur in all syntactical positions that may by occupied by nouns, of which the most frequent function are those of attributes of nouns, determinants of verbs and postpositions.

To analyse the Manchu-Sibe spatial system we have to turn first to written Manchu.

## 6.1 The spatial system in written Manchu

### 6.1.1 The spatial roots in written Manchu

The main roots, to which this set of suffixes may be attached to form spatial expressions, are:

*am(a)*- north, back
*ju*-    south, front
*wa*-    downwards, east
*we*-    upwards
*de*-    above, west
*feji*-  below, down
*do*-    inside
*ca*-    behind, further
*tu*-    out(side)

---

[1]  See Kapišovská 2003, as well as *Études Mongoles etsibériennes centrasiatiques et tibétaines* 2005–2006.

Some of these roots are found as roots of verbs with the meaning of 'movement in a particular direction'. The derivational verbal suffix is -*si*/-*ci*.

***do-si*-** to enter
***tu-ci*-** to go out
***wa-si*-** to descend
***we-si*-** to ascend

## 6.1.2 The spatial suffixes in written Manchu

The main suffixes used with spatials are -***la***$^3$, (-***ri***), -***rgi*** a -***si***. The suffix -***r-gi*** may be divided into ***r*** + ***gi***, of which -***r*** is possibly identical with the locative suffix -ri and related to the Mongolian ancient suffix -***r***, while -***gi*** is related to the Mongolian (and generally Altaic) adverbializer -**ki** (**h/h**" in Modern Khalkha).

Listed below are the combinations of roots and suffixes used in written Manchu:

| root | -*la*$^3$ | -*ri* | -*r-gi* | -*si* |
|------|-----------|-------|---------|-------|
| *ama-* | *ama-la* | | *ama-r-gi* | *ama-si* |
| *ju-* | | *ju-le-ri* | *ju-le-r-gi* | *ju-le-si* |
| *wa-* | *wa-la* | | *wa-r-gi,* | *wa-si* |
| *we-* | | | | *we-si* |
| *de-* | *de-le* | *de-le-ri* | *de-r-gi* | *de-le-si, de-si* |
| *do-* | *do-lo* | *do-lo-ri* | *do-r-gi* | *do-si* |
| *tu-* | *tu-le* | | *tu-le-r-gi* | |
| *oi* | *oi-lo* | *oi-lo-ri* | *oi-lo-r-gi* | |
| *ca* | *ca-la* | | *ca-r-gi* | *ca-si* |
| *feji-* | *feji-le* | | *feje-r-gi* | |

Besides these forms, which are derived regularly from the roots through a set of special suffixes, we can find a number of expressions derived from secondary stems through regular case suffixes. The stems are petrified spatial forms and the suffixes attached to them are the basic case suffixes (-*i*,-*be*, -*de*, -*ci* in written Manchu texts and -***deri*** in the Sibe written texts). In most cases the stems behaving in this way are formed by the suffix -***r-gi***.

Examples of expressions formed in this way, which I have encountered both in classical Manchu and Sibe written texts, are:

**Genitive**: *ama-la-i* (temp.) of the later (one)
**Dative-locative**: *ama-r-gi-**de*** 'in the north, on the northern side' etc., *julergi-**de*** 'in front, on the front/southern side', etc., *tulergi-**de*** 'outside', *dorgi-**de*** 'inside' *dele-**de*** 'above'
**Ablative -*ci*** (written Manchu): *dergi-**ci*** from above, *dorgi-**ci*** from inside
**Ablative -*deri*** (written Sibe): *tulergi-**deri*** from outside
**Accusative**: *dorgi-**be*** the inside (Acc)

## 6.1.3 Meaning and use of the Manchu spatial suffixes

The meaning of the spatial suffixes, though somewhat unclear, can be roughly characterized as locational (*-la³*, *-ri*), directional (*-si*) and attributive (*-r-gi*). In the Manchu sentence structure the spatials function mostly as verb-determinants(*la³*, *-ri*, *-si*) or as attributes of nouns (*r-gi*).

### The suffix *-la³*

Forms with this suffix are used mainly as verbal determinants. This suffix designates static relative location (for example, outside, inside, at the front side/back side), but may be, according to the context, understood in the lative meaning as a goal of the movement being expressed.

In its existing forms, the suffix -ri is added only to a stem extended by the suffix *-la³ amala* (*juleri amala* – 'one after another'), *jule-* (petrified as a stem), *dolo* 'inside' *dele* 'above', *fejile* 'under', *tule* 'outside'.

Ex. 1:   *age deo juwe niyalma **juleri amala** yabu-fi* ...
　　　　Lit.: Elder brother younger brother two person **in-front at-the-back** walk-CP ...
　　　　The two brothers were going **one after another**...

Ex. 2:   *gaitai **alin-i fejile** emu moo saci-re jilgan be donji-mbi* .
　　　　Lit.: Suddenly **mountain-GEN. below** one wood chop-NI. sound-ACC. hear-IMP.
　　　　Suddenly she could hear a sound of wood being cut from **beneath the mountain**.

Ex. 3:   *yeye aifini **duka-i tule** aliya-me te-hebi*
　　　　Lit.: Grandfather long-time **gate-GEN. outside** wait-CI. sit-PERF.
　　　　Grandfather has already been sitting **outside the gate** and waiting.

Ex. 4:   ***mini dolo** gūni-me waji-ha.*
　　　　Lit.: **My inside** think-CI. finish-NP.
　　　　I have found it (**inside**).

Ex. 5:   ***dele** emu biraki moo sinda-habi.*
　　　　Lit.: **Above** one rolling.pin wood put-PERF.
　　　　**Above** there lies a rolling-pin.

### The suffix *-ri*

The meaning and use of this suffix is virtually the same as that of the suffix *-la³*. In the attested forms it occurs only after stems extended by *la³* (*juleri* 'on the front/southern side', *dolori* 'inside', *oilori* 'on the outer side').

Ex. 1:   ***duka-i juleri** emu da amba hailan bi-mbi.*
　　　　Lit.: **Gate-GEN. in front** one NUM. big tree be-IMP.
　　　　**In front of the gate** there is a big tree.

117

Ex. 2: *siyan-i hafan ilan či golmin silenggi aldabu-fi **dolori guni-me**...*
Lit.: Prefecture-GEN. chief three inch long slaver loose-CP. **inside think-CI** ...
The Prefecture governor lost a three-inch spittle and **thought to himself** ...

Ex. 3: *aika hutu waka o-ci mini **juleri** tuci-me jio!*
Lit.: If ghost not be-CC. my in front **go out-CI. come-IMPER.**
If you are not a ghost, appear here **in front of me**.

### The suffix *-r-gi*

The complex suffix *-r-gi* is probably formed by the locative *-r* and the nominalizing suffix *-gi*.

The suffix *-r-gi* expresses a static location as well, but is used mainly to determine nominal expressions. Sometimes the form with *-rgi* is followed by a genitive suffix and thus seems to be used in place of the expression *-rgi ba* 'place in a certain location' (Ex. 2), **amargi** 'northern', **julergi** 'southern', **dorgi** 'internal', **tulergi** 'external'.

Ex. 1: *mini boo o-ci **amargi siyan-i julergi duka-i** giya-de tehe.*
Lit.: My house to become-CC. **northern prefecture-GEN. southern gate-GEN.** street-DL. sit-PERF.
My home is in the street of **the southern gate of the northern prefecture**.

Ex. 2: ***duka-i julergi-i** amba hailan-de doo-ha.*
Lit.: **Gate-GEN. in front of-GEN.** big tree-DL. land-NP.
He sat on the big tree in **front of the gate**.
Note: Here the use of a genitive suffix (*julergi-i*) suggests that the word *julergi* is used instead of *julergi ba* – 'the space in front'.

Ex. 3: *abka-i **fejergi** geren hacin ucun-be bahana-mbi.*
Lit.: **Heaven-GEN. below** all kind song-ACC. know-IMP.
He can sing all kinds of songs which exist in the world (lit. **below the Heavens**).
Note: Here the genitive suffix should probably be used too, but seems to be have been omitted, as is often the case.

Ex. 4: *bi **julergi** alin-de toro gaji-me gene-ki.*
Lit.: I **southern mountain-DL.** peach bring-CI. go-VOL.
I will go to the **Southern mountains** to bring the peach(es).

### The suffix *-si*

This is a lative suffix which exclusively designates the direction of a movement. It is thus always used as a verb-determinant.

Ex. 1: ***desi wasi** tuwa-ci emu hūwaita-ra jaka be baha-r-kū.*
Lit.: **Westwards eastwards** look-COND. one tie-NI. thing-ACC. find-NI.-NEG.
She looked **in all direction**s, but could not find anything to tie (them).

The linguistic apparatus for orientation in space in written Manchu is formed by several expressions which lack the morphological peculiarities of spatials. These expressions are mainly the words for lateral orientation *iči* 'right' and *hashū* 'left', and expressions for location in relative proximity: *dalbade* 'beside, aside, next to', *dade* 'by, near, next to', *jakade* 'close to, next to', etc.

## 6.2 The spatial system in spoken Sibe

### 6.2.1 Spatial roots in spoken Sibe

In the spoken Sibe language most of the roots correspond to those of written Manchu with specific phonetic changes:

*am-/ɛm-* back, north
*ju-* front, south
*vie-* east
*də-/di-* west
*fəji-* beneath, under
*dø-* inside
*če-* over, further
*nuŋ-* above

The main differences as compared to written Manchu are as follows:
1) The semantic field of 'above' is fully taken over by the root *nuŋ* (written Manchu *ninggu*), which tends to behave as a spatial (I have encountered the forms *nuŋś* and *nuŋurh* in the spoken language). The root *də-* then remains only as a desigation for '*west*'.

2) The expressions for east and west are, for reasons that are not sufficiently clear, used inversely: While in written Manchu *dergi* means 'eastern' and *wargi* means 'western', in spoken Sibe the *dirh* is used for 'western' and *vierh* for 'eastern'. In Sibe written texts, moreover, the use of the two terms varies according to the cognition of the author.

### 6.2.2 Spatial suffixes in spoken Sibe

The system of Sibe spatial suffixes presents a slightly different picture than that of written Manchu.

The suffix *-rh*, apparently the oral form of the complex suffix *-r-gi*, tends to behave as a regular nominal stem, which designates a point or direction in space, and to which regular case suffixes are added, forming a locational and directional determination. This suffix has an alternative form *-lh* which occurs only with the stems *ju-* > *juɹh* (Lit. Ma. *julergi*) and *ɛl-* > *ɛl'h* (Lit. Ma. *oilorgi*), which can probably be explained as a result of elision.

The suffixes *-la³* and *-ri* do not occur in the spoken language and are replaced in their function by the forms mentioned above *-rh + case suffixes*. (E.g. Lit. Ma. *dukai juleri* – S. *duqa(i) juɹyut* 'in front of the gate'.)

Unlike *-rh*, the suffix *-s'*, an oral form of *-si*, retains its productivity in the spatial system as well as its original function as a verb-determinant.

## 6.2.3 The use of Sibe spatials

Concerning the semantic fields of spatials, in Sibe, as in Manchu, there are two basic and related spheres of use – *relative positions* in space and *cardinal points*.

### Expressions for cardinal points

The expressions for cardinal points require several comments. While in written Manchu they essentially form a regular part of the spatials, in spoken Sibe it seems reasonable to view them as aseparate sub-group.

The roots of the Sibe cardinal points are as follows:
*ju-* south, southern side
*ɛmi-* north, northern side
*vie-* west
*di-* east

The expressions for *north* and *south* are identical with the expressions for *back* and *front* respectively, while the expressions for *east* and *west* are etymologically connected with the directions *up* and *down* – the western with the root *di-* 'upwards, above' and the eastern with the root *vie-* 'downwards, below'. While the roots for north and south are also used for back and front, the roots for east and west have lost their original meanings and are used only for the cardinal points. As mentioned above, the meaning of the expressions for east and west is reversed as against written Manchu.

### Expressions for relative positions in space

*fəji- fəjə-* below, under
*nuŋ-* above
*dø-* inside
*ɛ-* outside
*čɛ-* behind, further

#### The suffix *-rh* (*lh*) (*Spatial nouns*)

Expressions formed by this suffix may be designated as *spatial nouns*. Their nominal character results from the essentially attributive use of the Manchu form *-r-gi*. Case suffixes are added to the basic form of spatial nouns, creating either attributive expressions (genitive) or adverbial determinations (dative-locative, ablative, lative, accusative).

### Spatial nouns in the genitive

Spatial nouns in the genitive are used to determine nouns. In the spoken language the genitive often has a zero suffix.

Ex. 1:  *ər mamə da juɹh qarən-t aɹvən bi-yᵊi.*
Lit.: This gandmother ACT. **southern** fortress-DL. duty be-PERF.
This old woman used to work in the **southern** fortress.

Ex. 2:  *təs ňi o-mə **dirh vierh bo** bi-yᵊi.*
Lit.: They F. become-CI. **west east house** be-PERF.
They were neighbors (their houses were next to each other).

Ex. 3:  ***tais nuɳu-i baitə-f** bi iškʲa-ʁᵊi*
Lit.: **Stage above-GEN. matter-ACC.** I arrange-PERF.
I took care about the **matters on the stage** (about the performance).

Ex. 4:  *ər yilaⁿ samən ňi da izanč mamə-i **calə fəjərgᵊ-i** am samən ňi.*
Lit.: The three shaman-NI-ACT. Isanju mamə-GEN. **hand-0G. below-GEN.** big shaman POSS.
These three shamans are the three high shamans who **help** Isanju mamə.

Ex. 5:  ***ərᵊ-i diørgᵊ-i baitə-f** məji aɹm-bu-ki.*
Lit.: **This-GEN. inside-GEN. matter-ACC.** little tell-CI.-give-VOL.
I will explain something **related to this matter**.

Ex. 6:  *mangiⁿ zəyəɳ da, tər **am əndüri fəjərgᵊ-i** əndür ňi.*
Lit.: Mangin say-NP.II ACT. that **big deity below-GEN.** deity POSS.
Mangin is a deity whose rank is **below [that of] the high deity**.

### Spatial nouns with other case suffixes

Spatial nouns with the dative-locative, ablative, lative and accusative are used as verb-determinants.

### Spatial nouns in dative-locative

Ex. 1:  ***juɹyu-t ɛmirgi-t** gum bujaⁿ bi.*
Lit.: **Front-DL. back-DL.** all forest is.
There was forest **on all sides**.

Ex. 2:  *amś tavə-v-ûqᵘ̇. **ɛmirgi-d ňi** hut yivaʁəⁿ bi.*
Lit.: Northwards look-CAUS.-NI.-NEG., **Northern-side-DL.-POSS.** devil ghost is.
It is not allowed to turn to the North, in **the North** there are evil beings.

Ex. 3:  *šuda śieⁿ fanyi gəɹ mətər **hafsəi fəjərgᵊ-t** vəilə-m.*
Lit.: Absolutely good interpreter(Chin.) still the.same **boss-PL.-GEN. below-DL.** work-IMP.
Even the best interpreter still only works under **the bosses**.

### Spatial nouns in the ablative

Ex. 1:  *εmirgi-dəri am uduⁿ dam.*
Lit.: **Northern.side-ABL**. big with blow-IMP.
A strong wind started blowing **from the North**.

### The spatial nouns in lative

Ex. 1:  *fəjərgᵊ-či ta!*
Lit.: **Down-L**. look-IMPER.
Look **down**!

Ex. 2:  *diorgi-či tə!*
Lit.: **Inside-L**. sit-IMPER.
(Come and) sit **inside**.

Ex. 3:  *bo εmirg-i-d ňi am bujaⁿ bi.*
Lit.: **House north-GEN.DL. POSS**. big forest is.
There is a large forest **north of their house**.

Ex. 4:  *mədəri dørg-i-dəri či-či-maq ji-ɣᵊi.*
Lit.: **Sea inside-GEN.ABL**. go out-CONV.PERF. come.PERF.
She came out **of the sea**.

Ex. 5:  *əraɴ χᵘas-k naⁿ tər kəmən-t gənə-mə gəɹ fəjərgᵊ-i nanə-f gida-m.*
Lit.: Thus grow-NP. person that level-DL. go-CI. too **below-GEN. person-ACC**. press-IMP.
Somebody who has grown in this way, when he reaches the same level, would also oppress his **subordinates**.

## 6.2.4 The suffix -bi

Ex. 1:  *ər-bi-t gəɹ o-m, tər-bi-t gəɹ o-m.*
Lit.: **This-side-DL**. still become-IMP. **that-side-DL**. still become-IMP.
It is possible **either on this side or on that side**.

Ex. 2:  *juɹ-bi-t tə!*
Lit.: **Front-side-DL**. sit-IMPER.
Sit **in front**!

## 6.2.5 The suffix -ś

The forms derived from the suffix *-ś* (an oral form of *-si*) are adverbial in nature and are used for expressing direction of movement. In the contemporary spoken language this suffix is used only with some of the spatial roots, while others form equivalent expressions by adding the regular lative suffix -*či* to a spatial noun (e.g. *fəjərgə-či* 'downwards'). The forms most frequently used with -*ś* are: *am-ś* 'backwards/to the north', *ju-ś* 'forwards/towards the south', *vie-ś* 'westwards'*di-ś* 'eastwards', *nuŋ-ś* 'up', *če-ś* 'further'.

Ex. 1:   **am-ś** *tavə-v-ûq$^{\hat{u}}$.*
        Lit.: **Northwards** look-CAUS.-(NI).-NEG.
        **It is forbidden to look to the north**.

Ex. 2:   **nuŋ-š** *ta!*
        Lit.: **Upwards** look!
        Look **up**!

Ex. 3:   *śi-maq χ$^{\hat{u}}$aliazû$^n$ banjə-mεie, ə-dəri* **če-ś** *afš banjə-mie.*
        You-IS. peace live-PROG., this-ABL. **further** how live-IMP.
        I live in peace with you, how should I live **further** (= **better**?)

### Other expressions for spatial relationships

In addition to using the grammatically distinct expressions from the subclass of spatials, the language system of expressing space relationships is complemented by several other nominal expressions, namely the stems *da.ɪvə-* 'beside, aside, next to', as well as the stems for lateral orientation *iśte* 'right', and *śoлʙo* 'left'. The morphological properties of these stems are close to those of spatials.

Furthermore, idiomatic expressions such as *da-t* (Lit. Ma. *dade*, lit. 'in the root') 'next to, beside' and *jaqə-t* (Lit. Ma. *jakade*, lit. in a thing) 'next to' are present. The words *da* 'root' and *jaq* 'thing' are widely-used auxilliary expressions, acquiring a sense of spatial determination only in the dative-locative .

Ex. 1:   **da.ɪvə-či** *yila!*
        Lit.: **Side-L.** stand-IMPER.
        Go **to the side** (and stand there)

Ex. 2:   **da.ɪvə-či** *ta-mεye.*
        Lit.: **Side-L.** look-PROG.
        He looks **aside**.

Ex. 3:   **da.ɪvə-i** *bo ňi yiqa$^n$ bi-y$^ə$i.*
        Lit.: **Side-GEN.** house-POSS. Chinese be-PERF.
        Their **neighbours** were Chinese.

Ex. 4:   *əňi amə* **da-t** *bi na?*
        Lit.: **Mother Father root-DL.** is QUEST.
        Does she live **with her parents**?

Ex. 5:   *duqa jaqə-t fot leikə-m.*
    Lit.: **Gate thing-DL**. fodo hang-IMP.
    **Next to the gate** they hang the *fodo*.

### Figurative description of location using the word ba – place

Another word with many auxilliary functions, and the only one whose basic meaning is connected with space, is the word *ba* 'place'. Most often it expresses the meaning 'at someone's place' or 'with someone'.

Ex. 1:   *ər bitkə **mi-ⁿ bat** bi.*
    Lit.: This book **my place-DL**. is.
    I have this book **at home**.

Ex. 2:   ***junglo laoχaⁿ ba-t** gənə-m na?*
    Lit.: **Zhonglu old man place-DL**. go-IMP. QUEST
    Shall we go to visit **Mr. Zhonglu**?

## 6.2.6 Temporal use of spatials

As in many other languages, spatial expressions are also used figuratively to describe relative positions in time. Contrary to what one might expect, however, we do not find the basic spatial opposition of the roots ***ama-*** 'back, north' and ***jule-*** 'front, south' functioning as a basic opposition in temporal relationships. While the root ***ama-*** 'back, north' has predictably undergone a shift in meaning and its forms ***amala*** and ***amasi*** are used in the sense of 'after, later', and 'from then' respectively, its opposite meaning is expressed by another root, apparently a loan from Mongolic – the root ***onggo-*** 'before, former'.[2] It occurs only in the petrified form ***onggolo*** (Si. *oноɹ*), from which other forms are derived by means of regular case suffixes.

In some expressions, however, the root *ju-* is used with a temporal meaning, namely in the starting formula in written narratives about the past. The most frequent of these formulas are ***julge-i fon-de*** (Lit. in-front-GEN. time-DL.) and ***julge-i erin-de*** (Lit. in-front-GEN. time-DL.).

Ex. 1:   ***aməle-i mudaⁿ***, *aн lim fienš-kə-də* ...
    Lit.: **Later-GEN. time** mouth open-CI. ask-NP.-DL.
    **Next time**, when I dared to ask ...

Ex. 2:   *ər gum **aməɹ** bait ...*
    Lit.: This all **later-0G. matter**.
    This all happened **later**.

Ex. 3:   *ərᵊ-i oноɹ əmdaⁿ ji-γᵊi.*
    Lit.: **This-GEN. before** once come-PERF.
    I have come once (**before this time**).

---

[2]   Its relationship to the Mongolian root *öm-* is supported by several similar cases: Ma. *angga* – Mo. *am* 'mouth', Ma. *enggemu* – Mo. *emeel* 'saddle'.

Ex. 4: **_guri-m ji-h oɴolə-i_** _baitə-f taqa-r naⁿ qoms._

  Lit.: **Move-CI. come-NP. before-GEN.** matter-ACC. know-NI. person little.

  There are few people who know anything about the **time before the migration**.

# 7 THE VERB

## 7.1 The verbal system of spoken Sibe

The system of verbal expressions in spoken Sibe functionally resembles the verbal systems of the Mongolic and Turkic languages. Formally it is comparatively simple. Relatively simple verbal forms seem to be a typical feature of the more prevalently oral Altaic languages existing within the sphere of the influence of the Chinese language.[1] Compared to written Manchu, spoken Sibe expresses actions in a simpler and more analytic way.

In comparison with other Altaic languages, including written Manchu, we find a lesser number of forms on every level of the verbal system. In all of the basic varieties of verbal expressions (finite verbs, verbal nouns and converbs) there is a pair of forms representing the basic opposition of tense and aspect – the **present/future** – **imperfectivity** (which can also be described as **indefinite time**) and the **past** – **perfectivity** (**definite time**). In his description of spoken Sibe, Jang Taeho (Jang 2008, p. 132) speaks of the opposition between **past** vs. **non-past**. From a certain point of view it can be even stated that the general present-future tense can even semantically include, in some instances, an action belonging to the past, and that the morphological formants of the past-perfective forms delineate a specific section of time within this general tense.

Apart from this opposition, which covers most communication needs, there is (in the case of finite verbs and verbal nouns) a third, less frequent form which expresses **progressivity** or **durativity**, as well as several secondary forms which have developed recently from analytic expressions.

The Manchu verbs distinguish various types of tense, aspect and modality, and (with the exception of imperatives) do not distinguish person and number. Concerning the types of verbal expressions (Rus. *glagol'noje slovo*), most of the authors agree on the definition of three types of verbs, which may be generally labelled as **finite verbs** (**verba finita**), **verbal nouns** (**nomina**) and **converbs** (**converba**). The finite verb class is often divided into two classes – the command forms and the tense or indicative forms.[2] The Russian authors use

---

[1]  Examples of this phenomena may be provided not only by the "small" and geographically isolated languages, like the Mongolic languages of the Gansu-Qinghai region, but also from Eastern Mongolian dialects such as Khorchin or Baarin, whose speakers, despite their knowledge of Written Mongolian, use a much more simplified way of describing actions in speech.

[2]  Although different terminology has been applied by various authors (e.g. Chingalttai 1965, p. 83) – "the command and desire class, the verbal noun class, the tense class and the copulative verb class", the classification remains the same.

a terminology which was developed for the Slavic languages: *glagol'nye naklonenija* (verbal moods), *pričastija* (participles, verbal adjectives) and *deepričastija* (gerunds, or converbs)[3]. Modern works in Chinese distinguish *shijian xingshi* (temporal forms), *qishishi xingshi* (lit. stimulating forms[4]), *xingdong xingshi* (forms of verbal adjectives), *xingming xingshi* (forms of verbal nouns) and *fudong xingshi* (forms of converbs).

In his Manchu Grammar, which to a certain extent follows traditional Manchu grammars, I. Zaharov (1879, p. 172) speaks of eight types of 'naklonenija', among which he lists the '*pričastie*' and '*deepričastie*'. According to him, the verbs of literary Manchu have three time levels and six tenses, which can be expressed in all '*naklonenija*'.

In his comparative work, O. P. Sunik (1962, pp. 200–214) corrects the Russian terminology and points out the substantial differences in content of terminology between Slavonic and Altaic linguistic analysis. He emphasizes as well the different character of verbs in Manchu-Tungus languages with respect to verbs in Turkic and Mongolic languages. After a detailed analysis and definition of each Russian linguistic term used for the Altaic verbal system, he seems still inclined to employ them and defines four basic verbal forms in Tungusic languages: *pričastie* (participle), *imennye formy glagola* (nominal verbal forms, among which he lists supine, conditional and several others, none of which, however, occurs in Manchu), *deepričastie* (gerund, or converb) and *naklonenija glagola* (verbal mood). He distinguishes three verbal moods (indicative, imperative and conditional) and three time levels (past, present and future). In his work he does not mention the verbal noun II with the suffix *-ng*, typical of Manchu as a separate form.

This profound comparative work, based on rich material of the living Tungusic languages, faces a certain lack of material of the spoken forms of Manchu in dealing with the problematics of Manchu grammar. It is based solely on Zaharov's Manchu Grammar, which, in turn, analyzes only the written form of Manchu.

In her Manchu Grammar Liliya Gorelova follows the threefold division of verbal forms in Manchu (**participles, converbs** and **finite verbal forms**). In the last group she includes indicative, oblique moods (optative, imperative and prohibitive) and, as a special part of the finite forms, complex verbal forms with epistemic modality. (Gorelova 2002, pp. 231–233)

In this respect, a great contribution to the study of Sibe verbs has been made by Li Shulan, Li Shulan, Zhongqian and Wang Qingfeng in their monoghraph (1984, pp. 45–62), which describes the grammar of spoken Sibe from a purely synchronic point of view and is therefore highly helpful in defining the communicative functions of the particular forms.

This work distinguishes the following forms:
1) **temporal forms** – eight temporal forms expressing two time levels (the past and the present-future)
2) **stimulating forms** – imperatives for 1st, 2nd and 3rd person
3) **converbs**
4) **verbal adjectives**
5) **a verbal noun**

From my own experience with Sibe I can attest that this classification reflects the situation of the spoken language as it is used in actuality today.

---

[3]  Cf. e.g. Poppe 1937, p. 105.

[4]  The Chinese expression *qishishi* means 'encouraging, urging, motivating'; in linguistic terminology, it is used for causative forms.

For the purposes of the present description the following classification of the verbal forms is proposed:

### 1. Functionally finite forms
- present/future finite verb (presens imperfecti) *-mie*
- past/perfect finite verb (perfectum) *-ʁ°i(-e)/-y°i(-ye)*
- progressive finite verb *-mɛ-ye/-ma-ʁ°i(-e)*
- a verbal form for expressing a action taking place in the future

### 2. Imperative and optative forms
- first person singular and plural imperative (voluntative) *-ki/-či,*
- second person singular and plural, formed usually by the simple verbal stem and in several cases by special irregular forms.
- third person singular and plural imperative *-kiňi*

### 3. Converbs
- present/imperfective[5] converb *-m(-ə)*
- perfective[6] converb *-maq*
- perfective converb *-fi*

### 4. Verbal nouns[7]
- present-future/imperfective verbal noun *-r*
- past/perfective verbal noun *-h*
- progressive verbal noun *-maχ*

### 5. Verbal nouns II
Verbal nouns II are formed by adding the suffix *-ŋ/-N* to all forms of verbal nouns
- present-future verbal noun II *-rəŋ*
- past verbal noun II *-yəŋ/-ʁəN*
- progressive verbal noun II *-ma-ʁəN*

## 7.1.1 The problem of definition of the finite verbs in Sibe

According to G. I. Ramstedt (Ramstedt 1957, p. 81) the term 'verba finita' in the Altaic linguistic sphere 'in broader sense may be used for all verbal forms which mark the finiteness of a sentence'.[8] However, only the **imperative** and **optative** forms are considered by him to be 'finite verbs proper' whereas the remaining verbal forms are in fact verbal nouns.

As for Manchu, I. Zaharov distinguishes between **verbal nouns** (*pričastija*), **transgressives** (*deepričastija*), and two **verbal moods** (*naklonenija*) – the indicative mood and the imperative mood.

---

[5] Sunik, p. 267: *deepričastie odnovremennoje.*
[6] Sunik, p. 280: *deepričastie raznovremennoe.*
[7] The term 'verbal adjectives' (*xingdong xingshi* – lit. adjectival verbal forms) is common in Chinese grammatical tradition. It has been used in the description of Altaic languages, in particular for Manchu and Sibe, where these forms (unlike the category above of Verbal Nouns II) function largely as attributes and are rarely declined.
[8] *V altaiskih že jazykah eto opredelenie, v širokom smysle slova, možet byť primenemo ko vsem tem glagol'nym formam, kotoryje ukazyvajut na zakončennosť predloženija.*

O. P. Sunik (Sunik 1962, p. 309) speaks of the 'verb in the narrower sense', which corresponds to the concept of the finite verb, or the *naklonenija* (verbal moods), whose main common feature is their ability to function as the predicate (these are the forms of so-called "terminative predication" (*zakončennaja predikacia*) Sunik 1962, p. 309).

All these forms possess the category of mood, most of them possess as well the category of tense and in most of the Tungusic languages the verbs express person and number as well.

Unlike the other Tungusic languages, the Manchu and Sibe verb usually does not express person and number. From one viewpoint (Sunik 1962, p. 309) it may be concluded that in Manchu and Sibe the only finite forms are the imperative and optative forms, and most of the predicates are in fact verbal nouns or converbs. However, both Manchu and Sibe possess morphological means which makes these non-finite expressions specialized predicative forms, which may then be considered as finite (see below).

The authors of *Xiboyu kouyu yanjiu* (Li Shulan 1984, p. 56) divide the forms in question into the "stimulating forms" (imperatives) and "temporal forms", and the indicative mood of the verb.

In the Manchu verbal system, unlike the systems of other Altaic languages, the finite verbs (with the exception of imperatives) do not have specialized forms, but are originally analytic forms (verbal noun or converb + copula *bi* 'is'; Zaharov 1879, p. 173)[9]. An analogical feature seems to be found in other Tungusic languages as well; Avrorin (1955, p. 23), for example, states, that in Nanai there are no finite verbs because all predicative forms are verbal nouns.

The situation is similar in spoken Sibe. Forms which could superficially be labelled as finite according to their function in the sentence as predicates, in most cases can be broken down into a verbal noun or converb, and the suffix *-ᵊi(-ye)* (with the respective vocalic variants). This suffix consists of the vowel *-i*, which is considered by native speakers as a remnant of the literary suffix/copula *-bi*, and the vowel *-e*, which is a compulsory part of the imperfect *-m-i-e* and durative *-mɛ-i-e*; its use in the perfective verb *-ʁ-i(-e)*[3] is facultative. This vowel, which only recently became noted in the native descriptions and records of oral Sibe,[10] certainly has a stylistic and prosodic function but may even be regarded as a component with a certain degree of grammatical function. The entire suffix *-i(-e)* has a clear grammatical function (a form with this suffix can never be a converb or a verbal noun, while a form without the suffix can be either one of these two or a finite verb with a zero suffix). The position of this suffix corresponds to the position of the component *-bi* in literary Manchu. The forms with this suffix may therefore be taken for finite forms, despite the fact that they do not express person and number, because they can neither function as an attribute nor precede another verb. Their sole function is that of a predicate. At the same time they cannot be considered analytic forms, since the component *-i(-e)* contains no lexical or (other) grammatical meaning.

It may be of interest to note the way native speakers themselves transcribe their language. Attempts have been made to record pronunciation either by using the Manchu alphabet (in song lyrics or incidental documentation of speech in literary texts, the creation of which has been a tradition since the beginning of the 20th century), or by the Latin alphabet in more recent linguistic works and in internet communication. It is worth noting that most of

---

[9] L. Gorelova maintains, that the component -bi (defined in her work as a predicative copula) is probably of non-verbal nature and should be distinguished from the existential verb bi- (Gorelova 2002, p. 232).

[10] I have encountered, in several collections of Sibe speech gathered by native speakers, instances where the imperfect was noted as *-mi* and the durative as *-mai*, which may mean that native speakers themselves perceive the final vowel as nothing more than a facultative emphasis.

the speakers either ignore the entire suffix (as in the case of the imperfect verb in *Xiboyu kouyu yanjiu* – 1984), or use the short form *-i* (imp. *-mi*, as in *yav-mi* 'goes' instead of the pronounced form in actual usage, *yav-mie*, perf. *-hai*/*-hei* instead of *-ʁi(ye)*[3], dur. *-mai* instead of *-mɛye*, to cite a few examples). This method of transcription seems to follow the tradition of the first attempts to record the spoken language. Certain specific instances, such as that of the form *oʁⁱ̯-i-ye* ('became, enough'), regularly transcribed as *ohoye*, bear evidence against the idea that native speakers themselves are not aware of the long forms they pronounce.

Examples of comparison in the spoken and written forms:

| Lit. Manchu | *yabu-* | *-m* | *-bi* |
|---|---|---|---|
| Spoken Sibe | *yav-* | *-m* | *-i-ye* |
| Meaning | stem of 'to go' | imperfective converb | finite verb suffix |

| Lit. Manchu | *yabu-* | *-ha* | *-bi* |
|---|---|---|---|
| Spoken Sibe | *yav-* | *-ʁⁱ* | *-i-(e)* |
| Meaning | stem of 'to go' | suffix nom. perf. | finite verb suffix |

| Lit. Manchu | *yabu-* | *-ma* | *-ha* | *-bi* |
|---|---|---|---|---|
| Spoken Sibe | *yav-* | *-ma* | *-ʁⁱ* | *-i-(e)* |
| Spoken Sibe | *yav-* | *-mɛ* | | *-ye* |
| Meaning | stem of 'go' | suffix conv. imp. | suffix nom. perf. | finite verb suffix |

## 7.1.2 The delayed personal pronoun

A feature typical of many Mongolian dialects – the addition of personal pronouns after a predicate – occurs occasionally in the speech of the Jungarian Sibe. This may be encouraged by their linguistic environment: the surrounding Turkic and Oirat languages. In Sibe their use is always accompanied by a certain degree of a modal or emotional shading, and they seem to retain their full lexical meaning as in, for example, the Khalkha Mongolian phrase *margaaš ireh uu, ta?* 'will (you) come tomorrow, you?' as opposed to the more grammaticalized use of the same procedure in the Oirat dialects.

Ex. 1: **sa-qⁱ̯ bi.**
Lit.: Know-(NI.)-NEG. 1sg.
I do not know (emphasized).

Ex. 2: **gən-ɣᵊi bi.**
Lit.: Go-PERF. 1sg.
(But) I went there!

Ex. 3:   ***gən śi!***
　　　　Lit.: Go-IMPER. 2sg.
　　　　Go away! (strictness)

## 7.1.3 Verbum existentiae

Manchu has two main productive roots of existential verbs:

1. The root *o-* 'to be (something or somebody), to become, to be possible' corresponds by its function and lexical range to the verbal root *bol-* in the Mongolic and Turkic languages. It has a wide range of possible translations both lexically and in its auxiliary and grammatical functions. The central lexical meaning is that of identity or identification (*bi śint uɣumə om*, lit. 1sg. 2sg.-DL. aunt **become-IMP.**' – '**I am [in the position of]** an aunt for you'), and the main auxiliary functions represent the expression of possibility (e.g. *təvat gənə-m o-m*, lit. 'there go-CI. **become-IMP.**' – '**it is possible** to go there', '**we can** go there' etc.) and of change (e.g. *χa ʁəji ñi ambu o-ʁⁱi*, lit. 'son POSS. **big become-PERF.**' – 'her son **grew up**'). As a grammaticalized component of complex verbal expressions it usually expresses perfectivity or readiness for an action (e.g. *aʁa da-m-ů-ʁⁱi*, lit. 'rain have.connection.with-CI.-**become-PERF.**' – 'it is going to rain').

2. The verb *bi-* 'to exist, to occur, to be situated somewhere, to be present, to be in possession of' covers a range of meanings similar to Mongolian *bai-* and Turkic *bar-*. Its peculiarity is that in oral Sibe its imperfective finite form does not take a tense suffix (*bo naʁəⁿ śiñi əvat bi*, lit. 'house kang 2sg.-GEN. **here is**' – 'your home **is here**'). In literary Manchu there occurs, apart from the defective form *bi*, a regularly formed expression *bimbi*. In the spoken language, however, it is difficult to identify a similar form. If there is any, it would be the form *biye*, whose second component *-ye* is functionally comparable to the suffix *-bi* of the literary language (see above). The other forms of the verb *bi-* are formed regularly.
　　In literary Manchu verbal forms which are regarded as finite always include the suffix *-bi*, which might have a connection to the verbal root *bi-*.

The verb *bi*, like the Mongolian form *baina*, functions as a copula in nominal sentences and its use is facultative except when expressing 'presence' or 'location', in which case it is obligatory (*urumči-t ai bie* lit. 'Urumchi-DL. **what is**' – '**what is** in Urumči').

## 7.1.4 Negation of verbal forms

### Negation by means of the particle (*a*)*q̊u*

In most cases the verbal action is negated by attaching the particle (*a*)*q̊u* to a the verbal noun. In contemporary spoken Sibe the connection between the negative particle and the verb is so close that it seems more appropriate to speak of a suffix. The first syllable of the particle *a-* either elides or merges with the final vowel of the verbal form. In the imperfective verbal noun finishing in *-r* the suffix *-r* usually elides and the negative suffix *-q̊u* is attached directly to the verbal stem (e.g. Ma. *sara-q̊u* Si. *sa-q̊u* 'does not know'). In speech the final vowel *-ŭ* is usually reduced to a labialization of the preceding consonant *q* (> *-qᵘ*), and the vowel preceding the suffix *-qŭ* is often labialized (e.g. *mute-qŭ* 'can not' > *mutŭ-qᵘ*). Under the influence of the uvular pronunciation of the suffix the last stem syllable of the verbs with front vowels often acquires uvular pronunciation (*gən-ʁə-qŭ* 'did not go' > *gən-ʁa-qᵘ*).

### 1) Negation of finite verbs

The negative counterparts of the finite verbs are formed either by attaching the suffix *-i(ye)* to the negated verbal noun (thus resulting in a negative finite form), e.g. *gən-ʁa-qᵘ-i(-ye)* 'did not go (PERF)', or simply by the negated verbal noun, which is more common, e.g. *gən-ʁa-qᵘ* 'did not go (NP.)' The form with the finite verb suffix corresponds to the written Manchu form with the suffix *-bi* (*gene-he-kū-bi* 'did not go').

Ex. 1: *čimar gənə-m na? gənə-qᵘ.*
Lit.: Tomorrow go-IMP. QUEST. – go-(NI.)-NEG.
Will you go there tomorrow? – I **will not go**.

Ex. 2: *sadə-mɛi na? sadəmaʁ-a-qᵘi.*
Lit.: Be.tired-PROG. QUEST. **Be.tired-PROG.-NEG.**
Are you tired? (No), **I am not tired**.

Ex. 3: *ji-yə na? ji-ʁa-qᵘ-i.*
Lit.: Come-PERF. QUEST. – **Come-NP.-NEG.**
Did he come? (**No**), **he did not come**.

### 2) Negation of verbal nouns

The negative counterparts of verbal nouns are simply the negated forms of the verbal nouns.

Ex. 1: *gənə-r naⁿ* 'the person who will go' – *gənə-qᵘ naⁿ* 'the person who will not go'

Ex. 2: *ji-h saʁənč* 'the girl who came' – *ji-ya-qᵘ saʁənč* 'the girl who did not come'

### 3) Negation of converbs

The negative counterpart of a converb was originally an analytic form (the negated verbal noun plus the imperfect converb of the verb *o-* 'to be, to become'.

Ex. 1: *ji-qŭ-mə (< ji-qŭ o-mə) ainə-mie?*
Lit.: **Come-(NI.)-NEG.-(become)**-CI. do what-IMP.
What will you do **if not coming**? (= Why should you not come?)

Ex. 2: *śim-b sav-ʁa-qŭ-maq (< sav-ʁa-qŭ o-maq) yav-ʁə.*
Lit.: 2sg.-ACC. see-NP.-NEG. (become)-CP. go-PERF.
I **did not see** you there **and so** I left.

Ex. 3: *jə-qů-či (< jə-qů o-či) o-jůqᵘ!*
      Lit.: **Eat-(NI.)-NEG. (become)-CC**. become-(NI.)-NEG.
      It is impossible **not to eat** (= you have to eat).

### 4) Negation of verbal nouns II

The negative counterpart of the verbal noun IIs is formed by attaching the negative suffix to the verbal noun before the nominalizing suffix -$N^2$.

Ex. 1:   *əm jaq baʁənə-qůN da bi.*
      Lit.: One thing **know/can-NI.II.-NEG**. ACT. 1sg.
      I am the one who **knows nothing**.

### Negation by means of the particle *əm*

Negation of verbal forms by means of the prohibitive particle *əm* in Sibe occurs only with imperative forms. Moreover, while in literary Manchu the prohibitive particle *ume* occurs with second- and third- person forms (e.g. *ume yabukini*) the material collected for this analysis yielded only negative forms of the second person imperative. The particle *əm* in the negative form of the second person imperative is always followed by an imperfective noun.

Ex.:    *əm yavə-r, davɹ iśta-ʁᵊi.*
      Lit.: **PROH. go-NI**. too become.late-PERF.
      **Do not leave**, it is already too late.

## 7.1.5 Question

It is typical of Altaic languages (as well as of Chinese) to formally distinguish two types of questions – "wh- questions" (all questions that use question words) and questions which can be answered by "yes" or "no". This distinction is expressed by using different types of interrogative particles. Sometimes interrogative particles are not used in the first question type marked by the interrogative wh- word.

In literary Manchu there are several interrogative particles, of which *nio* (or, in verbal predicates, sometimes only the particle -*o* attached to the verb) are used for yes/no questions while other particles express various modal differences of wh- questions.

Spoken Sibe uses a single interrogative particle *na* for yes/no questions, while wh-questions are marked only by the interrogative vicaria (the interrogative pronouns *ai* 'what', *və* 'who' in all case forms, the interrogatives *afs* 'how', *ailiaN* 'what like', *aitiN* 'when', *yavat/ɛvit* 'where', *yam(kəⁿ)* 'which', the interrogative verb *ainə-* 'do what' and the like). Interrogative particles come at the end of the sentence and usually no sandhi changes occur,[11] but in verbal predicates the finite verbs drop their marker of finiteness.[12]

---

[11] In the speech of the younger generation the suffix of the imperfective verb is often dropped before the interrogative particle, e.g. instead *gənəm na?* Will you go? the form *gən na?* is pronounced.

[12] When the particle *na* follows the longer form of the finite verb, or is separated by a pause from the previous verb, it usually has a modal meaning which may be rendered as 'requiring confirmation or approval', e.g. (*śieⁿ gizermɛye, na?* 'she speaks well, **doesn't she?**').

Ex. 1:  *ənəN diøvr ji-m **mutə-m na**?*
Lit.: Today night come-CI. **be able-IMP. QUEST.**
**Can you come** tonight?

Ex. 2:  *ər baitə-f śi **dønji-m** duɹ-ɣ-a-qᵘ̈ na?*
Lit.: This matter you **hear-CI. pass-NP.-NEG. QUEST.**
**Have you not heard** about it?

Ex. 3:  *čimar aitiN ji-m **mutə-mie**?*
Lit.: Tomorrow **when** come-CI. **be able-IMP.**
**What time can you come** tomorrow?

Ex. 4:  *ər baitə-f śi **və-dəri** dønji-m **duɹ- yᵊi**?*
Lit.: **This matter-ACC. 2sg. who-ABL**. hear-CI. **pass-NP**.
**Whom did you hear** it from?

*Common use of the yes/no question*

## 1. Presens imperfecti

The suffix *-i(e)* is dropped before the particle *na* in the present-future finite forms.

Ex. 1:  *ər nanə-f **taqə-m na**?*
Lit.: This person **know-IMP. QUEST.**
Do you **know him**?

## 2. The progressive verb

In the progressive verb *-mɛye* only the last vowel of the suffix is dropped before the interrogative particle.

Ex. 1:  *hoŋlin ju naⁿ śieⁿ bo **banjə-mɛi na**?*
Lit.: Honglin two person good house **live-PROG. QUEST.**
Do Honglin and her husband **live happily** in their home?

Ex. 2:  *mim-b **taqə-mɛi na**?*
Lit.: 1sg.-ACC. **recognize-PROG. QUEST.**
**Do you recognize** me?

## 3. Nomen perfᵉcti (-ɣ/-ʁ, -k/-q) and the longer form of the durative verb- -m-a-ʁ-i(e)

Ex. 1:  *gizum-b ňi **ulⁱ-h-ə na**?*
Lit.: Word-ACC. POSS. **understand-PERF. QUEST.**
**Did you understand** him?

Ex. 2:   *ər učur əksə-m **yav-m-a-ʁ-ə na**?*
         Lit.: This section hurry-CI. **go-PROG. QUEST**.
         **Are you busy** these days?

*Figurative use of the interrogative constructions*

a) A gentle call or invitation is often expressed by the use of an imperfective verb with the interrogative particle. This question may be either an invitation to a common action, or a mild suggestion to the interlocutor, sometimes intended as an advice.

Ex. 1:   *avśe, məs **yav-m na**?*
         Lit.: How, 1pl.(incl.) **go-IMP. QUEST**.
         So **shall we leave**?
         Note: A usual question in any situation before leaving.

Ex. 2:   *ərəčuⁿ-zə bo-t əmdaⁿ **doźi-m na**?*
         Lit.: Erečun-PART. house-DL. once **enter-IMP. QUEST**.
         **Shall we drop** in at Erečun's place? (= Let us go and see Erečun.)

Ex. 3:   *śi-ⁿ fienji-r baitə-f tə **fienji-m na**?*
         Lit.: 2sg.-GEN. ask-NI. matter now **ask-IMP. QUEST**.
         Now you should **ask your questions**.

b) In the first person singular this question usually is used as an inquiry as to whether an action is appropriate.

Ex. 1:   *bi tə **gizərə-m na**?*
         Lit.: 1sg. now **speak-IMP. QUEST**.
         **Should I speak** now?

c) The imperfect verb with the interrogative particle is sometimes (as in Mongolian) used to express a polite suggestion which, however, anticipates refusal.

When the case in point is a question about a service or obligation by the speaker to the interlocutor, the question may imply a significant measure of hesitation or reluctance. In Sibe society an offer which is seriously intended is expressed by the use of an indicative sentence, or – as is more often the case –not even mentioned. An explicit commentary gives more room for a polite refusal.

Ex. 2:   *śi-ⁿ jiʁa-f śin-t ənəɴ **bu-m na**?*
         Lit.: 2sg.-GEN. money-ACC. 2sg.-DL. today **give-IMP. QUEST**.
         **Should I be giving** you your money back today?
         Note: Such formulation of a question anticipates a negative response and thus is only a sign of willingness to give the money back at some future time.

Ex. 3:   *bi śin-t ňinəɴə bədə-f **vənjəv-m bu-m na**?*
         Lit.: 1sg. 2sg.-DL. day rice-ACC. **heat-CI. give-IMP. QUEST**.

**Shall I heat up** the lunch for you?

Note: As in the previous case this is merely a polite rhetorical question in a context where the serving food is unnecessary.


## 7.2 Finite verbs

For the sake of greater clarity I deal only with the indicative mood in this chapter. The imperative forms are described in a separate chapter.

In the Altaic languages, the grammatical category of tense is invariably ascribed to the indicative verbal mood. Certain authors mention three temporal levels – past, present and future. According to V. I. Sunik, the present and future tenses form, by their dynamic character, an opposition to the static and perfective nature of the past tense.

A different classification seemingly better suited to the actual linguistic situation in the Altaic tongues, occurs in more recent works: this is the division into two temporal levels. It is employed, among others, by B. Sechenbaatar in his description of the Chahar dialect of Mongol (Sechenbaatar 2003, p. 137), in which he classifies all forms of the indicative mood into two groups- "past" and "non-past"). The same division is employed by Jang Taeho (Jang 2008, p. 132). G. R. Li also classifies the finite verbs of literary Manchu into two groups – "perfective (past)" and "imperfective (non-perfective)" (Li 2000, p. 358). Li Shulan speaks explicitly about two temporal levels in spoken Sibe – the past (*guoqu*) and the present-future (*xiandai-jianglai*).

Generally speaking, in comparison with Khalkha Mongolian, a certain general simplicity and straightforwardness of expression is characteristic of the spoken Sibe language as a whole. This quality also manifests itself in the verbal system. The two tense forms, which represent the basic opposition between the present-future and the past and thus satisfy most communicative needs, are supplemented by a third form that expresses progressivity.

The authors mentioned above all agree on the existence of two indicative verbal forms in Manchu – the imperfective form *-mbi* and the perfective form *-habi³/-kabi³*. Among the indicative forms, certain authors also enumerate a varying number of analytic forms, expressing mostly aspects of duration and continuation. (For example, G. R. Li recognises three synthetic forms *-mbi*, *-ra³ and -ha³* –, as well as twelve analytic forms.) The authors of *Xiboyu kouyu yanjiu* distinguish five synthetic forms – three forms of the past tense: *-heng*,[13] *-he*,[14] and *-hei*,[15] and two forms of the present tense: *-m*[16] and *-mahei*.[17] In addition to these synthetic forms they list four analytic forms.

I have decided to include only the synthetic paradigms that include the marker of finiteness – the suffix *-i(e)* – among the finite forms. This concerns three verbal formants:

1. Imperfect verb *-m-(i-e)* (or general present, praesens imperfecti, abbreviated as IMP.)
2. Imperfect durative verb *-mɛye*, *-maʁ³i-(e)* (progressive, abbreviated as PROG.)
3. Perfect verb *-ʁ³i-(e)*, *-y³i-(e)* (past tense, abbreviated as PERF.)

---

[13] A verbal noun II, which is often used as a predicate.
[14] A form which may be regarded either as a verbal noun used as a predicate, or as a past finite form with a zero suffix of finiteness.
[15] A short form of the past finite verb.
[16] A short form of the imperfect finite verb.
[17] A short form of the durative verb.

## 7.2.1 The imperfect verb -m(-i-e) (praesens imperfecti)

This verbal form, like the corresponding form in Mongolian (*-na*/Lit. Mo. *-mui*), is usually treated as the basic form of a the verb, and verbs in dictionaries are often given in this form. This form of the verb is most frequently designated as the present tense, present-future, aorist, indefinite tense (Sunik 1962, p. 313), or praesens imperfecti (Poppe 1955, p. 261).

### Meaning and forms of the imperfect verb

The imperfect verb is the most general tense form, which under various conditions can express both the general and concrete present tenses, the future tense and the past tense. It is sometimes also used analogically with the infinitive as we understand it from an Indo-European linguistic context. Etymologically (this point is also reflected in the linguistic interpretation of native speakers themselves) it derives from the written form *-m-bi*. The full form *-m-i-e* is more often used for the future than the other forms. In his article about the Manchu verb D. Sinor calls this form a "timeless" form, a general denotation of an action (Sinor 1949, p. 147).

### Use of the imperfect verb

**a) The full form *-m-i-e***

1. The full form of the imperfect expressing concrete present

Ex. 1:  *śi yet gənə-mie?*
       Lit.: 2sg. where **go-IMP**.
       Where **are you going**?

Ex. 2:  *tašqŭ-t gənə-mie.*
       Lit.: School-DL. go-IMP.
       **I am going** to school.

Ex. 3:  *aⁿ əksə-mie?*
       Lit.: Why **hurry-IMP**.
       Why **are you in a hurry**?

2. The full form of the imperfect expressing a general present action

Ex. 1:  *bi ər nanə-f taqə-mie.*
       Lit.: 1sg. this person-ACC. **recognize-IMP**.
       **I know** this man.

Ex. 2:  *śi ai uču<sup>n</sup> baʁənə-mie?*
       Lit.: 2sg. what song **know/can-IMP**.
       Which song **can you sing**?

137

Ex. 3:   *so-ⁿ təvat ai jə-mie?*
Lit.: 2pl.-GEN. there what **eat-IMP.**
What **do you eat** in your country?

Ex. 4:   *śi-ⁿ agə ai arə-mie?*
Lit.: 2sg.-GEN. elder brother **what do-IMP.**
**What does** your elder brother **do**?
Note: This formulation implies a general question (about, for example, a job). For a more concrete inquiry as to the present moment a durative would be used.

Ex. 5:   *śi-ⁿ gəvə-f ai zə-mie?*
Lit.: 2sg.-GEN. name what **say-IMP.**
What is your name?

Ex. 6:   *so-ⁿ bo śidəⁿ yask guidam yav-mie?*
Lit.: 2pl.-GEN. house between how much take time-CI. **go-IMP.**
How long does it take to **get** to your home?

Ex. 7:   *əraɴ oš da əǐi amə toruɴ ǐi ačəna-mie.*
Lit.: Thus become-CC. ACT. mother father abuse NI.II. POSS. **agree-IMP.**
In this case his parents **are right** to scold him.

Ex. 8:   *aⁿ saʙər-mie?*
Lit.: Why **catch.cold-IMP.**?
Why does one **catch a cold**?
Note: A humorous expression of discontent.

3. The full form of the imperfect expressing future actions

Ex. 1:   *ənəɴ məs ai jə-mie?*
Lit.: Today 1pl.incl. what **eat-IMP.**
What shall we **have for dinner** today?

Ex. 2:   *taqa da iʐinə-mie.*
Lit.: Instantly ACT. **reach-IMP.**
We will **be there** in a short while.

Ex. 3:   *aitiŋ boči məda-mie?*
Lit.: When house-LAT. **turn back-IMP.**
When are you **going home**?

Ex. 4:   *tə aitiŋ ji-m mutə-mie?*
Lit.: Now when come-CC. **can-IMP.**
When **will you be** able to come next?

### b) The short form -*m*

The short form -*m* is used in all the semantic paradigms listed above as well as for the expression of the past. While the future is more often expressed by the full form, the shortened form is used mainly to describe an action or condition in the past. This form is also often used in the narration of an event, in which case it enlivens the story or serves to accelerate the cadence of the narrative (Ex. 5).

1. The short form of the imperfect expressing the past

Ex. 1:   *dači mo-ⁿ bo-t gul **ji-m**.*
         Lit.: Originally 1pl.-GEN. house-DL. often **come-IMP**.
         Formerly **he used to visit us** often.

Ex. 2:   *dači mo-ⁿ ju naⁿ yinəŋ yinəŋ **sav-m**.*
         Lit.: Originally 1pl.-GEN. two person day day **see-IMP**.
         Formerly we **used to see** each other every day.

Ex. 3:   *jaq jə-r ərin-t gənkəndi əm naⁿ uči **fierə-m**.*
         Lit.: Thing eat-NI. time-DL. suddenly one person door **pound-IMP**.
         Suddenly somebody is **pounding** on the door.

Ex. 4:   *tər naⁿ dači nanə-f **χafsə-m**.*
         Lit.: That person originally person-ACC. **tell-IMP**.
         He used to **report** people.

Ex. 5:   *ər baitə-f **tačiv-m**, tər baitə-f **tačiv-m**, tači-m vajə-mə da tər čaqŭr **tavənəv-m**.*
         Lit.: This matter-ACC. **learn-CAUS.-IMP**., that matter-ACC. **learn-CAUS.-IMP**.,
         learn-CI. finish-CI. ACT. that *čaqŭr* **ascend- CAUS.-IMP**.
         They **teach him** various things and when he finishes the study, he **climbs** on the *čaqŭr*.
         Note: From an account of the initiation of a shaman.

2. The short form of the imperfect expressing the general present

Ex. 1:   *mo-ⁿ təvat ňimʁa laft **jə-m**.*
         Lit.: 1pl.-GEN. there fish much **eat-IMP**.
         In our place people **eat** mainly fish.

Ex. 2:   *mi-ⁿ agə **uźiⁿ vəilə-m**.*
         Lit.: 1sg.-GEN. elder.brother **field work-IMP**.
         My elder brother **is a peasant**.
         Note: The expression *uźiⁿ vəiləm* 'to work in the field' is, in addition to its concrete signification, is used as well to designate the typical way of life of the Chabchal peasants.

Ex. 3: *śivə set guruⁿ təraɴ **gizərə-m**.*
      Lit.: Sibe old folk thus **talk-IMP**.
      The old Sibe people **usually say** this.

Ex. 4: *saməⁿ ňi yivaʁəⁿ **gida-m**.*
      Lit.: Shaman F. evil.spirit **press-IMP**.
      The shamans **suppress** evil spirits.

3. The short form of the imperfect expressing future

Ex.: *čimar **yav-m**.*
      Lit.: Tomorrow **go-IMP**.
      **I will leave** tomorrow.
      Note: The short form of the imperfect is used for the future mainly in responding questions.

### Verbum existentiae

The verb *bi*, which mainly signifies the existence or presence of something or someone, has a zero form in the imperfect, formally identical with the root *bi*. The longer form *biye* is used mainly in questions and to create emphasis.

Ex.: *uigur-sə ňi omə da bakši zə-m, birχůⁿ, bakši, ju yilaⁿ gizuⁿ **biye**.*
      Lit.: Uighur-PART. POSS. become-CI. ACT. *bakši* say-IMP., *birhůⁿ bakši*, two three word **is**.
      The Uighurs use the word bakši … they **have** two or three expressions like *birhůⁿ*, *bakši* and so on.
      Note: From an account about shamans. The speaker uses here (as is often the case) the longer form bi-e to make his speech slow and distinct.

## 7.2.2 The progressive verb -*mɛye*

### Meaning and forms of the progressive tense

The main signification conveyed by this suffix is that of ongoingness and durativity. The form expresses an action in progress either at the moment of speech or in parallel to another action.

The most common form is -*mɛye*, which is a shortened form of the older suffix -*maʁ⁰i(e)*. It is a linguisticdevelopment of recent times (the authors of *Xiboyu kouyu yanjiu* – list only the suffix -*maʁi(e)* – Li Shulan 1984, p. 56). But when younger speakers transcribe the phonetic shape of their speech, they use the form -*mai*. The pronunciation of older speakers tends to lean towards the expression *maye*. The reason for treating the forms -*mɛye* and -*maʁ⁰ye* as separate endings is that in my experience a certain division in their use has already occurred: the older form is now used only to emphasize the ongoing quality of the action or state in question.

This verbal form does not have a direct correspondence in the written language and its meaning is reflected in the two suffixes -*mbi* and -*mahabi*.

### Use of the progressive verb

1) Expressing an action in progress at the moment of speech

Ex. 1:  *ai arə-mɛye? bitkə ta-mɛye.*
Lit.: What **do-PROG**. book **look-PROG**.
What **are you doing**? **I am reading** a book.

Ex. 2:  *aⁿ bait-aqᵘ baitə-f iški̯a-mɛye?*
Lit.: Why matter-NEG. matter-ACC. **arrange-PROG**.
Why **are you doing** unnecessary things?

Ex. 3:  *śi-ⁿ əñi śim-b χůla-mɛye.*
Lit.: 2sg.-GEN. mother 2sg.-ACC. **call-PROG**.
Your mother **is calling** you.

Ex. 4:  *uju-d ñi durvo qaɹtur-mɛye.*
Lit.: Head-DL. POSS. fly **slide-PROG**.
The **flies are sliding** (around) on his head.
Note: A humorous note about pomaded hair.

2) Expressing durativity in the past

Ex.:  *tər əm ñinəɴ yinhua dianhua ji-maq śim-b bia-mɛye.*
Lit.: That one day Yinhua telephone come-CP. 2sg.-ACC. **look.for-PROG**.
The other day Yinhua **was asking** about you on the phone.

## 7.2.3 The progressive verb -*m-a-ʁ-ᵊi*(*e*) (PROG.II)

### The form of progressive II

The suffix consists of the composite verbal noun -*m-a-ʁ*- and the suffix of finiteness -*i*(*e*)
It corresponds to the written form -***ma-ha-bi***/-***mo-ho-bi***.

### Use of the progressive II

The suffix expresses ongoingness and duration with emphasis on the "movement" and continuity of the action. The use of this verb may make reference to the moment of enonciation or to an action occurring in parallel with another action.

Ex. 1:  *mi-ⁿ əñi śieⁿ fienji-m-a-ʁ- ᵊi.*
Lit.: 1sg.-GEN. mother well **ask-PROG.II**
My mother **is sending her regards** to you.
Note: The use of this form adds a shading of urgency to the conveyed message.

Ex. 2:  *əm yavə-r, jaq **ara-m-a-ʁ-ᵊi**.*
   Lit.: PROH.-go-NI., thing **make-PROG.II**
   Do not leave, the food **is being prepared**!

Ex. 3:  *tər, **tavənə-m ji-m-a-ʁ-ᵊi**.*
   Lit.: That, **ascend-CI. come-PROG.II**
   It is him, he **is climbing** the stairs.

Ex. 4:  *ɢoškᵘ **əksə-m-a-ʁ-ᵊye**.*
   Lit.: Terribly **hurry-PROG.II**
   **I am too busy** right now.

## 7.2.4 The perfective verb -ʁᵊi(e), -ɣᵊi(e) and its alomorphs

### Forms and significance of the perfective verb

The perfective verb is a composite of the perfective verbal noun and the finitive suffix *-ᵊi(ye)*. It corresponds to the written form *-habi, -kabi, -hebi, -kebi, -hobi -kobi*. The suffix has three allomorphs, all with back and front variants: *-ʁᵊi(e)*, *-ɣᵊi(e)*, *-χᵊi(e)/-hᵊi(ye)* and *-qᵊi(e)/- kᵊi(e)*.

In the written language the allomorphs *-χᵊi(e)/-hᵊi()* and *-qᵊi(e)/-kᵊi(e)* exist as well, but their distribution differs from the spoken language. While in written Manchu the distribution of the four allomorphs (fricative-plosive in the velar and uvular variants) is strictly divided, in the spoken language the fricative-plosive distinction has disappeared and instead two variants with the voiced fricatives *-ɣ/-ʁ* are used (e.g. Lit. Ma. *dule-ke-bi* 'passed' x Si. *duɹ-ɣ-ᵊi* 'passed'). In concurrence with recent phonetic changes, a secondary allomorph *-kᵊi* has developed. In most cases this development is quite easy to trace, as its various stages are reflected in the language usage of the different generations.[18]

Distribution according to place of articulation is reflected in the fact that verbs with front vowels take the velar variant of the suffix, while the verbs with back vowels take the uvular variant. This rule is sometimes weakened in the allomorph with an explosive consonant. In the case of verbs with the vowel -o- in the stem the suffix is slightly rounded (e.g. *ohobi – oʁᵘ̊i* 'became', *daokabi – dooʁᵘ̊i* 'landed').

This verbal form expresses an action which has terminated in the past. It often reflects, however, an action with a result lasting up till the present moment. There is probably no contradiction of the two meanings, but it calls for two variations of rendition into English.

The finite suffix *-ᵊi(ye)* may be omitted and the form does not differ from the perfective noun. This form usually expresses a single and intensive action.

---

[18] The most frequent process of the development of the secondary *-ki* may be observed in verbal stems ending in a syllable with *-j-* or *-č-* . Due to the reduction and elision of the final vowel the cluster *jh>čh* has developed, which was then subsequently assimilated into *-čk-* and dissimilated into *-šk-* (Ex. *banji-χa > banč-χa >banč-qa/ banč-kᵊi >banš-kᵊi* gave birth/was born).

### Use of the perfective verb

Ex. 1: *aitiŋ ji-ɣᵊye?*
Lit.: When **come-PERF**.
When **did** you **come**?

Ex. 2: *diøf dači əm śivə nanə-f ɛtəv-ɣᵊi.*
Lit.: Fox originally one Sibe person-ACC. **save-PERF**.
The fox once **saved** a Sibe man.

Ex. 3: *an išta-m ji-ɣᵊye?*
Lit.: Why be.late-CI. come-PERF.
Why are you coming late?

Ex. 4: *čəksə mo-ⁿ bo-t yint-kᵊi.*
Lit.: Yesterday 1pl.-GEN. house-DL. **stay.overnight-PERF**.
Yesterday he **slept** at my place.

Ex. 5: *mi-ⁿ saʁənji-f ənəŋ-dəri śin-t su-m bu-ɣᵊi.*
Lit.: 1sg.-GEN. daughter-ACC. today-ABL. 2sg.-DL. **engage-CI. give-PERF**.
Today **I am giving** you my daughter in marriage.

Ex. 6: *saʁənji ňi qᵘariaɴ banš-kᵊi.*
Lit.: Daughter POSS. beautiful **be.born-PERF**.
Their daughter **is** beautiful.

Ex. 7: *aⁿ əvəš-k səjəⁿ əm duruⁿ tə-ɣᵊye?*
Lit.: Why break-NP. cart one form **sit-PERF**.
Why **are you sitting** like a broken cart?
Note: Scolding of a child who was sprawled on a sofa in the presence of adults.

### The short form of the perfective verb

Ex. 1: *tuku-mə da yaf-χ.*
Lit.: Doing.so-CI. ACT **go-PERF**.
And then he **was** (suddenly) **gone**.

## 7.2.5 The verbal form expressing a forthcoming action – *m-ůʁᵘi.*

The colloquial Sibe suffix, which has recently developed from a complex verbal form *-m + oʁᵘi*, is used to express an action which will inevitably occur sometime in the future. While spoken Sibe, as probably most of the Altaic languages, has no real future verbal tense, the suffix- *m-ůʁᵘi* is one of the options for expressing an action in the future. This form, which can be interpreted as "the situation has developed so that the action will take place" is both etymologically and sematically close to the Khalkha Mongolian composite form *-h bol-*, which is also used to express a certain type of future.

143

The authors of *Xiboyu kouyu yanjiu* treat this verbal expression as a composite verbal tense with the meaning of a future action or state (Li Shulan 1984, p. 46).

Ex. 1:   *bo čimar **gənə-m-ůʁůi**.*
         Lit.: 1pl.(excl.) tomorrow **go-CI.(become)-PERF**.
         We **will surely go there** tomorrow. (We **have decided to go there** tomorrow.)

Ex. 2:   *yinχůa śieriⁿ **ara-qů-ʁů** ba.*
         Lit.: Yinhua wedding **make-(NI.)-NEG. become-PERF**. PROB.
         Yinhua **is not going to marry** (at all), is she?

## 7.3 Imperative and optative forms

Various scholars classify the imperative forms according to different criteria. G. I. Ramstedt maintains that they are the only true finite forms in the Altaic languages (Ramstedt 1957, p. 81), while N. A. Baskakov, in his commentary on Ramstedt's work, regards them as verbal nouns (as he does all other verbal forms) (Ramstedt 1957, see footnote 82). *Xiboyu kouyu yanjiu* (1984, p. 56) classifies them as a special category of verbal forms equivalent to verbal nouns, converbs and finite verbs. The main criteria for such classification is the absence of the grammatical category of tense. Most authors, however, describe them as a subgroup of finite verbs in view of their predicative function. O. P. Sunik defines them as various forms linked together by their common syntactic function and a certain unity of modal meaning: the expression of volition (Sunik 1962, p. 335). These differences mentioned above mainly concern formal classification; generally speaking, these scholars agree on the definition of the imperative forms and their position in the overall verbal system of the Altaic languages. For the sake of greater clarity I have opted to adhere to the classification proposed by Li Shulan, which is to treat the imperative forms as a separate category of verbal expression.

The system of these[19] verbal forms shares common features in all branches of the Altaic languages. The main types of the imperative forms are:
1) *plain imperative*,[20] the form of which is usually identical with the verbal stem,[21]
2) one or more *suffixed forms of the imperative*, which serve to express different modalities of the imperative,
3) *voluntative* (commanddirected at the first person),
4) *permissive, optative, desiderative* (command directed at the third person).

### 7.3.1 Command for the second-person – imperative

Literary Manchu has several suffixed forms (*-ki, -rao* and others) in addition to the simple stem imperative. These forms express varying degrees of politeness. The high frequency of

---

[19] L. Gorelova (2002, pp. 295–304) employs the term "oblique moods" as opposed to the indicative mood. She divides them into imperative, optative and prohibitive forms.
[20] The term "plain imperative" was introduced by B. Sechenbaatar (2003, p. 141) to refer to the imperative form of Chakhar Mongolian, which is identical with the verbal stem.
[21] O. P. Sunik maintains that the simple imperative forms in Tungusic languages are secondary.

these forms in the written language probably results from contacts with the Chinese cultural environment. Spoken Sibe, on the contrary, uses the **simple stem imperative** form rather than the suffixed forms. Two suffixed forms, however, are currently used: the **benedictive** *-mə* and the **voluntative suffix** *-ki*.

### Forms of the plain imperative

The plain imperative in the spoken language is in most cases identical with the verbal stem. But, as in literary Manchu, there are severals verbs, which instead of the plain imperative use forms with irregular suffixes. The imperatives of these verbs in written and spoken language are as follows:

|  | to be | to become | to take | to eat | to come | to ask |
|---|---|---|---|---|---|---|
| Lit. Manchu stem | *bi-* | *o-* | *gayi-* | *jə-* | *ji-* | *bayi-* |
| Lit. Manchu imperative | *bisu* | *oso* | *gaisu* | *jəfu* | *jio* | *baisu* |
| Spoken Sibe stem | *bi-* | *o-* | *gia-* | *jə-* | *ji-* | *biɛ-* |
| Spoken Sibe imperative | *bis* | *os* | *gias* | *jəf* | *ju* | *biɛs* |

O. P. Sunik relates these residual forms to the regular imperative forms in Nanai (Sunik 1962, p. 336). Interestingly, these irregular forms belong to the most frequent verbs employed in the language. In the actual spoken Sibe the forms *bis* 'be!' and *os* 'become!' are rare and are not even known to most speakers, while the rest of the forms are part of everyday vocabulary.

### The basic use of the plain imperative

This imperative form is used for a common or strict command, but when the command is used "for the sake" of the person who is being commanded (e.g. 'sit down', 'eat' etc.) it may have the implication usually conveyed by the polite form.

Ex. 1:  *gizuⁿ **gia-s**!*
      Lit: Word **take-IMPER**.
      **Be obedient!**

Ex. 2:  ***gən**, tər bo-t **sənda**!*
      Lit.: **Go-IMPER.** that house-DL. **put-IMPER.**
      **Go and put** it into that room!

Ex. 3:  *min-t məji **bu**!*
      Lit.: 1sg.-DL. little **give-IMPER**!
      **Give** me a little!

Ex. 4:  *tər nanə-f **biɛ-s**!*
      Lit.: That person-ACC. **ask-IMPER.**
      **Ask** that man.

145

Ex. 5: *ɢaɹ-f ɕač!*
>Lit.: Hand-ACC. **bring-IMPER.**
>**Give me** your hand!

Some of the plain imperative forms are particularly frequent in polite conversation:

Ex. 6: *dərə-či tə!*
>Lit.: Table-LAT. **sit-IMPER.**
>Sit at the table (= **come** and eat)

Ex. 7: *doš, tə!*
>Lit.: **Enter-IMPER. sit-IMPER.**
>**Come in and sit down.**

Ex. 8: *jəv-ə!*
>Lit.: **Eat-IMPER.**
>**Help yourself, eat.**

Ex. 9: *yaf!*
>Lit.: **Go-IMPER.**
>**Come along!**

### Specific use of the plain imperative

The plain imperative is idiomatically used in some constructions with the third person. The resulting meaning is twofold: a slightly disapproving commentary on a specific deed committed by someone and a suggestion to alter it (a), as well as a description of a quick succession of actions (b).

#### a) Suggestion to change behaviour

Ex. 1: *ər saʁənju-s məji **danə**!*
>Lit.: This girl-PART. little **care-IMPER.**
>**Let** those girls **take care** of him a little (Why don't the girls care about him?)

Ex. 2: *tuku-š ta gəɣə ňi gəɹ məji jiʁa **bu**!*
>Lit.: Thus doing-CC. ACT. elder.sister POSS. still little money **give-IMPER.**
>In that case his sister **should give** him some money!

#### b) Description of a quick succession of actions

Ex. 1: *skᵊi həh **qǔčirə-m gia-z-ə, uči-f so**... čorʁo-dəri latə-maq da ɕa-m yav-ʁə.*
>Lit.: That woman **digg-CI. take-IMPER., door-ACC. open-IMPER.,** ... neck-ABL. stick-CONV.PERF ACT. take-CI. go-PERF.
>That woman **dug out (the key), opened the door,** ... grasped his neck and took him away.

146

*Intensification of meaning by use of the particle* -di

In the conveyance of narrated events, a special form is used to express an intensity of insistence – a reduplicated plain imperative with a particle *-di* added to the first member of the reduplicated expression. The verb to which the particle is attached stands in its longer form with a prothetic vowel.

Ex. 1: *mi-ⁿ amə mim-b sav-mə da **ju-ə di ju** zə-mači-m.*
Lit.: 1sg.-GEN. father 1sg.-ACC. see-CI. ACT. 1sg.-ACC. **come-IMPER-EMPH-come-IMPER**. say-INC.-IMP.
Whenever my father sees me, he always **insists that I should visit** him.

## 7.3.2 Polite imperative -mə (benedictive)

This form, which does not have a corresponding equivalent in the written language, expresses a polite request, recommendation or advice.

Ex. 1: *jǔʙǔⁿ **ta-mə**!*
Lit.: Way **look-BEN**.
**Watch out** on the way!

Ex. 2: *məzə-f **qarmə-mə**!*
Lit.: 1pl.-ACC. **protect-BEN**.
**Protect** us!

## 7.3.3 Voluntative

*Forms of the voluntative*

The voluntative suffix has a basic form *-ki(e)*, and an alternative pronunciation *-či(e)*. The distribution of the two allomorphs seems to occur on an individual basis.

*Use of the voluntative*

The voluntative is a verbal form typical for the Altaic languages and has an significant role in daily communication. In the singular it is expressive of the speaker's will or intention, whereas in the plural it is understood as an invitation to a common action.

**1. Singular**

Ex. 1: *əm učuⁿ **učuɹ-kie**.*
Lit.: One song **sing-VOL**.
**Let me sing** a song.

Ex. 2: *śi tə, bi **iškʲa-kie**.*
   Lit.: You sit-IMPER, 1sg. **arrange-VOL**.
   You sit, **I will clean** it up.

Ex. 3: *śi-maq əm bait **gizər-kie**.*
   Lit.: 2sg.-IS. one matter **talk-VOL**.
   **I would like to tell** you something.

Ex. 4: *bi śim-b **ɛli-kie**.*
   Lit.: 1sg. 2sg.-ACC. **wait-VOL**.
   **I will wait** for you.

**2. Plural**

When used for plural the voluntative form may have two meanings:

a) a similar meaning as in the singular: the expression of the speaker's will or intention

Ex. 1: *bo **yaf-ki**.*
   Lit.: 1pl (excl.) **go-VOL**.
   We **will go**.

b) as an invitation to a common action

Ex. 1: *məs **yaf-ki**.*
   Lit.: 1pl. (incl.) **go-VOL**.
   **Let us go**!

Ex. 2: *śiram **aš-ki**.*
   Lit.: In future **meet-VOL**.
   **See you later**.

Some speakers use the phonetic variant -*či*:

Ex. 3: *jaq **səktə-m bu-čie**.*
   Lit.: Thing spread-CI.-**give-VOL**.
   **I will make the bed** for you.

## 7.3.4 Optative -*kiňi*

The suffix -*kiňi* expresses a command directed at the third person, or respectively a wish concerning the third[d] person.

Ex. 1: *śi tə, saʁənč **of-kiňi**.*
   Lit.: 2sg. sit-IMPER. girl **wash-OPT**.
   You keep sitting, let the girl (my daughter) **wash it**.

Ex. 2:  *əm śivə saʁənč **baχ-kiňi ʐ-əm ɢůňi-mɛye**.*
       Lit.: One Sibe girl **find-OPT. say-CI. think-PROG.**
       **We hope that he finds** a Sibe girl for himself.

## 7.4 Verbal nouns

Verbal nouns, which are characteristic of all Altaic languages, are referred to either as participles (Zaharov 1879, p. 183; Sechenbaatar 2003, p. 123), or as **verbal nouns** (Poppe 1955, p. 269). In the terminology of the Chinese grammarians they are known as **verbal adjectives** (Li 1984, p. 56). The general property of these forms are their nominal characteristics, namely, that they take case suffixes and function as adnominal attributes, while maintaining most of their verbal characteristics of tense, aspect and voice.

In Manchu and Sibe, verbal nouns proper are mainly used as attributes, adverbials and, in certain cases, as predicates of dependent clauses. In part, the nominal functions are governed by the verbal form described here as *verbal nouns II*.

Spoken Sibe has three verbal nouns: The **present-future verbal noun** *-r*, the **past-perfective verbal noun** *-h*/*-χ* and the **durative verbal noun** *-maʁ*.

From the point of view of frequency the pair *-r* and *-h*/*-χ* is the more significant. The present-future form *-r* has also conveys the meaning of general, indefinite time, and may designate a permanent feature (*jə-r jaq*, lit. 'eat-NI. thing' – 'food'), while the perfective form *-h*/*-χ* usually has the concrete meaning of a past or perfective (completed) action.

### 7.4.1 The imperfective verbal noun -*r* (nomen imperfecti)

#### Forms of the imperfective noun

The nomen imperfecti usually has the form *-r*, to which the emphatic vowel *-ə* is added only rarely. In the written language the imperfective noun, as well as the imperfective verb, are negated by adding the particle (*a*)*qů* to the verbal noun *-r*. In the spoken language, however, the nominal suffix *-r-* usually is elided (e.g. Lit. Ma. *gisure-re-kū* – Si. *gizərə-qů* 'will not speak'/'does not speak' etc., Lit. Ma. *yabu-ra-kū* – Si. *yavu-qů* 'will not go', 'does not go' etc.).

In literary Manchu several "irregular" monosyllabic stems (the same stems that form irregular imperatives) are obligatorily extended by a deverbal suffix before attaching the nominal suffix *-r*. The resulting forms are: *jetere* < *je-* 'to eat', *jidere* < *ji-* 'to come', *ojoro* < *o-* 'to become', *bisire* < *bi-* 'to be', *gaijara* < *gai-* 'to take'. In the spoken language this rule is usually observed by speakers with good knowledge of their language, while particularly younger and illiterate speakers often use forms without extension (e.g. *jər jaq* 'things to eat'). In the case of the existential verbs *bi-* and *o-* the use the imperfective noun is simply avoided.

#### Basic use of the imperfective noun

The form with the suffix *-r* is used as attribute (1), or independently with certain case suffixes (2), or as a part of more complex formulations, for the most part the prohibitive and constructions with postpositions (3).

### 1) Nomen imperfecti as an attribute

Form the viewpoint of translation the construction with the imperfective noun as an attribute can be interpreted as either active, as in phrases where the verbal noun determines the agent (a); or passive, as in phrases where it determines the object (b). Furthermore, it may express other determinations (of time, space, or purpose) (c).

a) Nomen imperfecti as determiner of the agent

Ex. 1: *ər baitə-f **taqə-r na$^n$** tə aqŭ-ʁ$^{ŭ}$i.*
Lit.: This matter-ACC. **know-NI.** person now NEG.-become-PERF.
There is **nobody** left now who **could know** this.

Ex. 2: *čimar **gənə-r na$^n$** laft ba.*
Lit.: Tomorrow **go-NI. person** many PROB.
Many people **will** probably go **there** tomorrow.

Ex. 3: *mi-$^n$ agə **bo banjə-r na$^n$** vaq ba.*
Lit.: 1sg.-GEN. older brother house **live-NI. person** not PROB.
My brother is not the kind of **person who should have a family**.

b) Nomen imperfecti determining the object

Ex. 1: ***išk$^i$a-r baitə** ñi gum aлč$^i$.*
Lit.: **Arrange-NI. matter** POSS.all on.the.edge.
He does everything by halves, he does not finish **what he does**.

Ex. 2: *ɢazn-t **taqə-r na$^n$** bi na?*
Lit.: Village-DL. **know-NI. person** is QUEST.
Do you **know anybody** in Chabchal?

Ex. 3: *mi$^n$ **taqə-r na$^n$** gum jiʁa aq$^{ŭ}$.*
Lit.: **1sg.-GEN. know-NI. person** all money NEG.
All the **people I know** are without money.

c) Nomen imperfecti expressing purpose and destination

Ex. 1: *yamsqŭ$^n$ **jaq jə-r ərin-də ñi** śiñi bo-či məda-m.*
Lit.: Evening **thing eat-NI. time-DL. F.** only house-LAT. turn back-IMP.
We used to come home only **at dinner-time**.

Ex. 2: ***ñuŋk ta-r ərdəmə ñi** śie$^n$ vaq ŭrŭ.*
Lit.: **Ilness see-NI. knowledge** POSS. good not PROB.
The **level of health care** was not good.

Ex. 3: *lam bəš-k nanᵊ-i bo-t ji-m **lom ara-r dor** aqů-ʁᵘi.*
Lit.: Lama die-NP. person-GEN. house-DL. come-CI. ***lom** make-NI. custom* NEG.-(become)-PERF.
**The custom in which** a lama comes to the house where someone has died and **performs the *lom*** has vanished.

## 2) Constructions with postpositions

The imperfect noun construes most often with the postpositions *ongoɹ* 'before, ago', *aməɹ* 'after', *śidəⁿ* 'between' and *diorgit* 'inside, in the course of'.

Ex. 1: ***yavə-r śⁱdəⁿ** ər ju yilaⁿ učuⁿ aɹ-m bu-ki.*
Lit.: **Go-NI. between** this two three song tell-CI. give-VOL.
**Before you leave**, I will teach you some of these songs.

Ex. 2: ***gizərə-r diorgidə** χaʁəč da ər əmbičⁱ jaləⁿ naⁿ, əmbičⁱ abbanš-k guruⁿ bi-yᵖye ...*
Lit.: **Talk-NI. inside** boy ACT. this maybe world person maybe how.born folk be-PERF.
**While they were talking**, the boy [was thinking]: Are these people from this world or what beings could they be?

Ex. 3: ***yavə-r oɴoɹ** bo-d ňi əmda døš-či o-m ba?*
Lit.: **Go-NI. before** house-DL. POSS. once enter-CC. become-IMP. PROB.
What about going to see him once **before you leave**?

## 3) Nomen imperfecti with case suffix (DL.)

Constructions of the imperfect verb with the dative-locative suffix convey, very similarly to the situation in Mongolian, the grammatical meaning of two parallel ongoing actions, or of one action occurring simultaneously with another action (a); or it conveys the sense of a characteristic of the given action, qualifying it for the most part as easy or difficult (b). Apart from this, the imperfective noun in the dative-locative may acquire a more nominal character and thus convey the meaning of "in the given action", e.g. *yavə-r-d ňi*, lit. 'in his walking', which then may mean either 'when he was going' or 'by his walking'.

If the subject of the action is marked, it mostly stands in the genitive case. When the subject is not expressed, it is often marked by the enclitic pronoun *ňi*. The impersonal subject remains unexpressed.

a) Paralell actions

Ex. 1: *śi-ⁿ **yavə-r-t** bi śim-b bən-ki.*
Lit.: 2sg.-GEN. **go-NI.-DL.** 1sg. 2sg.-ACC. escort.
I will see you off **when you are leaving**.

Ex. 2: ***yavə-r-də ňi** bi faɹ-χ əvəⁿ ara-m bu-ʁᵊi.*
Lit.: **Go-NI.-DL. POSS.** I heaved bread make-CI. give-PERF.
**When he was leaving**, I made a Sibe bread form him.

151

Ex. 3:  *čaqůr **tavənə-r-t** amś tavə-vǔ-q$^{ǔ}$.*
      Lit.: čaqůr **ascend-NI.-DL.** northwards see-CAUS.-(NI.)-NEG.
      **When climbing the** *čaqůr* he is not allowed to look to the north.

  b) Expression of purpose or goal

Ex. 1:  *śivə gizu$^n$ **tači-r-t maN** na?*
      Lit.: Sibe language **study-NI.-DL.** difficult QUEST.
      Is the Sibe language **difficult to study**?

Ex. 2:  *ər śok **ara-r-t** hən ja.*
      Lit.: This vegetables **make-NI.-DL** very **easy**.
      This dish is **easy to cook**.

Ex. 3:  *gira$^n$ **čiči-və-r-də ňi** gəɹ bait laft.*
      Lit.: Corpse **come.out-CAUS.-NI.-DL.** F. still matter many.
      There are many rules to be observed **during the burial**.

### *The imperfective noun as an attribute of certain words with general meaning*

The nomen imperfecti is often used with nouns of more 'abstract' meaning: *ba* 'place', *bait* 'matter', *duru$^n$*, *arvə$^n$* 'form, appearance', and can in this way form a great number of terms.

  a) Constructions with the noun *ba* place

Idioms with the word *ba* express (apart from the basic meaning of 'place') the meaning of space in the more abstract sense; for example, an opportunity for an action, among other meanings. In literary Manchu the word *ba* has also the purely grammatical function of substantivization of a verbal form (Zaharov 1879, p. 76), while in spoken Sibe it retains part of its lexical meaning. Its stylistic function corresponds to that of the Chinese expression *dian* 'point, place'.

Ex. 1:  *bo yaf-ki, ənəŋ gəɹ **gənə-r ba** bi.*
      Lit.: 1pl.(excl.) go-VOL., today still **go-NI. place** is.
      We have to leave now, we still have to **visit somebody** today.
      Note: In this case the word *ba* is used in its lexical meaning.

Ex. 2:  *si-$^n$ du-t **soNq$^{ǔ}$ aɹdəvə-r ba** gəɹ bi-y$^{ə}$ye.*
      Lit.: 2sg.-GEN. younger.brother-DL. **cry drop-NI. place** still be-PERF.
      You see, your younger brother has **moments when he cries**.
      Note: Here and in the following examples the use of the word *ba* generally signifies an opportunity or space for an action.

Ex. 3:  *ai ursu$^n$ banš-k$^{ə}$ye, šuda **ta-r ba aq$^{ǔ}$**.*
      Lit.: What ugly be born-PERF, completely **look-NI. place NEG**.
      How ugly she looks, it is not **possible to look at her**.

Note: Expressions like *ta-r ba aqᵘ̊* 'no place for looking', *ta-r duruⁿ aqᵘ̊* 'no form to look at' as well as *ta-m oju-qᵘ̊* 'impossible to look' are used as negative statements about the appearance of something or someone.

Ex. 4:   *qᵘ̊ariam-b ňi **gizərə-r ba aqᵘ̊**.*
         Lit.: Beautiful-ACC. POSS. **speak-NI. place NEG**.
         Her beauty is **hard to describe**.

b) Constructions with the noun *bait* 'matter'

Idioms with the noun *bait* can be generally rendered in two ways: a more 'static' rendition, which is related to the conception of the general tense, when the nominal character of the whole expression is more pronounced and can be translated as 'about' (Ex. 1); and a more 'dynamic' rendition which applies to the future, expressing the idea of 'appropriate, desirable' (Ex. 2).

Ex. 1:   *jai əm duaɹ-də ňi **yavə-r baitə-f** gizər-ʁᵊi.*
         Lit.: Next one strophe-DL. POSS, **go-NI. matter-ACC**. speak-PERF.
         The next strophe is **about the journey**.

Ex. 2:   *ər həɣə-f χafsə-r **bait** bi-yᵊi.*
         Lit.: This woman-ACC. **tell-NI. matter** be-PERF.
         One **should have reported** that woman.

c) Constructions with the nouns *duruⁿ, arvəⁿ*: 'form, appearance'

The imperfective verbal noun with the expressions *duruⁿ, arvəⁿ* is used to express the external aspect of an action. It should be rendered as 'it seems/appears that'.

Ex. 1:   *śi-ⁿ tər **yalə-r durum-b** ňi ta-mə bi gəɹ-yᵊi.*
         Lit.: Your **ride-NI. form POSS**. see I fear-PERF.
         When I saw the **way you rode** I was scared.

Ex. 2:   *təraɴ o-mə tər fayiŋə-v ňi **čiči-və-r duruⁿ** bie.*
         Lit.: Thus become-CI. soul-ACC. POSS. **come out-CAUS.-NI. form** is.
         **It seems that** in this way they **help the soul to get out** (from the body).

### Use of the imperfective noun in other grammatical functions

#### 1) Negation of the imperfective noun and the imperfective verb

The negated form of the imperfective noun serves to create the negative counterpart of the imperfective noun itself (a) and of the imperfective verb (b). As described above, the abbreviated form is largely used in the spoken language, although the full form at times does occur in the speech of the older generation.

a) Negation of the forms of the imperfective noun

Ex. 1: *ər jaq danə-q$^{ŭ}$, ačənə-m na **ačəna-q$^{ŭ}$** gizu$^{n}$ gizər-maq dut-k$^{ə}$i.*
Lit.: This thing care-NI.-NEG. agree-CI. QUEST. **agree-(NI.)-NEG**. word talk-CP. lay-PERF.
She keeps talking and does not care whether she speaks correctly or **not**.

Ex. 2: *na$^{n}$ **išk$^{i}$a-m mutu-q$^{ŭ}$** baitə-f əmda$^{n}$ išk$^{i}$a-kie zə-m ɕŭñi-m.*
Lit.: **Person arrange can-(NI.)-NEG**. matter once arrange-VOL. say-CI. think-IMP.
I would like to one time do **something that nobody else could do**.

Ex. 3: *dači ɕazn-t mi-$^{n}$ ɕorəyi-f **taqə-q$^{ŭ}$ na$^{n}$ aq$^{ŭ}$.***
Lit.: Originally village-DL. 1sg.-GEN. far-grandfather **know-(NI.)-NEG. person NEG.**
Formerly there was nobody in Chabchal **who would not know** my grandfather from Mother's side.

b) Negation of the imperfective verb

Ex. 1: *tiørʁŭ-m χorʁŭ-m ta-š gələ ji-də-r arvəm-b **savə-r-qŭ**.*
Lit.: Turn-CI. turn-CI. look-CC. still come-NI. form **see-NI.-NEG**.
I was looking and looking around but **I could not see** her coming.
Note: From the lyrics of a song written in the 1970s. The author was born into an educated family and his songs often employ literary forms which are still sung unchanged, even by speakers ignorant of the literary language, right up to the present day.

Ex. 2: *moχt faqar gəɹ arə-m **bana-q$^{ŭ}$**.*
Lit.: Short trousers still make-CI. **know-(NI.)-NEG**.
He **does not** even **know** how to make trunks (= he is manually inept)

## 2) Negation with an inserted particle

A special form of negative expressions is created by inserting the particles *gəɹ* 'still, too' or *χań(i)* 'little, at least' between the verbal noun and the negative suffix with the resulting meaning 'not even'. The verbal noun retains its full form. This type of constructions most often expresses a modal meaning of displeasure or disagreement.[22]

Ex. 1: *ər saʁanju-s **danə-r gəɹ aq$^{ŭ}$**.*
Lit.: This girl-PART. **care-NI. still NEG**.
These girls do not **even/at all care** about him.

Ex. 2: *mim-b sav-mə **śie$^{n}$ fienji-r gəɹ aq$^{ŭ}$**.*
Lit.: 1sg.-ACC. see-CI. **good ask-NI. still NEG**.
When she sees me **she does not even say hello**.

---

[22] This construction is formally and semantically analogical to the Mongolian construction *verbal noun+č+gui medeh č gu'i* 'I do not even know'.

Ex. 3: *ər naⁿ dor yozə-f taqə-qᵘ, naⁿ ji-š da vəra-f **tiki-r gəɹ aqᵘ**.*
Lit.: This person custom rule-ACC. know-(NI.)-NEG., person come-CC. ACT.
buttocks-ACC. **lift-NI. still NEG.**
He has no education, when somebody comes in, he **does not even lift** his buttocks.

Ex. 4: *yav-m vaš-kᵊi, bi **sa-r χaň aqᵘ**.*
Lit.: Go-CI. finish-PERF, 1sg. **know-NI. little NEG.**
He has left and **I even do not know about it**.

### 3) Constructions with the particle *indi*

The particle *indi* (Lit. Ma. *unde*) refers to an action which has been expected but has not yet occurred. The general meaning should be translated as 'not yet'.

Ex. 1: *ər uču-mb bi **dønji-r indi**.*
Lit.: This song I hear-NI. **not yet.**
**I have not heard** this song yet.

Ex. 2: *bi təzə bo-t **gənə-r indi**.*
Lit.: 1sg. they house go-NI. **not yet.**
I have **not yet visited** them.

Ex. 3: *ər bitkə-v **arə-m vajə-r indi**.*
Lit.: This book-ACC. **write-CI. finish-NI. not yet.**
This book is **not yet finished**.

## 7.4.2 Perfective verbal noun -h (nomen perfecti)

*Forms of the perfective verbal noun*

The basic form of the suffix is *-χ/-h*, distributed according to the place of articulation.
Some verbs have a variant *-q /-k* (in the modern language the velar/uvular distinction is gradually being lost). As in the case of the imperfective verb, the distribution of the allomorphs *-k/-h* differs from that of literary Manchu.

*Use of the perfective verbal noun*

The perfective noun is used in the same way as the imperfective noun. However, forms which are similar to the perfective noun may occur also in a predicate position, especially when a sequence of actions is being described. Therefore the use of the perfective noun may be described as (1) an attribute, (2) occurring in constructions with postpositions, (3) occurring in constructions with case suffixes, and (4) as a predicate.

### 1. Nomen perfecti as an attribute

In the similar fashion to the imperfective noun, is the nomen perfecti is used in both active and passive constructions as well as in other determinations.

a) Nomen perfecti as an attribute of the agent

Ex. 1:   *χanč **yafh guruⁿ** bəyə-v ňi ov-m.*
   Lit.: Close **go-NP. folk** body-ACC. POSS. wash-IMP.
   His **close friends** wash his body.

b) Nomen perfecti as attribute of the object

Ex. 1:   *sur **døš-k naⁿ** ňi əm bait aqᵘ̊ da soɴů-m.*
   Lit.: Sur **enter-NI. person F.** one matter NEG cry-IMP.
   **A person who was possessed** by the soul of a dead person cries without reason.

Ex. 2:   *suʌʙo **yila-χ ɢarʙəⁿ** dor arə-m.*
   Lit.: **Apple stand-NP.** branch custom make-IMP.
   **A branch with apples** bows.
   Note: A proverb.

c) Nomen perfecti in determination of circumstances

Ex.:   *haɴś **døš-k ňinəŋ** uduⁿ da-mə dih ňinəŋ uduⁿ da-m zə-r.*
   Lit.: *haɴś* enter-NP. day wind blow-CI. fourty day wind blow-IMP. say-NI.
   When a wind blows on the **first day of the *haɴś*** (a period in the Chinese agricultural calendar) it is said that it will blow for forty days.

### 2. Nomen perfecti with postpositions

The perfective noun is often combined with the postpositions *aməʌ* 'after' and *oɴoʌ* 'before', *śidən* 'between', as well as with some other postpositions.

Ex. 1:   *ər naⁿ **ji-ɣ aməʌ** śiňi ər baitə-ʃ sa-ʙ°i.*
   Lit.: This **person come-NP. after** only this mater-PERF.
   I have learned about the whole thing only **after he came**.

Ex. 2:   *əm gizuⁿ **gizər-h śidəⁿ** da aqů -ʙᵘ̊i.*
   Lit.: One word **say-NP. between** ACT. NEG-become-PERF.
   She disappeared **before I could say** a word.

### 3. Nomen perfecti used as an independent noun with case suffixes

Ex. 1:   *əva-t ɕaš-kə-də orʁŭ-i joʁŭ<sup>n</sup> yav-ʁ<sup>ə</sup>i.*
Lit.: Here bring-NP.-DL. grass-GEN. way go-PERF.
**When they were being brought** here, they went through the grasslands.

Ex. 2:   *ajigə nu<sup>n</sup>-bə daʁə-m **yav-ʁa-də** sav<sup>ə</sup>-i fatə<sup>n</sup> ñi man-ʁ<sup>ə</sup>ye.*
Lit.: Little younger sister follow-CI. **go-NP.-DL.** shoe-GEN. sole-POSS. wear. through-PERF.
**As I was following** my little sister (=beloved) the soles of my shoes got worn through.
Note: From the lyrics of a folk song.

### 4. Nomen perfecti as a predicate

Ex.:   *oɹʁŭ-i nanə-f **ar-ʁə**, arə-m vaji-maq da χošqŭ<sup>n</sup> utku-v ñi **utu-v-ʁə**, maʁaɹ-v ñi uju-d ñi **utuvʁə**.*
Lit. Rushes-GEN. person-ACC. **make-NP.** make-CI. ACT. son-in-law POSS. clothes-ACC. Cap-ACC. POSS. **put.on-CAUS.-NP.** head-DL. POSS. **put.on-CAUS.-NP.**
She **made** a human figure of rushes, **put** the clothes of her son-in-law on it, and put his cap on its head.

#### *Negation of the perfective noun*

As in the case of the imperfective noun, the negated form of the perfective noun serves to negate either (1) the perfective noun itself, or (2) the perfective verb.

The negation is achieved by attaching the negative particle *(a)q<sup>ŭ</sup>* to the verbal noun. In rapid speech the strongly uvular pronunciation of the negative particle causes, in cases of front vowel stems, an assimilation of the preceding suffix of the verbal noun. The result is a shift of pronunciation of the suffix to the back position, which, however, does not reach the degree of the usual pronunciation of uvulars and back vowels (e.g. *gən-ɣ<sup>ə</sup>i* 'went' – *gən-ʁa-q<sup>ŭ</sup>* 'did not go').

### 1. Negation of a verbal noun

Ex.:   *śi-<sup>n</sup> ji-m **jaft-qa-q<sup>ŭ</sup>** baitə-f min-t aɹ-m bu-ɣ<sup>ə</sup>i.*
Lit.: 2sg.-GEN. come-CI. **manage-NP.-NEG.** matter-ACC. 1sg.DL. say-CI. give-PERF.
They informed me that you **could not come.**

### 2. Negation of the perfective verb

In the negation of the perfective verb the negated form is sometimes followed by the marker of 'finiteness' *-i(-e)*. Such forms correspond to the literary forms *-he-kū-bi/-ha-kū-bi* (*yabu-ha-qū-bi* 'did not go').

Ex.: *bi śim-b sav-ʁa-q$^{ü}$-ye!*
Lit.: 1sg. 2sg.-ACC. **see-NP.-NEG.**
**I really did not notice** you.

### 7.4.3 The progressive verbal noun -*maʁ*

The complex suffix of the progressive noun -*maʁ(ə)* corresponds to the written form -*maha*. The frequency of use of this nominal form is considerably lesser than that of the previous two nominal forms. As with both of these forms, it may function as an attribute or as a specification of circumstances.

#### 1. The progressive verbal noun as an attribute

Ex.: *təvat yav-maχ na$^n$ ñi mi-$^n$ guč$^u$.*
Lit.: There **go-NPROG. person** POSS 1sg.-GEN. friend.
**The man who is walking** there is my friend.

#### 2. The progressive verbal noun in specification of circumstances

Ex.: *kəskə ma.ıtə-maʁ əm duru$^n$ čira ov-m.*
Lit.: Cat **lick-NPROG.** one form face wash-IMP.
He washes his face as carelessly as a cat **licks** itself.

### 7.4.4 Verbal nouns II

A feature typical of both Manchu and Sibe are the independent verbal nouns formed by the addition of the nominalizing suffix -*ŋ(ə)* -*n(ə)* (in literary Manchu this suffix has a single form -*ngge*) to verbal nouns, as well as the imperfective noun -*r-ə*, the perfective noun -*ʁ-ə/ y-ə* a and the progressive verbal noun -*maʁ-ə*. The epenthetic vowel -*ə*- is compulsory.

The independent verbal nouns usually refer to the agent, the patient (not in the grammatical sense of object) or the abstract denomination of an action. They may be also occur in a predicate position. This function is characteristic of the perfective verbal noun II, a fact which leads the authors of *Xiboyu kouyu yanjiu* to include this form among finite verbs (Li Shulan 1984, p. 46). Given the pronounced nominal character of these forms, their use slightly differs from the use of nominal predicates in Mongolian. This concept is supported by the correlation of the category of Manchu verbal nouns II with the Chinese verbal form with the genitive/adjectival particle *de*, which is generally used to translate the Manchu forms with -*ngge*.

The function of the category of Manchu and Sibe verbal nouns II is similar to Mongolian verbal nouns with the possessive (nominalizing) particle *n'*, which are actually used to translate Manchu verbal nouns II: *yavsan n'* 'his having left' or 'the one who has left'; *ireh n'* 'his arrival' or 'the one who will come' and so forth.

### The imperfective verbal noun II -rə-ŋ(ə)

#### 1. The imperfective verbal noun II as a nominal predicate

Ex. 1: *śivə naⁿ yiqaⁿ həh gia-m **ojǔ-qǔ-N** təraN.*
Lit.: Sibe person Chinese woman take-CI. **can-NI.II.-NEG**. like.that.
That is **why it is impossible** for the Sibes to marry Chinese girls.

#### 2. The imperfective verbal noun II expressing an immediately preceding action

The imperfective verbal noun II is often used in the descriptions of parallel actions, of which one conditions the other, adhering closely to the meaning of 'as soon as'. In this function the Sibe verbal noun II is regularly followed by the actualizing particle *da*, which implies a closer succession of the actions.

Ex. 1: *mim-b **savə-rə-ŋ da** bait fienji-mači-m.*
Lit.: 1sg.-ACC. **see-NI.II ACT**. matter ask-INC.-IMP.
**As soon as he sees** me, he starts to inquire about all possible things.

Ex. 2: *uči **jiлʁanə-rə-ŋ da** gətə-m vaš-kᵊi.*
Lit.: Door make.**sound-NI.II ACT**. wake-CI. finish-PERF.
**As soon as** the door **creaked**, I woke up.

#### 3. Imperfective verbal noun II in the function of a nominal sentence constituent

The imperfective verbal noun II most often functions as a subject or an object. It often takes the accusative suffix, which is never affixed to a plain verbal noun. On the other hand it does not take the dative-locative suffix, which is the only case suffix used with plain verbal nouns.

Ex. 1: *tər ərin-t **ivi-rə-N-ə** həⁿ šufu.*
Lit.: That time **play-NI.II** very pleasant(Chin).
In those times **playing** was so pleasant.

Ex. 2: *təraN ərin-də naⁿ bəčə-maq təraN lom **ara-rə-N-v** ňi sav-ʁᵊye.*
Lit.: Thus time-DL. person die-CP. *lom* **do-NI.II-ACC**. F. see-PERF.
At that time I saw **how** a lama **performed** the *lom* ritual after somebody's death.

The imperfective verbal noun II is typically used in a construction with another verbal form derived from the same stem. This construction defines a part of the members of a group, all of whom are referred to by the lexical meaning of the verb. (A similar linguistic device is familiar from Mongolian – e.g. *yavah n'yavna, suuh n'suuna* 'those who want to leave may leave, those who want to sit may sit'.)

159

Ex. 3:   *tuku-mə da saməm-b ňi va-rə-ŋəv ňi va-m, dielə-rə-ŋəv ňi dielə-m.*
Lit.: Thus.do-CI. ACT. shaman-ACC. POSS. **kill-NI.II. ACC. POSS. kill-IMP.,**
**drive-NI.II. ACC. POSS. drive-IMP.**
So they **killed part** of the shamans and **chased the other part** to other places.

### *The perfective verbal noun II*

In the spoken language the perfective verbal noun II is used mainly (1) in the function of a predicate, (2) in a function similar to that of a converb, and (3) in all nominal functions of the verbal nouns II (agent, object and denomination of an action).

In the spoken language the negative form of the suffix (Lit. Ma. *-haqūngge/-hekūngge*) usually carries an uvular pronunciation *-ʁa-qǔ-n(ə)*, caused by the uvular articulatory position of the negative suffix.

### 1. The perfective verbal noun II as a predicate

The perfective verbal noun II is frequently used as a predicate, but – as appears from the collected material – only with the first and second persons. This seems to refer to the grammatical category of evidentiality – the use of the perfective verbal noun II either expresses first-hand experience or emphasizes the speaker's personal interest.

Ex. 1:   *yet gən-yə-ŋ-ə?*
Lit.: Where **go-NP.II.**
Where **have you been**?

Ex. 2:   *bi təzə-f sav-ʁən, bi jiɹʁan-ʁaqǔn.*
Lit.: 1sg. 3pl.-ACC. **see-NP.II.**, 1sg. **make.sound-NP.II.NEG.**
**I did see** them, but I **did not address** them.

Ex. 3:   *jaq jə-kə-ŋ na? jə-kə-ŋ-ə.*
Lit.: Thing **eat-NP.II. QUEST. eat-NP.II.**
**Did you eat? Yes, I did.**

### 2. The perfective verbal noun II in a converbial function

The perfective verbal noun II occurs as a dependent member of a verbal construction more frequently than its imperfective counterpart. It may occur:
a) Directly preceding another verb.
b) Followed by the actualizing particle *da*. Such constructions express various time relationships and are interchangeable with converbs.
c) The perfective verbal noun II preceded by the word *əmdaⁿ* 'once' (< *əm mədaⁿ* 'one time') has a function similar to the perfective converb, expressing a more loosely defined temporal sequence than in the previous cases. The resulting meaning is either an action preceding another action, or a single action entering into a durative action. The word

*əmdaⁿ* adds a modal tint of intensity to the single action and is a frequent means of enlivening narrative.

a) Plain construction of the verbal noun II with another verb

Ex. 1:   *əñi ñi* **susχaɹ-ʁəŋ fienji-r śidə<sup>n</sup>da** *fa-dəri ñi χûɹɣʁa-m ta-m bi-yˀi.*
Lit.: Mother POSS. **whip-NP.II ask-NI. between ACT**. window-ABL. POSS. steel-CI. look-CI. be-PERF.
While her mother was **whipping and asking**, he was watching secretly from outside the window.
Note: From an account about healing a person possessed by a soul of the dead.

Ex. 2:   *ərči tərči* **amčə-m zə-ɣəŋ doʁûr-maq ta** *ulan-či tu-hˀi.*
Lit.: Here there **hunt-CI. say-NP.II roll-CP. ACT** hole-LAT. fall-PERF.
She was running here and there **to catch it, until she stumbled** and fell into a pit.

b) Construction with the perfective verbal noun II followed by the particle *da*

Ex.:   *bədərə-m* **jiɣəŋ da daʁə-v-maq,** *fayiŋ ñi gəɹ daʁə-maq ji-h bi-yˀi.*
Lit.: Return-CI. **come-NP.II ACT follow-CAUS-CP**. soul POSS. still follow-CP. come-NP. bi-PERF.
**When he was coming back** (from the graveyard) **he brought it** (unconsciously) with him – the soul (of the buried person) followed him back home.

c) Constructions with the word *əmdaⁿ* once:

ca) An action preceding another action

Ex. 1:   **əmdaⁿ gən-ɣəŋ,** *yivəŋ yivəŋ naⁿ.*
Lit.: **Once go-NP.II** *yivaŋ yivaŋ* (ONOM.) person.
**As I went there**, there were lots of people.

Ex. 2:   **əmdaⁿ fier-ɣəŋ,** *dəyi-maq yav-ʁˀi...*
Lit.: **Once hit-NP.II** fly-CP. go-PERF
**As she hit it**, it flew.

cb) An action occurring simultaneously with another action or state

Ex. 3:   **əmdaⁿ dǿźi-m ji-ɣəŋ** *bo-t jalu naⁿ bi.*
Lit.: **Once enter-CP. come-NP.II** house-DL. full person is.
**When I went in**, the room was full of people.

Ex. 4:   **əmdaⁿ ji-ɣəŋ,** *əm jiri sarʁaⁿ naⁿ.*
Lit.: **Once come-NP.II**, one pair female person.
**As they came nearer**, he could see that they were two women.

### 3. The perfective verbal noun II in the functions of subject or object

The perfective verbal noun II can denote the agent, the object or an abstract denomination of the action. The form of the verb *zə-* 'say, call' has a specific idiomatic function – the form *zəyəŋ* (*ə*) is used as a way of explaining the meaning of another word or of a statement. In literary Manchu the imperfective verbal noun II *serengge* is used in this function. In Mongolian the corresponding expressions are derived from the root *ge-* (*gedeg n', gesen üg,* and other derived forms.)

Ex. 1:  *śivə diørʁ̊ut huis, huihui-maq śieri<sup>n</sup> **ar-ʁəN** ňi bi.*
  Lit.: Sibe inside Uighur, Hui-IS wedding **make-NP.II F**. is.
  Among the Sibe people there are **those who have married** Uighurs and Huis.

Ex. 2:  *fa **mavəɹ-ʁəŋ ňi** əm bait o-ʁ̊<sup>u</sup>i.*
  Lit.: Window **wipe-NP.II F**. one matter become-PERF.
  **Washing** a window became an issue. (= He makes a problem of washing a window).

Ex. 3:  *hut **zə-yəŋ da**, əhśie<sup>n</sup> jaq.*
  Lit.: Ghost **say-NP.II ACT**. bad.good thing.
  The word 'hut' **means** an evil being.

***The progressive verbal noun II -maʁəN(ə)***

The progressive verbal noun II usually occurs in a predicate position.

Ex.:  *yava-dəri **ji-maʁəN-ə?***
  Lit.: Where-ABL. **come-NPROG.II**.
  Where **are** you **coming** from (right now)?

## 7.5 Converbs

The verbal forms usually designated as **converbs**[23] in most English-language analyses are usually referred to as ***deepričastija*** (gerunds) in the Russian literature and ***fu dong ci – adverbial verbs*** by Chinese linguists. The Mongolian grammatical term ***nöhcöl üil üg*** is close to the Chinese one. The main syntactical function of converbs is to join two and more verbs or verbal phrases in a sentence. Different types of converbs express different types of relationships between the respective verbal actions.

B. Sechenbaatar divides Chachar Mongolian converbs into two main groups – the **coordinative** and the **subordinative** converbs. The coordinative converbs "can take auxilliary verbs and be used repeatedly" while the subordinative converbs do not (Sechenbaatar 2003, p. 127–128). Sechenbaatar lists three coordinative converbs, ten subordinative converbs and one which may be classified as both in Chahar Mongol.

---

[23] "The converbs express actions characterizing other actions. They express manner or circumstances in which the action of the finite verb is performed." (Poppe 1987, p. 276)

In Manchu and Sibe, there are three converbs of the coordinative type and two converbs of the subordinative type. The coordinative converbs are also employed in defining the temporal relationship between two or more actions, while the subordinative converbs express other non-temporal relationships: condition and termination.

*Coordinative converbs*

Spoken Sibe uses two main coordinative converbs: the **imperfective converb** -*mə*, which, by means of its function, corresponds to the Mongolian imperfective converb -*ž/-č*; and the perfective converb -*maq*, which corresponds to the Mongolian perfective converb -*aad⁴*. A third converb, the perfective -*fi* of literary Manchu, is used as a variant.

The difference between the two main coordinative converbs -*mə* and -*maq* seems to adhere in the relative greater or lesser proximity of the junction between the described verbal actions, often involving as well a relative temporal determination. The perfective converbs, in particular the converb -*fi*, usually express the concrete temporal meaning of an action which precedes another action.

The main function of the coordinative converbs is the formation of verbal phrases; these are the most important means to describe verbal actions and their various aspects. Both of the coordinative converbs join with various verbs in their original lexical meaning, as well as with modal and auxiliary verbs to create different kinds of verbal phrases.

*Subordinative converbs*

The subordinative converbs in spoken Sibe are the conditional converb -*či*, which corresponds to Mongolian -*bal⁴* and the terminative converb -*čiňi*, which has a partial resemblance to the Mongolian converb -*tal⁴*.

The semantical characterisitics of the subordinative converbs is more specific than that of the coordinative converbs.

## 7.5.1 The imperfective converb -*m*(ə) (converbum imperfecti)

The imperfective converb (designated as ***deepričastie odnovremennoe*** byRussian scholars) has a single form in both the literary and spoken languages: the form -*mə*.

Given the frequency of occurrence of this converb, it may be concluded that formerly it played a more significant role in the language than its perfective counterpart. This fact is particularly evident in the literary language, where the perfective converb -*fi* is used only when the temporal succession or causal relationship of the actions is emphasized, whereas the greater abundance of all the differing verbal phrases is mainly formed by the imperfective converb -*me*.

In the contemporary spoken language the situation has changed somewhat, in large part because the use of the perfective converb -*maq* adds more vivacity to the spoken word, whereas the converb -*m* has a rather neutral tone.[24] Still it must be stated that the scale of the modal tints which may be expressed by the imperfective converb is so broad that a full enumeration is not attempted in the present work, let alone a complete analysis. I have

---

[24] A similar tendency may be observed in the Mongolian use of the imperfective converb -*ž/-č* and the perfective converb -*aad⁴*.

simply endeavoured to give a sense of the main ranges of use and meanings which the suffix *-m(ə)* may create, adding as well some specific observations which occurred in the collected material.

### Usage of the imperfective converb

The imperfective converb is used to **form verbal phrases** (linking two or more verbal forms immediately one after another). Often they are further developed into **dependent clauses**, in which the converb then functions as a predicate.

#### The imperfective converb in verbal phrases

From the point of view of semantics the most frequent verbal phrases with the imperfective converb are: (1) constructions with reduplicated converb, (2) constructions with verbs with full meanings, and (3) constructions with modal verbs.

#### 1) Reduplication

Reduplication of the imperfective converb usually expresses a repeated action which takes place during a certain period of time.

Ex. 1:  *min-či **ta-m ta-m** inji-mə...*
          Lit.: 1sg.-LAT. **look-CI. look-CI.** laugh-CI...
          **Peering** at me **from time to time** and laughing...

#### 2) Constructions with verbs with full lexical meaning

The significance of such constructions varies among that of the simple **connection of two or more actions, a resultative consequence, an action and its goal**, and others as well. The boundaries between these subtle shades of meaning are often quite difficult to define.

Ex. 1:  *tər, **fəksa-m fietə-m** jimɛye.*
          That, **cough-CI. fart-CI. come-PROG.**
          There he **comes**, (I can hear him) **coughing.**

Ex. 2:  *bi təzə-maq davɹ **gənə-m ji-q$^{\ddot{u}}$.***
          Lit.: 1sg. 3pl.-IS. too **go-CI. come-(NI.)-NEG.**
          **I do not have** frequent **contacts** with them.

Ex. 3:  *śim-b **bia-m ji-ɣ$^{ə}$i.***
          Lit.: 2sg.-ACC. **seek-CI. come-PERF.**
          I am **coming to see** you.

Ex. 4:  ***ainə-m ji-ɣ$^{ə}$ye, tači-m ji-ɣə na?***
          Lit.: **Do.what-CI. come-PERF, study-CI. come PERF. QUEST.**
          **What did you come for, did you come for study?**

164

### 3) Constructions with modal and auxiliary verbs

Most of the modal and auxiliary verbs require a construction with the converb -*m(ə)*, in particular:
– verbs expressing option, possibility or ability: *ba(ʁə)nə*- 'to be able, to know', *mutə*- 'to be able to', *o*- 'to be possible'
– the verb *čaʁa*- 'to like'
– verbs of initiation and termination of actions: *vajə*- 'to finish', *dəriv*- 'to start'
– verbs of giving and taking: *gia*- 'to take', *bu*- 'to give'
– verbs of movement and staying: *gənə*- 'to go there', *ji*- 'to come', *yila*- 'to stand'
– the verb *ta*- 'to look'
– the verbs expressing an achievement of a goal *javdə*- 'to hurry up [so as] to manage' and *baʁə* 'to succeed in, to get the opportunity to'
– the auxiliary verbs *o*- 'to be possible', *zə*- 'to say' and *bi*- 'to be'

All modal and auxiliary verbs – with the exception of *javdə*- 'to hurry up [so as] to manage' and *baʁə* 'to succeed in, to have the opportunity to', which appears on the first position in the phrase – follow the main verb.

Each of these groups of verbs (and possibly every single verb) has its own semantic range and its own function which is connected with its lexical meaning. The relative bounded or unboundedness of the connection with the main verb also depends on the original lexical meaning of the grammaticalized verb.[25]

a) **verbs expressing option, possibility, ability**: *ba(ʁə)nə*- 'to can, to know. to be able to', *mutə*- 'to be able to', *o*- 'to be possible'

Ex. 1:   *məs gələ-maq **banjə-m o-m na**?*
        Lit.: 1pl. fear-CP. **live-CI. can-IMP. QUEST**.
        **How can we live** in fear?

Ex. 2:   *čimar bi **gənə-m mutə-q$^{\ddot{u}}$**.*
        Lit.: Tomorrow 1sg. **go-CI. can-NI.-NEG**.
        **I cannot go** there tomorrow.

Ex. 3:   *uču$^n$ **učulu-m baʁənə-m**, **bəylə-m baʁənə-m**.*
        Lit.: Song **sing-CI. know-IMP, dance-CI. know-IMP**.
        **He can sing and dance**.

b) **The verb *čaʁa*- to like**

Ex.:   *bi əvat **ji-m čaʁəN**.*
       Lit.: 1sg. here **come-CI. like**.
       **I like to come** here.

---

[25] An analogical system of using the converbs with modal verbs to form phrases with a broad scale of meanings also exists in Mongolian and in the Turkic languages. What is conspicuous is the almost perfect agreement in the semantic fields of individual auxiliaries.

c) **Verbs of initiation and termination of actions**: *vajə-* 'to finish', *dərif-* 'to start'

Ex. 1: *jašqaⁿ ara-m vaš-kᵊi.*
Lit.: Letter write-CI. finish-PERF.
He **finished writing** the letter.

Ex. 2: *əmgəri učulu-m dəriv-yᵊi.*
Lit.: Already **sing-CI. start-PERF**.
They have already **started to sing**.

d) **Verbs of giving and taking**: *gia-* 'to take', *bu-* 'to give'

The verb *gia-* 'to take' expresses direction of the action towards the object or patient, whereas the verb *bu-* 'to give' expresses direction towards the subject or the agent of the action. The given concrete context determines whether the original meaning of giving or taking remains a part of the actual verbal signification.

Ex. 1: *ər bitkə gəvə-ʃ bi əjə-m gia-ki.*
Lit.: This book name-ACC. 1sg. **remember-CI. take-VOL**.
I will **note down** the name of the book.

Ex. 2: *jai əmdaⁿ ji-mə śin-t faɹ-χ əvəⁿ ara-m bu-ki.*
Lit.: Next time come-CI. 2sg.-DL heave-NP. **bread make-CI. give-VOL**.
Next time when you come I will **make** Sibe bread **for you**.

e) **Verbs of movement and staying**: *gən-* 'to go there', *ji-* 'to come', *yila-* 'to stand'

The verbs of movement, especially the verbs *ji-* 'to come' and *gən-* 'to leave', 'to go there' are often used in a partly grammaticalized meaning, which is mostly connected with their spatial semantics.

The verb *yila-* in connection with the imperfective converb expresses duration of an action.

Ex. 1: *bi təñi bodə-m ji-yᵊi.*
Lit.: 1sg. recenlty think-CI. **come-PERF**.
**I have** just **got** it.

Ex. 2: *śivə gizuⁿ mo-ɴ gizuⁿ-maq adašə-m gənə-m.*
Lit.: Sibe language Mongolian language-IS **resemble-CI. go-IMP**.
The Sibe language **is close** to Mongolian.

Ex. 3: *ali-mə yila!*
Lit.: **Wait-CI. stand-IMPER**.
**Wait a minute!**

f) **The verb *ta*-** to look

This verb expresses a short, single action, often implying the signification of an particular experience.

Ex. 1:   *əmdaⁿ **ta-m ta**.*
  Lit.: Once look-CI. **look-IMP**.
  **Just have a look**.

Ex. 2:   *Mi-ⁿ əñi-maq əmdaⁿ **gizərə-m ta**.*
  Lit.: 1sg.-GEN. mother-IS **once talk-CI. look-IMPER**.
  **Try to talk** to my mother.

g) 'Reversed' verbal phrases

While the most frequent types of verbal phrases are those with the modal or auxiliary verb following the main verbs, spoken Sibe has several verbs used as modal verbs, which are regularly used in the form of converbs preceding the main verbs. The most frequent of these are two verbs: *baʁə-* 'to hit (the mark), to reach' and *javdə-* 'to manage in time'. When these verbs come on the first position in a verbal phrase, they are modal verbs with the respective meanings of 'to have the opportunity, to succeed in' (*baʁə-*) and 'to do something quickly in order to manage it' (*javdə-*).

Ex. 1:   *śim-b **baʁə-m savə-qǔ-mə** afš azəɹ-m-ǔ-ʁᵘo?*
  Lit.: 2sg.-ACC. **reach-CI. see-NI.-NEG**. (become)-CI. how solve-CI. (become)-PERF.
  What shall we do if we **cannot see** you?

Ex. 2:   *javdə-m ta-mɛye!*
  Lit.: **Manage-CI. look-PROG**.
  **She is trying to read it quickly** (in my absence).

h) **The auxiliary verbs *zə*-** 'to say' and ***bi*-** 'to be'

The verb *zə*- with an imperfective converb usually expresses the meaning 'to plan, to be about to do'.

Ex. 1:   *ainə-m zə-mɛye?*
  Lit.: **Do. what-CI. say-PROG**.
  **What are you going to do?**

Ex. 2:   *śim-b ta-m **ji-m zə-či** solo aqᵘ.*
  Lit.: 2sg.-ACC. **see-CI. come-CI**. say-CC. free time NEG.
  **I have** always **been thinking about coming** to see you but I have no time.

The perfective form of the verb *bi-* is used as an auxiliary verb. It expresses an action to which the speaker was a witness, or an action about which he reminds the hearer. It corresponds to the Mongolian particle of verbal origin *bilee*.

Ex.:   *śi yiŋ gizuⁿ* **baʁənə-m bi-ɣᵊi**.
   Lit.: 2sg. English word **know-CI. be-PERF.**
   **But you know** English!

*The imperfective converb as a predicate of dependent clauses*

Dependent clauses with the imperfective converb most often specify time, circumstances or cause. Such constructions differ from the type described above by use of the longer form *-mə*, which prosodically separates the converb from the following part of sentence.

Ex. 1:   **ɛrk dolo-m-bu-mə** *nənəm da mavə-d ňi dolo-m-bu-m.*
   Lit.: Liquor **pour-CI.-give-CI.** formerly original forefather-DL. F. pour-CI.-give-IMP.
   **When** the liquor **is offered** to the ancestors, it is first of all offered to the clan ancestor.

Ex. 2:   **ɛli-m gia-m vajə-mə** *śiňi səf bia-m.*
   Lit.: **Receive-CI. take-CI. finish-CI.** only teacher look.for-IMP.
   Only **after he agrees** to become a shaman, they look for a teacher for him.

Ex. 3:   *naⁿ* **gizərə-mə** *daɹjⁱ-aqᵘ.*
   Lit.: Person **speak-CI.** relation NEG.
   He does not care **when people talk** about him.

Ex. 4:   *məji* **bait bi-mə** *śim-b bia-m ji-ɣᵊi.*
   Lit.: Little **matter be-CI.** 2sg.-ACC. look.for-CI. come-PERF.
   I come to you **because I need your help**.

Ex. 5:   *daɹvət naⁿ* **yila-mə** *gizərə-m mut-qa-qᵘi.*
   Lit.: Nearby person **stand-CI.** talk-CI. can-NP.-NEG.
   I could not talk to him **because there were** people around.

Ex. 6:   *nanᵊ-i ňonʁǔⁿ mi-ⁿ duqa-t* **ji-m dudu-mə** *ɢaɹvaɴ.*
   Lit.: Person-GEN. dog 1sg.-GEN. gate-DL. **come-CI. lay-CI.** bad.
   **When** a neighbour's dog **comes and lies** down at my gate, it is a bad omen.

Ex. 7:   **śi ji-mə** *əli śieⁿ.*
   Lit.: You come-CI. still good.
   **If you come**, [it is all] the better.

*Other syntactical specifics of the imperfective converb*

### 1) Phrases with the actualizing particle *da*

In the spoken language the imperfective converb is often followed by the actualizing particle *da*. This particle is at times used only to emphasize the converb; at times it makes the temporal designation more precise, or indeed limits it. Often it does not influence the meaning, and functions only as an interjection, which prosodically separates two parts of a sentence.

Ex. 1:  *uči **døži-mə** da śie^n va baʁə-v-ʁ^əi.*
       Lit.: Door **enter-CI. ACT**. good smell hit-CAUS-PERF.
       **As soon as I entered** the door I smelled a nice smell.

Ex. 2:  ***gənə-mə da** baχ^əi.*
       Lit.: **Go-CI. ACT**. hit-PERF.
       I found it **as soon as I got there**.

Ex. 3:  ***døži-mə da** čiš-k^əi.*
       Lit.: **Enter-CI. ACT**. come out-PERF.
       He **just dropped** in (did not stay long inside).

### 2) The imperfective converb at the end of a sentence

The imperfective converb sporadically occurs at the end of a sentence. Usually this occurs in the case of a rhetorical ellipse, or when the speaker, wishing to topicalize or place emphasis on the verb, inverts the order of the clauses. In all such cases the longer form *-mə* is used.

Ex. 1:  *əm ňinəŋ fəkš-kə, śim-b **bia-mə**.*
       Lit.: One day run-PERF, 2sg.-ACC. **seek-CI**.
       I was running around the whole day **looking for** you.

*Temporal determinations originating from imperfective converbal forms*

Certain petrified forms of the imperfective converb express temporal determination adverbially. The degree of grammaticalization of these expressions varies. The most frequent are the fixed expressions *śiramə* 'later, in future' (1) and *nənəm* 'first, before' (2). The expression *vajimə* 'in a while' (3) seems to retain more verbal characteristics than the previous two, which by their character resemble Indo-European adverbs.

### 1) The expression śira-m(ə) '*later*'

The word *śira-m(ə)* 'later, in the future' is the imperfect converb of the verb *śira-* 'to continue, to succeed', which is an important cultural term in and of itself (*jalə^n śira-* 'to continue the clan'). This expression in the modern language occurs both with verbs and nouns; native speakers are often not aware of its verbal origin.

169

Ex. 1:    *šira-m aš-ki.*
       Lit.: **Later** meet-VOL.
       See you **later**.

Ex. 2:    *tər ňi gum šira-m bait.*
       Lit.: This F. all **later** matter.
       These are all future matters.

### 2) The expression *nənəm(ə)* 'before'

The word *nənəm* 'first, before' is a converb derived from the verbal stem *nənə* - from which a petrified derivative is employed in written Manchu – the perfective noun *nənə-hə* – 'former, preceding'. The stem itself is probably related to the verb *nənə-/ŋənə-* 'to go' (cf. Ma. *gene-*) of the Evenki and other Tungusic languages.

Ex. 1:    *so tə, bi nənə-m yav-m-ů̆-ʁⁱ̊o.*
       Lit.: 2pl. sit-IMPER., 1sg. **first** go-CI.-become-PERF.
       I am leaving (with your permission).
       Note: A polite formula used in the Chinese cultural environment when somebody is leaving a group of people: it notifies the others not to be disturbed by his departure.

Ex. 2:    *ši nənə-m døš.*
       Lit.: 2sg. **first** enter-IMPER.
       Go **ahead**. (You first.)

### 3) The expression *vajəme* 'in a while'

The expression *vajəmə*, lit. 'finishing' is used as an idiom in the sense of "after a while". It is mostly used in a context which corresponds to the original meaning (i.e., when the present action is finished), but in the linguistic cognizance of younger speakers it seems to be perceived as an adverb designating the near future.

Ex. 1:    *vajə-mə məs yavm na?*
       Lit.: **Finishing** 1pl.(incl) go-IMP QUEST.
       Shall we leave **slowly**?

Ex. 2:    *vajə-mə bait aqⁱ̊ ba?*
       Lit.: **Finishing** matter NEG. PROB.
       Are you free **after**?

## 7.5.2 The perfective converb -*maq* (converbum perfecti)

The suffix -*maq* is a peculiarity of spoken Sibe which does not have a equivalent in the written language.

## Use of the perfective converb

The perfective converb expresses **an action which precedes another action** (1).

Generally speaking, the connection between the two actions is more loosely defined than in the case of the imperfective converb. In the spoken language, however, it is often used as a variant of the imperfective converb without affecting the sense of the temporal relationship of the actions. It adds a more plastic and colloquial character to the flow of speech and therefore it occurs in many cases in which the imperfective converb -*mə* would be used in the written language, expressing **the simultaneity of two or more actions**[26] (2).

The construction with the converb -***maq*** is obligatory. Its use is favoured in many phrases with **modal or auxiliary verbs** (3).

Due to its more loosely defined relation to the following verb, it is more often used as a **predicate of a dependent clause**. In this function it is particularly favoured in narration or story-telling, where long chains of converbs may often occur (4).

### 1) Converbum perfecti in expressing successive actions

Ex. 1:   *baijihua o-mə da **bəčə-maq** čənl-h, giraⁿ dəri čənl-h naⁿ bi-ɣᵖi.*
Lit.: Baijihua become-CI. ACT. **die-CP. originate(Chin)-NP.**, corpse-ABL originate(Chin)-NP. person be-PERF.
Baijihua was a person **who arose from a corpse**.

### 2) Converbum perfecti in expressing paralell actions

Ex. 1:   *ňur bəri ɢač, ɢaft, **ɢaftə-maq tuɣə-f**, zə-r.*
Lit.: Arrow bow bring-IMPER, **shoot-IMPER, shoot-CP. fall-CAUS.-IMPER.**, say-NP.
They say: Bring the bow and arrows and **shoot him down** (lit. shooting let fall).

Ex. 2:   *ɛli-ʁə ɛli-ʁə **vⁱelə-maq yav-ʁⁱi.***
Lit.: Wait-NP. wait-NP. **throw-CP. go-PERF.**
I was waiting and waiting and then I **left**.
Note: The phrase *vieləmaq yav-* 'throwing leave' is used to express the abandonment of something or someone.

### 3) Phrases with modal verbs

The frequency of use of the perfective converb in the spoken language is markedly higher than in the written language. It is used either alternatively with (a) the imperfective converb, or (b) obligatorily in phrases with certain modal verbs.

---

[26] The same tendency can be observed in the usage of the Khalkha Mongolian converbs -*ž.-č* and -*aad.*, when in the colloquial language the perfective converb -*aad* is often used in a phrase where the imperfective converb -*ž.-č* would be used in a more literary style.

171

a) Alternation with the imperfective converb

In the spoken language some modal and auxiliary verbs may occur with both converbs without a differentiation in the temporal relationship. In this case the use of the perfective converb -*maq* is distinguished by its greater expressivity and vivacity.

Ex. 1: *əmfalən śidən da ju əriⁿ gizər-maq gⁱɛ-m.*
Lit.: One while between ACT. two hour **speak-CP. take-IMP.**
In a short while he **speaks** for two hours.
Note: A humorous critique of a talkative person.

Ex. 2: *tər saməⁿ ñi dači da ulav-maq ji-ɣᵊi.*
That shaman F. originally ACT. **hand.down-CP. come-PERF.**
The shamanic practices **have been handed down** from the olden times.

b) Fixed expressions with modal verbs

The modal verbs *sənda*- 'to put' and *dut*- 'to lay' are always used with the perfective converb. The use of these verbs as modals is strongly expressive and is limited to the spoken language.

### Phrases with the verb *sənda*- *'to put'*

The modal verb *sənda*- conveys the sense of a quick, intensive and single action.

Ex. 1: *kaošə-v ñi maitoɹ-maq sənda-ʁᵊi.*
Lit.: Examination(Chin)-ACC. POSS. **flail-CP. put-PERF.**
He did the examination test by **guessing**.
Note: The expression *maitoɹ*- (to flail) is a humorous metaphor of guessing the correct answers in examination tests by chance.

Ex. 2: *mətəraɴ da z̧ə-maq sənda.*
Lit.: Just like this ACT. **say-CP. put-IMPER.**
**Just say** it in this way.

**Constructions with the verb *dut*- 'to lay'**

The modal verb *dut*- adds the sense of intensity, insistence and long duration to the main verb.

Ex. 1: *fiɣə ñi tiørʁŭ-maq dudə-m.*
Lit.: Brains POSS. **turn-CP. lay-IMP.**
Her brains are **working all the time.** (She does not leave anything in peace.)

Ex. 2: *əm jaq da.ɹjⁱ aqŭ yav-maq dudə-m.*
Lit.: One thing relation NEG. **go-CP. lay-IMP.**
He does not care about anything and just **keeps walking.**
Note: This expression describes energetic end determined gait of a certain individual.

Ex. 3:  *aⁿ śi-ⁿ gəγə **soNů-maq dut-kᵊye?***
Lit.: Why 2sg.-GEN. sister **cry-CP. lay-PERF**.
Why is your sister **crying all the time**?

### 4) The perfective converb as a predicate of a dependent clause

Ex. 1:  *jaq **arə-maq** śim-b ɛli-mɛye.*
Lit.: Thing **make-CP**. 2sg.-ACC. wait-PROG.
We are waiting for you **with the dinner**.

Ex. 2:  *miⁿ bo-t **ji-maq** mi-ⁿ gizum-b gia-s.*
Lit.: 1sg.-GEN. house-DL **come-CP**. 1sg.-GEN. word take-IMPER.
**Once you have come to my house** you have to listen to me.

Ex. 3:  *χaʁəji-f da šašqəɹ-mə **gətəv-maq** bo-či ñi ɢajə-m ji-γə.*
Lit.: Boy-ACC. ACT. slap-CI. **wake-CAUS.-CP**. house-LAT. POSS. bring-CI.-come-PERF.
She **woke** the boy with a slap and brought him home.

### *Other syntactic peculiarities of the perfective converb*

#### 1) The perfective converb at the end of a sentence

The converb *-maq* occurs at the end of a sentence more frequently than the imperfective converb. It is used to express cause or circumstance, just like the Mongolian converb *-aad⁴*, used in similar types of incomplete sentences.

Ex. 1:  *juzə-v ñi danə-m vaq aie, bəy ñi banjə-m **banə-qů-maq**.*
Lit.: Children-ACC. POSS. care-IMP. not what, body give birth-CI. **know-(NI.)-CP**.
Of course she cares about their children, **since she was not able to** give birth.

#### 2) The perfective converb in constructions with the particle *da*

The perfective converb is often separated by the particle *da* from the following parts of a sentence. This particle, when used with the perfective converb, always marks an end of a clause and is never used as a part of a verbal phrase.

Ex.:  *bait iškⁱa-m **vajə-maq** ta tiorʁů-maq ji-qů na?*
Lit.: Matter arrange-CI. **finish-CP. ACT**. turn-CP. come-NI.-NEG. QUEST
Why don't you come back **after you finish** your work?

### *Idioms formed with the perfective converb*

In the spoken language the perfective converb often forms a part of an idiomatic phrase expressing a more complicated set of ideas. Many of these expressions are typical in the spoken language and have no written equivalents.

Ex.: **yila-maq ta** əm gizuⁿ gizərə-m.
Lit.: **Stand-CP. ACT**. one word say.
He is speaking **discontinuously**.

### 7.5.3 The perfective converb -f(ie)/-f(ə)

The perfective converb -f(ie)/-f(ə) is typical of written Manchu (the form -fi). In the spoken language its use is limited to the older generation of speakers who are literate in Manchu. It often occurs in song lyrics. Its meaning generally overlaps that of the perfective converb -**maq**, but it is used more frequently in the sense of temporal succession (Ex. 1).

Ex. 1: jaq **jə-fə** aičⁱ!
Lit.: Thing **eat-CP**. move-IMPER.
Have something to **eat before** you leave.

Ex. 2: tŭχtaⁿ śi mim-bə tuнaɹ-χ ərin-də damjiⁿ **migər-fie** daвə-m ta-χ bi-yə.
Lit.: First.time 2sg. 1sg.-ACC. meet-NP. time-DL, scale.beam **shoulder-CP**. folow-CI. look-NP. be-PERF.
When I saw you for the first time, I turned after you and kept watching **with my scale beam on my shoulders**.

### 7.5.4 The conditional converb -či (converbum conditionale)

#### Forms of the conditional converb

The conditional converb -či has two variants – the basic form -či and the form -š before stops. This variant occurs frequently due to two widely used particles with an initial stop – the particles da and gəɹ, which often follow the conditional converb.

The negative form of the conditional converb, like the negative forms of other converbs, is formed by the negated form of the imperfective noun followed by the conditional converb of the auxiliary verb o- 'to become'. In literary Manchu these forms exist as analytic expressions, while in the spoken language they are pronounced as one word and seem to be perceived as synthetic (e.g. Lit. Ma. generkū oči > Si. gənəqᵘči 'if he does not go').

Ex. 1: amə **taqə-qᵘ-či** və taqə-mie.
Lit.: Father **know-(NI.)-NEG.(become)-CP**. who know-IMP.
Who should know it **if not you**, Father?

Ex. 2: čiškə **fietə-mə-š** gəɹ udun-t tuza.
Lit.: Sparrow **fart-CI.-become-CC**. still wind-DL. help.
**Even a sparrow's fart** can help the wind.
Note: A proverb.

### Usage of the conditional converb

The conditional converb *-či* always functions as a predicate of a dependent clause which expresses the condition for the main clause. Apart from this conditional meaning it is often used to simply express a sequence of actions (Ex. 1).

On the syntactical level a specific construction is used to express a condition in the past: the main verb is in the form of the perfective noun, followed by the conditional converb of the existential 'to be' (Ex. 5).

#### 1) The conditional in the present and future

Ex. 1: *ər əm daivə-f ɓaš-či χoj o-jůqᵘ, tər əm daivə-f ɓaš-či χoj o-jůqᵘ.*
Lit.: This one doctor-ACC. bring-CC. good become-(NI.)-NEG, that one doctor-ACC. **bring-CC**. good become-NI-NEG.
They were **calling** all possible doctors but she did not get better.

Ex. 2: *ərə-f gəɹ **jə-m vajə-qᵘ-či** banjə-qᵘ ta o-ʁᵘi.*
This-ACC. still **eat-CI. finish-(NI.)-NEG.-become-CC**. live-(NI.)-NEG. ACT. become-PERF.
**If you cannot finish** up even this, there is no need for you to live.
Note: Humorous encouraging of a bashful guest to eat.

Ex. 3: *ərt **yi-qᵘ-či** jaq ba-ʁəm jə-qᵘ.*
Lit.: Early **get.up-(NI.)-NEG.-become-CC**. thing hit-CI. eat-(NI.)-NEG.
**If you do not get up** early, you will not have time to eat breakfast.

Ex. 4: *naⁿ ňi dači mo-maq **avələ-či**, tə ňi ňur bəri bi o-ʁᵘi.*
Lit.: Person F. originally wood-IS **hunt-CC**. now F. arow bow is become-PERF.
People **were first hunting** with wooden sticks and now they acquired the bow and arrow.

Ex. 5: *śi jih **bi-či** laft śieⁿ biɣᵊi.*
Lit.: You **come-NP. be-CC**. very good be-PERF.
It would have been nice **if you came**.

### Other syntactical peculiarities of the conditional converb

The conditional converb seldom occurs at the end of a sentence. It may express a regret about something one did or did not do (a).

The conditional converb is often followed by the particles *da* (b) and *gəɹ* 'still' (c).

a) The conditional converb at the end of a sentence

Ex. 1: *əmdaⁿ **gən-h bi-čie**, zə-m ɓůňi-m.*
Lit.: Once **go-PERF. be-CC**. say-CI. think-IMP.
**Had I gone** there just once …

b) Constructions of the conditional converb and the particle *da*

This particle is often used without a change of meaning in the verbal expression. It may slightly emphasize the verb, or place it into light contradictory opposition to the other part of the sentence. It has often only a prosodic function – native speakers appear to prefer finishing a verbal form by using the syllable *da* as opposed to concluding with the syllable *-či*.

Ex. 1:   *bait **bi-š ta** dianhua tant.*
   Matter **be-CC. ACT.** telephone hit-IMPER.
   **If you need** anything, call me.

Ex. 2:   *jə-m **mutə-qŭ-š ta** jə-qŭ da o-ʁŭi.*
   Lit.: Eat-CI. **can-(NI.)-NEG. become-CC. ACT**. eat-NI.-NEG. ACT. become-PERF.
   **If you can not** eat it, you are not obliged to.

c) Constructions of the conditional converb and the particle *gəɹ* 'still, also'

Like the Monglian particle *č*, the particle *gəɹ* has the meaning of either addition or diminishment, depending on the positive or negative context of the utterance. In a positive sentence it should translated as 'too, also', while in the negative sense as 'nor, neither, not even'. The construction of the conditional converb with this particle has the resulting signification of 'even if' or 'even if not'.

Ex. 1:   *urai amtiŋ, saⁿ **mitə-mə-š gəɹ** sa-qŭ.*
   Lit.: How much tasty, **ear cut-CI.-become-CC.** still know-NEG.
   It is so tasty that I would not feel it **if someone cut off my ear** (while eating).
   Note: Humorously praising a dish.

Ex. 2:   *śim-b **unča-maq sənda-š gəɹ** śi sa-qŭ.*
   Lit.: 2sg.-ACC. **sell-CP. put-CC.** still you know-(NI.)-NEG.
   **If she had sold you**, you would not even notice it.
   Note: A humorous characteristic of a clever young girl who is good at dealing with people.

### *Idiomatic expressions with the conditional converb*

The by far most frequent idiom with the conditional converb, used in both the spoken and written languages, is a construction of the negative converb *-či* and the verbal form *ojŭqŭ* 'it is not possible'. The construction as a whole expresses an inevitable need.

Ex. 1:   *jə-f, **jəqŭ-či o-ju-qŭ**.*
   Lit.: Eat-IMPER. **eat-(NI.)-NEG.-become-CC. become-(NI.)-NEG.**
   Eat, **you have to eat.**

Ex. 2:   *ənəŋ gənə-qᵘ-či o-jŭ-qŭ-ʁᵘi.*
Lit.: Today **go- (NI.)-NEG.-become-CC. become-(NI.)-NEG.-(become)-PERF.**
Today we **have to go** there **in any case**.

## 7.5.5 Terminative converb -čiňi

Literary Manchu possesses a group of combined suffixes which distinguish fine modal shades of meaning (*-čiňi, -čina, -čibe, -biňi* , as well as others). Only one of these suffixes, the suffix *-či-ňi*, which is composed of the conditional converb and the particle *ňi*, is currently in use in the modern spoken language.

### The basic meaning of the terminative converb -čiňi

While in the grammars of the written language the meaning of this suffix is rendered as vaguely as is the case with many other verbal suffixes, in the spoken language it has developed a relatively clear and concrete use – the terminative meaning which ought to be translated as 'until' and corresponds to the Mongolian terminative converb *-tal⁴*.

Ex. 1:   *mim-f **giri-f-čiňi** gizər-mɛye.*
Lit.: 1sg.-ACC. **shame-CAUS.-CT.** speak-PROG.
You are **making me blush** (by your words).

Ex. 2:   *naⁿ **gələ-f-čiňi** azəɹ-m.*
Lit.: Person **fear-CAUS.-CT.** behave-IMP.
He is running riot **so that one would be scared**.

### Idiomatic use of the terminative converb

The terminative converb in a construction with the three auxiliaries (*o-* 'to be, to become', *zə-* 'to say' and *bi-* 'to be') and the vicarious adverb *tut* 'thus, this much' conveys the meaning of contradiction, which may best be translated as 'though, although, but'. These constructions correspond to Mongolian phrases with the verbal root + *-vč*.

Ex. 1:   *təzə-i saməⁿ ňi alla alla zə-m, **tut bi-čiňi** baitə ňi saməⁿ bait.*
Lit.: Their shaman-POSS. alla alla say-IMP. **thus be-CT**. matter-POSS shaman matter.
Their shamans are turning to Allah in their invocations, **but** their rituals are shaman rituals.

Ex. 2:   ***tut o-čⁱňi** islamə ňi ɢoškᵘ.*
Lit.: Thus **become-CT**. Islam F. terrible.
**But** Islam is strong.

177

## 7.6 Deverbal suffixes

The number and function of deverbal suffixes in written Manchu and spoken Sibe differs significantly. While in the grammars of written Manchu we find a number of derivational suffixes which express various aspects of an action, in spoken Sibe these suffixes are mostly unproductive and occur as petrified parts of fixed forms.

In written Manchu, according to Zaharov, there is one passive-causative suffix *-bu-* as well as eleven suffixes of aspect, of which three (*-nggi-, -na-* and *-ji-*) are in fact grammaticalized verbs *unggi-* 'to send', *gene-* 'to go' and *ji-* 'to come'. In comparison with the Mongolian suffixes of aspect (Sechenbaatar 2003, pp. 116, 145), which are phonetically heterogenous, etymologically unclear and, but for a few exceptions, a productive part of the verbal system, almost all the Manchu deverbative suffixes have the shape CV. Zaharov, in compliance with the traditional Manchu grammars, relates them to various grammaticalized words: the suffix *-ča³-* to the verb *ača-* 'to meet', the suffix *-nu-* to the adverb *yooni* 'all', the suffix *-ndu-* to the noun *ishunde* 'mutually'.

Although this etymologization is verified only in the case of the three suffixes of movement (*-nggi-, -na-, -ji-*), whereas concerning suffixes expressing other aspects it may be only of secondary importance, it is clear that the deverbal suffixes in literary Manchu should be grouped among grammatical means that were artificially developed and maintained. Zaharov himself comments on the suffixes, noting that they are only one of many options to express aspects of verbal actions, and that among those literate in written Manchu a tendency towards the use of analytic expressions prevails (Zaharov 1879, pp. 164, 168).

In the spoken language these derivational suffixes of aspect (unlike the causative marker *-bu-*) are fixed in particular verbal forms and are not recognized by native speakers with the exception of those educated in Manchu grammar:

*tan-də* 'to beat': *tan-* 'to hit' + *-de* – suffix of repeated action

*ɢa-jə-* 'to bring', lit. *ga-ji-*: *gayi-* 'to take'+ *ji-* 'to come'.

In modern colloquial Sibe there are two fully productive deverbal suffixes:
1. **the causative-passive suffix *-v***
2. **the suffix expressing the commencement of an action (inceptive) *-mači-***

### 7.6.1 The causative suffix -v

#### *Form and meaning of the causative suffix*

This derivational suffix, originally a grammaticalized verb *bu-* 'to give' (in literary Manchu the form of the suffix is *-bu-*), is one of the most frequent word-forming means in spoken Sibe.

Its range of meanings, viewed through the prism of Indo-European grammatical categories, encompasses two basic meanings, the ***causative*** and the ***passive***. This classification is, however, not entirely suitable for the Altaic languages.[27] Manchu and Sibe do not seem to make a distinction between the two categories.

---

[27] The Mongolian suffix *-gd-*, which is often classified as the passive voice, is in fact a suffix with a highly specific use (mainly with verbs connected to sensual and intellectual perception, e.g. *bod-* 'to think' *bodo-gd-* 'to come to mind').

On the other hand, in Mongolian the so-called causative suffixes are used in certain contexts which from the point of view of Indo-European grammar, would most likely be classified as passive, e.g. (*zod-uul-* lit. 'beat-CAUS'. –

**The category of causativity** in the Altaic languages is an essential way of expressing the relation between the agent, the action and the object or patient of the action. Manchu and Mongolian in particular prefer the causative constructions to other constructions. The causative relationship is marked even when it can be clearly understood from the context, as seen in the following example:

Ex.: *aнəv ňi yaqsə-v-ʁᵊi.*
Lit.: Mouth-ACC. POSS. **shut-CAUS.-PERF**.
He **shut** his mouth.

In several cases the causative suffix *-v-* has lost its causative meaning and formed a secondary stem with a new meaning (e.g. *sa-v-* 'to see, to be seen' < *sa-* 'to know').
The object of causative constructions is either in the dative-locative or in the accusative. Often it is possible to use both:

Ex. 1: *ujᵘ ara-maq ta yenjir-v ňi utkᵘ utu-v-m.*
Lit.: Head make-CP. ACT. **doll-ACC. C. dress put.on-CAUS.-IMP**.
After we had made the head of the doll we **put clothes on her**.

Ex. 2: *aɹh bos čaн čaн iza-v-maq ta yenjir-d ňi utkᵘ ara-m utu-v-m.*
Lit.: Coloured cloth lots gather-CP. ACT. **doll-DL. C. dress make-CI. put.on-CAUS.-IMP**.
We were collecting lots of coloured rags/cloths, making dresses and **putting them on the dolls**.
Note: These two variants occurred in the speech of one speaker in immediate succession.

Although any attempt to classify the so-called semantic range of the various causative constructions risks the introduction of Indo-European grammatical categories into a linguistic context where they are simply not present, the following can nonetheless be concluded from the collected material: in the formulations which are closer to the category of the **causative** (1) the object is more frequently in the accusative, whereas in those closer to the passive the agent (i.e., the grammatical object) tends to be in the dative-locative (2).

### 1) Causative type constructions

Ex. 1: *giraⁿ čiči-v-m vajə-maq əmbat jaq jə-m.*
Lit.: Skeleton **go.out-CAUS.-CI**. finish-CP. together thing eat-IMP.
**After the burial** ('taking out the bones') they eat together.

Ex. 2: *nanᵊ-i cůňim-b daʁə-v-m mutə-m.*
Lit.: Person-GEN. mind **follow-CAUS.-CI**. can-IMP.
He can **attract** other people. (He can **make** people **like** him.)

---

'to get beaten' and so on). Therefore it may be very correct to state that the Altaic languages distinguish only one *causative-passive* voice.

Ex. 3:   *ər učum-b mi-ⁿ amə **banjə-v-ʁᵊi.***
      Lit.: This song 1sg.-GEN. father **be born-CAUS.-PERF.**
      My father **composed** this song.

Ex. 4:   *ɕaš, bi śin-t **uluf-kie.***
      Lit.: Bring, 1sg. 2sg.-DL. **eat-CAUS.-VOL.**
      Come here, **I will feed** you.

### 2) Passive type constructions

Ex. 1:   *χara śin-t **maχtə-v-mie.***
      Lit.: Hara 2sg.-DL. **throw-CAUS.-IMP.**
      **Hara is not as good as you.**
      Note: The causative form *maχtə-v-* 'to let oneself being thrown' is used idiomatically
      in the meaning 'to be worse than' in knowledge, abilities, and the like.

Ex. 2:   *śi fəkśi-mə bi jaf-š da śi **ətə-v-ɣᵊi.***
      Lit.: 2sg. run-CI. 1sg. catch-CC. ACT. **2sg. win-CAUS.-PERF.**
      When you run and I catch you, you **have lost.**

Ex. 3:   *saʁůrun-t **baʁə-v-ʁᵊi** ba!*
      Lit.: Cold-DL. **strike-CAUS.-PERF.** PROB.
      You most probably **have caught** a cold.

Ex. 4:   *sər zə-r tərə udun-də ňi śidəⁿ uči ňi **li-v-ɣᵊye.***
      Lit.: Ser say-NI. that wind-DL. C. between door C. **open-CAUS.-PERF.**
      In gust of wind the inside door **opened.**
      Note: From the lyrics of a folksong.

Ex. 5:   *tər jaq huizə-t **tandə-v-maq** qor ba-χᵊi.*
      Lit.: That thing Uighur-DL. **beat-CAUS.-CP.** harm get-PERF.
      He **was beaten** by the Uighurs and injured.

### *Negation of the causatives*

The negative forms of the causatives are particularly important in communication. Apart
from the meaning of prohibition (1) they often designate the **unnecessary quality** of a given
action (2).

### 1) The meaning of prohibition

Ex. 1:   *əvat daməŋ **ɕůči-v-ůqů.***
      Lit.: Here tobacco **smoke-CAUS.-(NI.)-NEG.**
      It is not **allowed to smoke** here.

Ex. 2:   *χalə-i diørʁůt **sadulə-v-ůqᵘ***.
Lit.: Clan-GEN. inside **make.relatives-CAUS.-(NI.)-NEG.**
It is **not allowed to marry** inside a clan.

Ex. 3:   *čaqůr tavənə-r-t amš **tavə-v-ůqᵘ***.
Lit.: Čaqůr ascend-NI.-DL backwards **look-CAUS. (NI.)-NEG.**
When ascending the *čaqůr* he **must not look** back.

**2) Meaning of unnecesity**

Ex. 1:   *gizərərə-ŋə-f **bia-v-ůqᵘ***.
Lit.: Speak-NI.II.-ACC. **look for- CAUS.-NI.-NEG.**
It is **not necessary** to talk about it

Ex. 2:   *əm nan ňunkuŋ biš da, ... if χᵘarən-t bənə-m vajə-maq da śinaq **utu-v-ůqᵘ***.
Lit.: One person sick be-CC.-ACT. ... tomb yard-DL. escort-CI. finish-CP. ACT.
mourning **put.on-CAUS.-(NI.)-NEG.**
When somebody is sick, he is **not obliged to wear** mourning after the end of the
burial.

These two suffixes are attached to a verbal stem, which is often extended by the older
petrified deverbative suffixes.

## 7.6.2 Beginning of an action: the suffix -*mači*-

This verbal form expresses the beginning of an action and is considered to have developed
from the imperfective converb -*m(ə)* and the verb *a(i)či*- 'to move' by native speakers.
In the perfective forms the final vowel of the inceptive suffix is dropped and it results in
a dissimilation of the cluster thus formed: *čh/čχ>šk/šq* (e.g. *gənə-maš-kᵊi* 'started going').
This suffix is used for **marking a beginning of an action** (1) and for **expressing parallel
actions** (2).

**1) Suffix -*mači*- designating the beginning of action**

A verb with the suffix -*mači*- conveys this meaning when it is a finite predicate of
a sentence.

Ex. 1:   ***bi fančə-mači-mie!***
Lit.: 1sg. **angry-INC.-IMP.**
**I will get angry!**

Ex. 2:   *amə-v ňi əmdaⁿ sav-mə da **bait čiči-mači-m***.
Lit.: Father-ACC. POSS. once see-CI. ACT. **matter come out-INC.-IMP.**
Whenever she sees her father, **something happens** to her.

Ex. 3:  *śivə dongbəi-dəri ji-maq əvat **banjə-maš-kʰi**.*
Lit.: Sibe northeast-ABL. come-CP. here **live-INC.-PERF**.
The Sibe people came from Manchuria and **began** living here.

Ex. 4:  *tər həh əm ňinəŋ saʁənč banjə-maq jai ňinəŋ bo-t jaq **ara-maš-kʰi**.*
Lit.: That woman one day daughter give birth-CP. next day house-DL. thing **make-INC.-PERF**.
That woman gave birth to her daughter and the next day she already **started cooking** for her family.

### 2) The suffix *-mači-* in the meaning of parallel actions

When the suffix *-mači-* forms part of a converbal predicate of a dependent clause, it expresses the first of two simultaneous actions.

Ex. 1:  *yiqaⁿ guruⁿ śim-b **bia-mači-mə** goškᵘ azəɹ-mači-m.*
Lit.: Chinese folk 2sg.-ACC. **plea-INC.-CI**. terribly behave-INC.-IMP.
**When** the Chinese are **asking you** a favour, they would do anything.

Ex. 2:  *so-ⁿ təvat jaq **jə-mači-mə** liaoča baitələ-m ba?*
Lit.: 2pl.-GEN. there thing **eat- INC.-CC**. drag use-IMP. PROB.
In your place, **when you eat**, you use a pitchfork, don't you?

Ex. 3:  *gizuⁿ **tači-mači-mə** laft gizərə-mə śiňi o-m.*
Lit.: Word **learn-INC.-CC**. much speak-COMV.IMP. only become-IMP.
**When one studies a language**, it is possible only when one speaks a lot.

Ex. 4:  *bi jaq **ara-mači-mə** daməɴ laft ɢuči-m.*
Lit.: 1sg. thing **write-INC.-CI**. tobacco much smoke-IMP.
**When I write** something, I smoke a lot.

## 7.7 Vicarious verbs

In Manchu and Sibe, as in many other Altaic languages, vicarious verbal expressions are present. In comparison with the Mongolian system of three verbs with full paradigms (interrogative *yaa-*, proximal *inge-* and distal *teg-*) the Manchu system is defective. It can, however, be assumed, that a full system existed in the earlier stages of the language and was partially lost.

Literary Manchu has only the interrogative verb *aina-* 'to do what'. Spoken Sibe has, besides its oral form *ain-/ɛn-* 'to do what', the demonstrative vicarious verb *ək-* 'to do that', which is used for both proximate and distal deixis. An important aspect of the semantic range of these verbs is the implicit referral to an action known both to the speaker and interlocutor from a previous context ('to do what both of the communication partners already know about').

I have in one instance recorded the use of the vicarious verb *tək*, which might have originally been the distal-deictic equivalent of the verb *ək-*, as is suggested by the regular occurrence of the pair of vicarious roots *ə-/tə-* for distal and proximate reference. The phonetic correspondence to the Mongolian distal vicarious verb *teg-* is worth noting. In view of the long lasting contacts and the multitude of mutual borrowings, the Mongolian origin of this vicarious verb cannot be excluded.

One more vicarious verbal stem should be probably listed from the purely synchronic point of view. Literary Manchu has no direct correspondence to the Mongolian pair of demonstrative vicarious verbal stems *teg-* and *inge-*; an analogical meaning is however conveyed by the complex expressions *uttu o-* lit. like.this become, 'to be in this way' and *tuttu o-* lit. like.that become, 'to be in that/such way.' In colloquial Sibe, however, the expression *tuttu o-* has developed into what should be regarded instead as a verbal stem *tuku-* 'to do so', which is, however, used only with converbal suffixes.

At the same time, in the speech of the elder generation, there occur the forms *tutof* or *tutᵊfie*, which are the genuine equivalents of the literary form *tuttu ofi* , lit. like.this. become-CC.

Some of the vicarious verbs, in addition to their use on the basic lexical level, are also used to create phrases with other verbs, which usually renders their meaning more abstract.

### *Vicarious verbs in their basic meaning*

In the spoken language two vicarious verbs are frequent – the interrogative – *εn-/εin-* 'to do what' (a) and the demonstrative *ək-* 'to do this/that' (b).

a) The vicarious verb *εn-/εin-* 'to do what'

Ex. 1:  *tər saʁənč təvat **εnə-maq** dut-kᵊye?*
       Lit.: That girl there **do.what-CP**. lay.down-PERF.
       **What is** the girl **doing** there all the time?

Ex. 2:  *εnə-m ji-ɣᵊye?*
       Lit.: Do.**what-CI**. come-PERF.
       **Why** (to do what) did you come?

Ex. 3:  *εn-ʁᵊye?*
       Lit.: **Do.what-PERF**.
       **What happened**?
       Note: An idiom analogical to the Mongolian expression *yaasan (be)*? 'What happened?'

Ex. 4:  *əňi ňi **εn-ʁᵊi** zə-m fək śi-m čiš-kᵊi.*
       Lit.: Mother-POSS. **do.what-PERF**. say-CI. run- CI. do out-PERF.
       Her mother ran out to see **what happened**.

b) The demonstrative vicarious verb *ǝk-* 'to do this/that'

This verb stands either for an action which can be understood from the actual context (Ex. 1), or an action known to both partners in communication from the previous context (Ex. 2). In everyday speech it is often used as an interjection with the function of slowing down the flow of speech or anticipating the utterance of a fact that for some reason should actually not be pronounced in the normal course of speech (Ex. 4). In colloguial Mongolian both meanings are usually expressed by the interrogative vicarious verb *yaa-* or the idiom *yuu yaa-*.

Ex. 1:  *ɕaš, bi ǝkǝ-m bu-ki.*
  Lit.: Bring-IMPER. 1sg. **do.that-CI**. give-VOL.
  Let me **fix** it for you.
  Note: A frequent phrase introducing detailed manual assistance.

Ex. 2:  *ajiguruⁿ gǝlǝ-mǝ, mǝtǝraɴ ǝkǝ-m vaq na?*
  Lit.: Children fear-CI. just thus **do.this-IMP**. not QUEST
  When children are scared, people **usually do the same**, you know?

Ex. 3:  *čǝksǝ ǝkǝ-m ta-ʁǝ na?*
  Lit.: Yesterday **do.that-CI**. look-PERF. QUEST
  Did you try **it** yesterday?

Ex. 4:  *ut ǝkǝ-maq da, ǝñi ñi aɹ-m bu-m vajǝ-maq da bǝy ñi χaišgǝɹ nanǝ-i aɹvǝⁿ bači ñi vǝilǝ-mǝ yav-ʁⁱi.*
  Lit.: Thus **do.that-CP. ACT**. mother POSS. tell-CI. give-CI. finish-CP. ACT. body POSS. still person-GEN. service place-LAT. POSS. work-CI. go-PERF.
  After **having done like this** – her mother, after having explained everything, went back to the place of her service.

c) The vicarious verb *tuku-* 'to do so'

The three forms encountered in the collected material are *tuku-mǝ* 'do.so-CI.', *tuku-maq* 'do.so-CP.' and *tuku-či* 'do.so-CC.' The former two are used to express the meaning 'after that' analogically to the Mongolian verbal form *tegeed*, lit. 'do.so-CP.', while the third has the meaning of 'in that case' as in the Mongolian form *tegvel*, lit. 'do.so-CC.'

Ex. 1:  ***tuku-mǝ** da baijihua ñi bǝy ñi ɕam-ʁǝi.*
  Lit.: **do.so-CI**. ACT. Baijihua F. body POSS. take.away-PERF.
  **And so** Baijihua took him away herself.

Ex. 2:  ***tuku-maq** da skⁱi baijihua tom.*
  Lit.: **Do.so-CP**. ACT. that Baijihua abuse-IMP.
  **Then** Baijihua started abusing her.

Ex. 3:     *tu-maqa?*
           Lit.: **Do.so-CP**.
           **And? So what?**

Ex. 4:     *tuku-č śi əmzaq gənə-müʁü na?*
           Lit.: **Do.so-CC**. 2sg. alone go.there-CI.(become)-PERF. QUEST.
           **So it means** that you are going there alone?

### *Vicarious verbs in a phrase with a verb with full meaning*

Ex. 1:     *tuku-mə təvat banjə-maq εni-m, gizuⁿ tači-maq εni-m...*
           Lit.: Do.so-CI. there live-CP. **do what-IMP, language study-CP. do what-IMP.**
           Then he was **living there, studying the language and so on.**

Ex. 2:     *ɣav-ʁə εn-ʁə da əm bira-t iźin-ɣ°i.*
           Lit.: **Walk-NP. do what-NP. ACT**. one river reach-PERF.
           He **went on and on** and he came to a river.

Ex. 3:     *buddizm ye samanjiao goškuli av-m təkə-m...*
           Lit.: Buddhism(Rus.) and shamanism(Chin.) terribly **fight-IMP. do that-IMP.**
           Buddhism and shamanism were **fighting [each other]** hard.

# ACKNOWLEDGMENTS

I wish to thank Prof. Jaroslav Vacek, my teacher and PhD. supervisor, who introduced me into the study and description of the Altaic languages and without whose guidance my thesis would never have been accomplished. I owe thanks to Mr. Kicengge, my teacher of spoken Sibe, Mr. Guoqing and his family, and all my Sibe advisors and friends without whose kindness and help the present work would have been impossible. I should like to thank all my colleagues who helped me by their precious advice and, in particular, Ms. Rachel Mikos for proofreading and corrections of my English. I am deeply grateful to my parents and uncle Dušan for their unceasing support of my work.

# APPENDIX

## An example of a text in spoken Sibe with English translation

The following two texts were recorded by Mr. Kicengge in the winter of 1993. Both of the texts are examples of real speech and therefore repetitions, ellipses and other characteristics of spoken language are frequent. Both texts belong to a genre which may be termed "oral history". The events described are situated in concrete locations and definite historical periods. The first text is of further interest in its description of certain shamanic practices. The second text is an account of a historical event that took place during the great Muslim rebellion in the 19th century – a period considered as heroic among the Sibes.

*Recorded 13. 1. 1993 in Chabchal.*

*baijihua baiyüśiaŋəi juvə*

ər əm əyi mamət da əm χaʁəč biᵞi. χaʁəjᵊi
gəvuv ňie kičətu zəm. ər χaʁəč tačirt, tačir
diorgit əm ňinəŋ ər χaʁəč tašqə ainʁə, ɢaitai əm
ňinəŋ afqai suvdun yečin udun dam, aʁa dam,
əraɴ turgun fəjiɹ da ər χaʁəjif am udun dəyivmaq
ta ɢam yavʁə. diyɣə, diyɣə, diyɣə, ut əmə da tof
səm da ɛmirgi birai əkčint bujan diorgit gənəmaq
ta tuhᵊi. ər χaʁəč tuh aməɹ, əm jalənt uči duqa
čičim mutqaqů. tašqůdəri giamaq boi naʁən śiňi
banšk nan. ər χaʁəč bujan diorgit tuɣumaq ta tof
zəm da məzəi vəɹgien dundar soo ər ňi da bujan
diorgit, gəɹ əm gurh ɢasχəi qaičar jiɹʁan da
lahčəqů. əraɴ turgunt da ər χaʁəč da,
-ai, ər ərint da fanjəŋ da yuh yindaʁůⁿ kəvəɹt

*Free translation into English*

*The story of Baijihua and Baiyuxiang*

An old man and an old woman had an only son. The boy's name was Kičetu. This boy went to school and studied – the boy was studying and suddenly one day strange weather came – a black wind[1] and rain, and the boy was taken by the strong wind and blown away. He was flying and flying and at the end he fell down right in the middle of a forest on the northern bank of the river. This boy had lived his whole life between his home *kang* and school, he had no chance to go even a stone's throw away. Now suddenly he fell down in the middle of the forest, right to the place near our pig-trough. He could hear only the unceasing sounds of wild animals and birds.

---

[1]  The expression "black wind" is used to mean a storm with rain or snow.

døźimɐ̌ɐ̌iə,

zəm da ɢɐ̌ňim. əraɴ turguⁿ fəjil afśe, ər χaʁəč bujan diorguf hirgim yavərdə əmgəri šun tuhə,

šun tuɣəmə da gəɹ ɢɐ̌ňim bodəm,

-χaišɢəɹ ərgəⁿ χairin.

tut of bujan diorgit yavərdə əm am χaliⁿ baʁəm savm.

-ər χalint tafšəm døš ta, yuh yindaʁɐ̌ndəri guəm barə.

zəm da. ər χaʁəč da ər χalint tafšəm təmaq ta diovr dulindəri amirgidəri ju duŋlo dəyir gəs ta jiɣəi. ər χaʁəč,

-ər ai jaq biɣəye

zər.

-ərvadə nanəi dəvərgəⁿ aɢɐ̌ ai dəŋjəⁿ əɹdəⁿ biɣəye.

taʁəŋ da ər dəŋjəⁿ əɹdəⁿ

-χaliⁿ yedie

zəmaq da tof ər χalimf biamaq jiɣəi. əmdaⁿ jiɣəŋ, əm jiri sarɢan nan, əmkən ňi gəvəv ňi baijihua, əmkən ňi gəvəv ňi baiyüśiaŋ zər.

ər ju nan omə da, ɢɐ̌ňiχaqɐ̌ ta alin bira diovr saršər čiŋkuaŋ bi. tutof ta ər jaq da χalin bat jim sarɢašəm, čai muku emim, əraŋ ərimb ňi duluvm. baijihua omə da bəčamaq čəŋlh, giran dəri čəŋlh nan biɣəi. baiyüśiaŋ omə da jalən nan. əralian əjunnun aʁɐ̌ndo jafhəi. tutof, əmkən ňi bira dəri muku ɢajəm yavʁə. əmkən ňi dišk hədərkie zəm da məiməňi guŋzuo anpailh aməɹ məiməňi juʁɐ̌nči yavʁəi. dietti gənəmaq ta baijihuar ňi dišk ɢajəm jih, baiyüśiaŋ ňi muku ɢajəm jih. čait da muku. čoʁot da muku fəyivm, əraɴ da čai gəɹ fəih aməɹ da χaliⁿ fəjild gənəf ta ju nan da čai muku emim təh ərint da gizərər diorgidə χaʁəč da

-ər əmbič jalən nan, əmbič abbanšk guruⁿ biɣəye,

əmdaⁿ gələmaq əm savdəⁿ śik aɹdəvʁəi. ər śikə ňi tof səm da baijihua uju nuŋud ňi jimaq tuhəi. tukumə da baijihua gizərəm: –ai yono, ərai fərgoško, śi əmdaⁿ tam ta, tuksə aʁa dam na, min uju nuŋut əmdaⁿ aʁa daʁəye,

zəmə da baiyüśiaŋ ňi,

-ai gəɣə, urai foliŋə, tuksə aɢɐ̌, ut duruⁿ uśiχai čaɴ gəɹ aʁa dam na?

zəm. oi śi taqɐ̌ na, min ujuf əmdaⁿ biləm tam ta. min uju nuŋut əm savdəⁿ aʁa savdkəye,

In such conditions the boy said to himself: "Oh no, now I will surely get into the belly of a wolf or another wild animal."

What should he do in such a situation? While wandering about in the forest, the sun set. After sunset he was thinking: "After all life is precious." As he was wandering through the wood, he saw a big tree. "If I climb on this tree, I could escape the wolves," he thought.

The boy climbed on the tree and was sitting there. In the middle of the night two lanterns came from the north as if flying. The boy thought: What could this be, there is not a living soul around here, what lanterns could be here? As he was watching, the lanterns said: "Where is the tree?" and came looking exactly for this tree. As they came, they were a pair of women. One was called Baijihua and the other Baiyuxiang. These two were wandering surprisingly at night through mountains and rivers. And so these two came to the forest to drink tea, this is the way they were passing their time.

Baijihua was dead, a being which rose up from a corpse. Baiyuxiang was from this world. Thus they made friends as sisters. And so one went to the riverside to bring water and the other went to collect fuel. So they arranged their work and each went her way. In a moment Baijihua brought the fuel and Baiyuxiang brought the water, water for tea. They boiled the water in the tea pot, after the tea boiled they went under the tree and were drinking tea together. As they were sitting and talking, the boy thought: "Are these people from the human world, or some other beings?" And as he became frightened, he dropped a drop of urine and the drop fell exactly on Baijihua's head. Then Baijihua says: "How funny, how strange, look, is it raining? A raindrop fell on my head!"

Baiyuxiang said: "Oh sister, why do you talk so much, no clouds, so full of stars, how can it rain?"

"Just touch my head, a raindrop dropped on the top of my head," she says. As she touched it, it was wet indeed, how strange. Both were looking up and down and suddenly noticed the boy.

zəm da, əmdaⁿ biləm taʁəŋ da jəŋkən uśikuⁿ,
urai ɢañiŋ baitə. ju nan vešhun fosχǔn tam
yilaʁədə skəi χaʁəjif savmaq giaʁə. baijihua da
-śi ai nan, śi hut na, maɴus na, χǔduduⁿ uvm ju
śi, uvm jiqǔš ta śin ərgən ər yemji vajəm, aiqa
uvm jiqǔš ta.
ərəi śidəⁿ da baijihua da ərsuⁿ, uvm jiqǔš ta
ojǔqǔ,
-ər χaʁəjie, oi vaq, uvuqǔči vaqa, əmbič abbanšk
gurun taqaqǔ,
 əraɴ turgunt da ɢǔñində ñi kənɣunjəm.
tukumə da ər ju saʁənč, ər ju həɣəi qaičir əhər
turgun da fəjilda, χaʁəč da fosqǔⁿ uvm jiɣⁿi. ər
ju saʁənč,
-ər χaʁəč uvmaq jiɣə
zəm da ju nan əm nan əm oʁədəri qavčimaq
giaʁⁿi, giamaq ta əmgəri da dəyivmaq da udun
jiɹʁan li donjim. śan zər jiɹʁaⁿ, ər χaʁəč da əmə
li jaqəf taqǔqǔ. tukumə da śinčəŋei juɹh duqai
louzə nuŋui bohton bat da gənəmə da tof səm
yilaʁⁿi. yilamə da baijihua bo ñi omə da tərəi
amirgit bi. baiyüśiaŋ omə da χotun diorgut,
tukumə da ju nan omə da juɹh duqat yilamə da
bəy bəydəri diurnumaškⁿi,
-gəɣə bi ɢamki,
oi ər əmkən ñi
-bi ɢamki,
ər antqəf bi ɢaməm śi ɢaməm ju nan da
diurimaškⁿi. diurivɣədə baijihua ñi omə χaiškəɹ
ər jaqəi bəšk jaqə dəri čənlh jaq vaq na, ər
baiyüśiaŋ anəvmaq ta
- oi čimar yamsqǔⁿ bi ɢaməm
zəmaq da anəvmaq da yavʁⁿi. tukumə da
baijihua ñi bəy ñi ɢamʁⁿi. ər ɢaməm gənər ərint
da tof səm da čoqo χǔlar əriⁿ oʁǔi. təvat ər χaʁəč
əm gulɣun ñinəŋ udunt diyɣə, aʁat fičavʁə,
anʁə da, gulɣuⁿ ñinəŋ amʁəm mutkaqǔ, diovr
gəɹ čoqo χǔlah, tukumə da əmdaⁿ gənɣəŋ əm
fonqət døžimaq əm, oi əm nanə li dudur li orⁿ,
fonqəi diorgit. tukumədа

Baijihua: "What kind of man are you? Are you
an evil spirit[2] or a *mangus*,[3] quickly come down,
if you do not come down, your life will end this
night, if you do not come immediately!"
While Baijihua was calling the boy down
angrily, the boy was thinking: "No, no, it is not
that I don't want to come down, but I do not
know what beings they are."
At the end, as the two girls, two women kept on
shouting, the boy climbed down. The two girls
(were happy) that the boy came down, each one
took him by one armpit and flew, he could hear
only the sound of wind. A whistling sound.
The boy did not know anything. Then they
reached the bumpy place near the southern gate
of Xincheng.[4]
As they stopped, Baijihua's house was to the
north from that place and Baiyuxiang (lived)
inside the town, and so the two stopped in front
of the southern gate and started to fight over the
boy.
"Oh sister, I will take him," the other said,
"I will take him," so they were struggling, who
would take this guest home. And so they were
fighting – Baijihua was after all a revived corpse
and so Baiyuxiang gave up and said, "all right,
I will take him tomorrow," and left.
So Baijihua took him home herself. When she
was taking him away, it was just the time of the
rooster's crow.
The boy had been flying in the wind and
was lashed by the rain, he did not sleep for the
whole day and now the rooster crowed, and so
they entered a pit, but there was only a place for
one person inside the pit. Then (she said) "You
sleep in the house and I will sleep here on the
ground." The boy (said) "Oh no, Aunt, you sleep
in the house, I will sleep on the ground." "How
can a guest sleep on the ground? You sleep
inside."

---

[2] The word *hut* (Ma. *hutu*) usually means a soul of
a dead person which causes evil to living people.

[3] *Mangus* (mo. *mangas*) is an evil being known
mainly from Mongolian (and other Mongol-related,
as Mongghul) folklore. This figure is known for the
most part from Mongolian fairy-tales and legends,
so one can probably speak of a Mongolian influence
in this case. The *mangus* is most often depicted as an
old woman who eats human flesh.

[4] Xingcheng is one of the villages in the Chabchal
territory.

-ər bot da, śi ər bot dudə, bi ər nad ňi dutkie,
zəm da, ər χaʁač

-naqə, gəɣə ər bod ňi dudə, bi nat dudki zəm da.
oi ojuqǔ, jir antq aibi nat dudər gian biɣəye, śi
əmdan bod ňi dudə

zəm da ər χaʁač da nanᵊi favənt doškəi, arʁaqǔ
da skəi χovə diorgit qotoŋ zəm da doškᵊi.
dǿzimaq dudərəŋ da amʁəmaškᵊi. əməli jaq
taqəqǔ. gulɣun ňinəŋ sadəm čukəm diyɣə,
diovr dulin śidəⁿ amχaqǔ, əraŋ turgundə səkəi
həɣə χaʁəji amh turgun fəjildə śergəi śidənbə
ňi əmdan biləm taʁᵊi. əmdan biɹɣəŋ, ər χaʁəji
məməi orun bie, məmə aqǔ biɣᵊi. tukumə da
təmə da soNǔmaškᵊi.

-hei, bi veiɣun jalən də yiɣiⁿ zəm giaʁəNə, gəɹ
əm vaq jaqəf tuNaɹʁəye, uv səɣəŋə, ai nəkəlien,
bəšk jalənt əmkən tuNaɹm baχəŋ gəɹ əm ərən
jaqət tuNaɹʁᵊi. miⁿ uf hondəvʁəN da mərəŋə,
zəm soNǔm. soNǔm vašqəye, arʁaqǔʁᵘi. ər
baiyǔśiaŋ ňi əm əňi biɣᵊi. ərəi əňi da juɹh qarənt
aɹvən biɣəi. tof səm da śinqiliu yamsqǔⁿ oh
biɣᵊi. diovr ər mamə tičim taʁəN da tiuɹgut
soNor li jiɹʁan.

-ai, ər ai zəm soNǔmεie,
taʁəN da baijihuai soNor jiɹʁan taχə. əzə ňi omə
da əyun nun, əzə bod ňi gənəm jimə da taqəm.
tukumə da

-baijihua ňi an soNǔmaχ biɣəye, bot dǿzim takie,
zəm.

-ai saʁənjie, so əyun nun ju nan bučunh bait
bi na, ainχ bait biɣəye, an śin gəɣə soNǔmaq
dudkəye, bi śitəm čiśkəŋ gəɹ soNǔmaq dudkᵊi,
qorsum nazəm soNǔmaq dudkəye,
zəm. ai baitəi čiśkəye, zəm.

-ai bait tičimie, yeye bait čiśqaqǔye,
zəməq ta saʁənji ňi aɹʁaqǔʁᵘi. oi tər mamə tuttut
da əɹəi soNǔr jiɹʁan əɹəi uzat donjim. tumaq ta ər
mamə jaqəi utumaq da tivmo sujamaq da ər

The boy had no choice and followed her
command, tumbled into the coffin and
immediately fell asleep, and did not know
anything. He had been flying the whole day
and was tired after having not slept till the deep
night. At this time, as the boy was sleeping,
the woman tried to touch his crotch, and as she
touched it, there was a place for a penis but there
was no penis. She sat down and started crying:
"Oh, in my human life the one whom I had taken
as husband was also a mistake. A fate, how lowly
it is, when I found another one after my death,
I have encountered the same thing. It must be my
fate," she cried. But there was no help and she
stopped crying.

Baiyuxiang had a mother. Her mother was on
duty at the Southern fortress.[5] It was Saturday
evening. At night the old woman[6] went out and
suddenly she heard somebody crying. "Why is
she crying," she thought and then she recognized
the crying voice of Baijihua. She knew her,
because they were friends and (Baijihua) used
to visit their house. "Why is Baijihua crying?"
she thought, "I should go home and see". —
"Oh daughter, did you two sisters quarrel?
What happened, why is your sister crying?
When I went out to piss, she was still crying
heartbrokenly, what happened?" Her daughter
did not tell: "What should happen, nothing
happened at all."

But the crying sound was still more pitiable. Her
mother dressed up, took her stick and went there.
"It seems that the two had quarreled."
As she got there, the woman was sitting beside
(the grave) and crying. "Why are you crying?
Why are you crying, my girl?" "Oh, damn it,
when I had a husband in my human life, it was
like this, and today when I found another one

---

5   *qarən* (Ma. *karūn*) – watchpost – is a term from the
times of the Manchu Dynasty. A chain of border
fortresses was built along the whole western and
northern border of the Manchu empire. In Xinjiang
their importance was greater than elsewhere, because
on one hand, they prevented Russian expansion into
the Manchu territory, and on the other, they controlled
the frequent unrest among the Muslim inhabitants of
Xinjiang, The qarens in the Ili area were manned by
the Sibe soldiers and played an important role in the
lifeand culture of the Sibe community until 1911.

6   The expression mame grandmother, old woman is
a polite address to a woman of 40 years and older.

mamə ai əmdan gənɣⁱi.
-kənəŋ da ər ju jaq bučunur arvən bi. əmdaⁿ
gənɣəŋ da skəi həh da daɹvət da təf sonǔm.
-ei, an sonǔm? an sonǔmɛie, saʁənjie? – aia naqa
čiźie, vəiɣun jalənt əm yiɣin zəm giaʁəŋə əran
bait tunaɹɣəye, ənəŋə gəɹ əmkən baʁəm ɢaškəŋ,
gəɹ əran bait. miⁿ uf da məranə,
zəmaq sonǔm təɣⁱi.
-osaʁənč, təran banšk bait.
tukumaq da skəi χaʁəjif:
-ye,
zəm, ujudəri šašqaɹm.
yaf, mon boči yaf, səɣⁱi. mamə da χaʁəjif da
šašqaɹmə gətəvmaq boči ňi ɢajəm jiɣə. ɢajəm
jimaq ta saʁənjif:
-ye, saʁənje, ye, muku fəyif, χǔdǔduⁿ, zəm da
muku fəyivm, anim. emim vajimaq mamə skəi
guizədəri skəi vans oχtəf da čičivm ɢajəm, əm
yilan faχ ɢajəm jimaq ta ər χaʁəjit da
-emmie,
zəm,
-emmaq da dudəm amʁə. tukumə da jai ňinəŋ,
ər mamə da šanbaɹm yavmǔʁǔ. saʁənjid ňi
avəvʁⁱi.
-saʁənjie, nanəi ərɣənmaq əm ivirə. ər χaʁəč bi
taʁənə ər jalən nanⁱi arvən bi. so əyun nun
ju nan śidər χodur yavm. čiŋkuaŋ əraŋ banšk
bait oʁǔie. əňi jai əm śiŋči jir śidəⁿ da yaya
χačin baitəf əm čičivər. ər χaʁəjivə əm uči duqa
čičivər, zəmə, əňi učivə tiɹɣudəri yozuɹmaq uči
anqəf tər uči bioʁǔn bat ummaq yavʁⁱi.
-aiqa baijihua jiš da əm aɹmburə,
zəm da,
-tər nanəi ərɣənmaq əm ivirə. tutof ta čira
avəvmaq da mamə da yavʁə, ju nan da əyun nun,
aʁǔn do əm durun da injim ivm, uttu ainʁə da
sunja ňinəŋ yafh oh biɣⁱi. sunja ňinəŋ omə da
səkəi baijihuadə čik səm ɢǔňint doškⁱi.
-ər mamə χaʁəjif ɢamʁə ainəmah biɣəye, əsk
guidam əm məjig aqǔ,
-zəm da
-bi əmdan gənəm taki.
baijihuai yavər ərin omə da, diovr li yavm, ňinəŋ
sun yavm mutəqǔ, ərəi giraŋ ňi tərəŋ banšk
bait ǔrǔ. tukumaq da ər jaq diovr duliⁿ yimaq
ta əmdaⁿ gənɣəŋ da ju nan ňi tof səm, baijihua
ər χaʁəjimaq ju nan bəy bəymaq vəh giam ivm,
naʁənt injim ivm təɣəye. tukumaq ta skəi fai
fonqǔdəri əmdan gulɣuŋ da ju jaq ta injim ivm.
tukumaq ta skəi baijihua tom,

and brought him, it is the same, my fate is just
like this," she said and cried.
"Oh I see, my girl!" Then she slapped the boy
and said: "Get up, let us go to our place." She
woke him up by slappping and brought home.
When she brought him, she said: "Get up,
daughter. Quickly boil water, quickly!" They
boiled the water and when (the boy) drank it,
the old woman took out pills of medicine from
a coffer and gave three pills to the boy. "Take it
and then go to sleep".
The next day the old woman had to leave for
work. She ordered her daughter: "Daughter, do
not play with people's life. As I see, this boy is
from our human world. You two sisters are close
friends. But now the matter turned up like this.
I will come home next week. Before that, do not
do any mischief. Do not let the boy out of the
door."
Mother locked the door from outside and burried
the key into the soil in front of the door. "If
Baijihua comes, do not tell her about it. Do not
play with the boy's life".
Thus the old woman, strictly commanding, gave
a strict order to her daughter and left. The two
were laughing and playing like siblings, and this
way five days had passed. When it was five days,
a thought suddenly occurred to Baijihua. "What
is the old woman doing with the boy? For such
a long time there is no news from her, I have to
go and see."
The time when Baijihua could travel was
only in the night, she could not walk in the
daylight. It was because of her body. So she
got up at midnight and went to see them. The
two, Baijihua and the boy, were just playing
at 'claws', they were sitting on the kang and
playing and laughing. She peeped in through the
window and saw how the two were playing and
laughing, and she started abusing them: "Are
you not ashamed, you have brought this boy here
and live with him having good time, you are
enjoying the life. Open the door!" Thus she was
shouting angrily. Baiyuxiang said: "I do not have
the key, our mother took it with her." "Oh you
have to open, just open it. If you do not open,
I will kick the door out!" At that time the boy
saw her and started trembling in fear. He huddled
up in the corner of the *kang* and kept trembling
like this.

-oi girim banaqᵘ jaqə, śi gəɹ ər aštaf ɕajəmjifə,
bəyi səbjən səlačuqa banjən duluvm, injim ivm.
śi jaq səm banjəm. so, učif so!
əmdaⁿ ərsun qačim. oi, tukumaq ta baiyüśiaŋ ňi
gizərəm,
-oi uči anqə ňi mint aqᵘ, məzəi əňi ňi ɕaməm
yavʁᵊi,
zəm da. tukumə
-śi soqǔči ojǔqǔ,
zəm da
-so, uči so! uči soqǔš ta uči χᵘa fuskulum, zəm
da, ər tərᵊi śidən da tər χaʁɔč da skəi həh əmdaⁿ
jimə da dart dart suryunum, gələm. ər maf da
naʁɐⁿ χozət kokormaq ta dart durt suryunum, oi
təraŋ. tərəi śidən da qaičim, ursun, tukumaq ta
baiyüśiaŋ ňi gəɹ gələmaq ta,
-oi oi tər uči anqə ňi uči χozət bi, bioʁɐnt umyᵊi.
skəi həh qǔčirəm giasə, učif so, jih jiyədə,
čorʁodəri latəmaq da ɕam yavʁə. tukumaq ta
skəi mamə omə da əm χačin feiančaobi ərdəm
biyəliaŋə, yaz anə ňi tatəvm, ər mamə juɹh
qarənt əm śiŋči əm śiŋčiliu əm śiŋčidəri śiňi
bod ňi jiməči sunjač ňinəŋ omə da ňiŋun śiňi
omə da yaz an tatəvm. əmdaⁿ śiumyuⁿ hədəmə
ər χaʁəjif əmgəri da ɕam yavʁə zər. tə ju ňinəŋ
gənəqǔš ta ərgən jalən ňi vajimǔʁǔ. tukumaq
ta ər mamə solo biamaq da fars səmaq iźinmaq
jiyᵊi. jimaq saʁənjif tom,
-bi ai zəyə, śint affə gənh biyə. nanᵊi ərgənmaq
ivm na śi? ər abbanšk jaqə, zəmə da tom. tumə
da saʁənji ňi gəɹ,
-oi nanᵊi gizun gum taqaqǔ ujandaqᵘ azəɹm,
tumaq aɹmaq buyəŋ. ɕam yavʁəye,
zər. səkəi mamə jih jiyə saʁənjif vajirdə tivmo
sujamaq ta yavʁə. gənəmaq da dieləmaq
ɕajəmaq jiyəi. əmdan jiyəŋ, ər χaʁɔč da, tə ju
ňinəŋ da ərgən vajəmǔʁǔ, ərgən da śiqai gəskə
fənškᵊi. tutof tər saʁənjif
-χǔdǔn muku fəyif!
muku fəyivm anim, muku fəyivmaq ta gəɹ əm
χačiⁿ oχțəf čičivmaq χaʁəjit əmdaⁿ emivmaq
ta da duruⁿ oʁᵘi. tukumə da da duruⁿ omə da
mamə da gizəryᵊi:
-śi gələ əvat guidam banjəm ojuqǔo, ər ju bo
guanśi ňi omə da čalabun ňi čaləvm yilayəye, śi
taqəm yilaʁəye. bo zəyəŋə jalən nan, tər zəyəŋə
bəčəmaq čənlh jaq. tutof əraŋ turgun da śidər
χodur aqǔ banjəm. tutof da śi əvat yinəŋ guidam
banš da śin amə əňit gəɹ ačəm mutaqǔ, bəyzəi
ərgəⁿ jalⁿ gum vajəvm. tutof da ənəŋdəri min

The woman kept shouting and raving, and
Baiyuxiang was seized by fear and said: "The
key is in the corner of the door, she burried it in
the ground."
The woman dug it out, opened the door, broke
in, grabbed the boy at his neck and took him
away.
The old woman seems to have some sixth
sense, her eyes and mouth started jerking. This
old woman used to go home for Saturday and
Sunday. This was the fifth day and on the sixth
day her eyes and mouth started jerking. She
counted with her fingers and saw that the boy
had already been taken away, there were two
days left and his life would finish.
So the granny took a leave and in a flash reached
her home. She abused her daughter: "What did
I tell you, I gave you orders, how can you play
with people's lives? You!" The girl said: "Oh she
did not listen to me, she was acting like crazy so
I told her and she took him away." The granny
finished with her daughter, took her stick and
went off. She went there and drove the boy back
When the boy came, (it was clear that) in two
days his life would finish, there was as much
life as a horsehair left in him. So she said to her
daughter: "Quickly boil the water!" While she
was boiling water, (the granny) took out yet
another medicine, gave it to the boy and when
he took it, he became as he had been before. The
old woman said: "You cannot stay here long.
Our two families have special relatioship, they
are not the same, you know it – we are people
from this world, but that one is a revived corpse.
So there are problems in between. If you stay
here too long, you could not see your parents
any more, you would even break their own lives
short. So from today I am engaging my daughter
to you, you go and tell your mother and father.
On the fifteenth of the eighth month hitch a cart
and come to take your wife," thus she ordered
him.
The boy thanked her, bowed in front of her, she
gave him some silver and saw him off.
The boy came home. His parents were blinded
from crying. When he came, they were crying
and sobbing, they were hugging each other and
crying. The boy was licking his mother's eyes,
licking his father's eyes until they recovered.
Only then his parents started asking him,

saʁənjif śint tə sum buɣᵊi. śin əňi amət gənəm al, jaqŭn biya tofχon yamji səjən toʁŭmaq ju, zəm da. tukumə da śin həɣəf ɢam gənə, zəm da əralian avəvʁᵊi. tukumə da ər χaʁəje -ambu baňiχa zəmə da yaqŭrum hiŋkəlf ta, tut fančan moŋun buf ta aičivʁᵊi. χaʁəji ňi bod ňi əmdaⁿ iźinəm jiɣəŋ da əňi amə ňi soʁko faʁə, yaz ňi gum doʁovʁᵊi. tut χaʁəč ňi jif ta soɴŭm fam, yilan anəɹ bəy bəyəf tivələm tivələm soɴŭm. χaʁəj ňi əňiŋə yazəv ňi yiləm, aməyiŋ yazəv ňi yiləm, ərən of ta yaz ňi gulɣun omaq jiɣᵊi. tut omaq ta śiňi əňi amə ňi bait turgun fienjim, -afš banšk baitə, yeči yafh zəm fienjim. -ər yilan duyin biya yəči yafh zəm da, ər ňi da baitai turgumf gum gian giaňie aɹʁəŋ, bəy ňi təvat gənəmaq afš həh buɣᵊi, afš tərɑn baitət tunaɹʁᵊi, bəyiŋə əm jalən baitəf bodombuʁᵊi, tərɑn zəm da, əňi ňi oi zəm usun bailəm, təri śidən da amə ňi jil banjəm. -urai, ai jaqəi hut maɴŭzəi banjəm jimaq urai lɔvlə vaqa, zəm tom χaʁəjif. tukumə da əňi ňi yiɣimb ňi fienjim, -vaqa, set, toroɴəf baivŭqŭ, jiɣəŋ da oʁᵘi. hut na, maɴus biɣə na, śin χaʁəji əm jalən baitəf bodombuɣᵊi. ərəv ňi an tomie. toroɴəf biavŭqŭ. məs da jaqŭn biya tofχoⁿ yemjif əški. tudtu, məs orunbə ňi ɢajəmjiki, zəm da tər set ňi gəɹ ojuqŭ. yavʁə gənɣədə jaqŭn biya tofχoⁿ iźinɣə. tər əňi ju nan təŋəm tof, əňi ju nan tumaq ta gənh, əmdan gənɣə da skəi mamə saʁənjif ənduri gəs dazəmaq ta, jaqəi utumaq ta duqai pai juɹbit əmdaⁿ alimə yilaʁəye. o, əmdan gənɣəŋ, -oi śi bot døźirəŋəf biavŭqŭ, śin həhəf təf. tuvmaq ta aiči aiči. tər baijihua tər jil ujandaqŭ baitədə, zəm da, tər mamə ňi gəɹ tər həɣət sərəvuqŭ zəm da aič zəm da. jaq jamun məji maɹɣŭⁿ tuvmaq da aičivʁᵊi. tut bot ɢajəm jimaq ta o, jai ňinəŋ da śierin aramŭʁŭ, zəm da uɣuri gučču aɣŭndof śoɹm. śien ňinəŋ tamə da śierin aram, ju yilan ňinəŋ śieriⁿ araʁᵊi. tut banškə gənɣə ainʁə da əm aňi aməɹ da həɣə ňi əm χaʁəč banšk ᵊi. mašqŭⁿ χaʁəjie, banjəmə da əňiv ňi gəɹ gurivm ɢaškᵊi. əňiv ňi da gurivm da, jaq jamun da ju śiŋči śidən da əňiŋ ňi gurivm ɢajərəŋ da guizəli, am guizəli. ər guizət gəm am yoz tavʁᵊi. ai biɣəŋəf saqᵘ.

what happened, where he was. He told them everything step by step, how he got there, how he got engaged, what he saw there, how they arranged his life for him.

His mother was pleased, but his father flew into rage: "What, are you going to bring ghosts and *manguses* home? What nonsense!" he was scolding his son. His mother said to her husband: "Oh no, man, there is no need to abuse him, it is enough that he is back. And wheather she is a ghost or a *mangus*, she arranged the whole life of your son, why should you abuse him? Let us remember the fifteenth day of the eighth month, on that day we bring our daughter-in-law." The old man still did not agree.

The time passed and the fifteenth day of the eighth month came, the mother and the son agreed among themselves and went there. When they arrived, the old woman had dressed up her daughter, so that she was looking like a fairy, and was awaiting them in front of the gate. When they arrived, she said: "Do not enter, take your wife and go quickly, otherwise Baijihua will get furious". The old woman did not want Baijihua to know, so she told them to leave quickly. She gave them some presents and saw them off. So they brought her home, invited all the friends and relatives, chose an auspisious day and prepared the wedding. The celebration lasted for two three days. Then they lived on and after a year the wife gave birth to a boy, a thin boy. When the boy was born, they brought her mother too. When they were moving her property, they were bringing it for two weeks, many big coffers. All the coffers had big locks and nobody knew what was in them. They were bringing them one after another, until there was no space to put them. The old woman was holding the keys.

After the wedding, one night, the old woman told her daughter: "Daughter, now you have come to a new family. You have to serve your parents-in-law and live in peace and love with your husband. Do not ever think about the old wild things, never mention Baijihua. Never play with human lives. This is the most important." She was talking to her all night, but she was still not sure about her daughter, so she pulled off three pieces of her hair, packed them in a piece of paper and gave them to the girl:

səndaʁə səndaʁə bod ňi gəɹ baχtəqů. ər da ər
mamə gum anqəv ňi jafhəi. tutof ta əs śierin
aram vajəmaq da əňi ňi saʁənjid ňi əm yemj
avəvʁ°i:

-saʁənjie, śi əmgəri nan°i duqat doškʰi. ʋnandaf
śien giŋul. yiɣin həh śien χač χǔaliasůn banč. śin
tər bigan bodorənəf biavəqů. jai əmdan baijihuaf
jonorənəf biavəqů. śi nan°i ərgənmaq əm ivərə,
śiňi ər baitə,

zər. tutof, əm diovr gizun tačivm vajəvmaq gəɹ
saʁənjiv ňi eiduqů, uju finɣəv ňi yilan da finh
tatəm giafə, χoźint χoźim buɣ°i.

-manət tunaɹχ ərində ňi tičivm diźie,
tut ər yilan da finɣəf χoźim giaf saʁənjid ňi
azərəvʁ°i. tutof da banškə gənɣə əm mašqůn
χaʁəč banšqa əm aň oʁo. tumə da əm diovr da ər
həɣə ňi gəɹ gizərmaq giaʁə. yiɣinmaqə ňi:

-he! χaʁə nan da liaŋxin bail aqů.

-Ui! bi ai liaŋxin aqů bait bi. śimaq χǔaliazůn
banjəmɛie, ədəri češ afš banjəmie, ai liaŋxin aqů
bait bie,

zəm da, ər hutu ňi tər baitəf oʋůmaq səndaʁə,
zər. ər həɣəvə.

-tə baijihua əmgəri χaʁəč banškʰi. śim da liaŋxin
aqů bait əvat bi vaq na? śi əmdan tam ojuqů, śi
əmdan cǔňint døźivm ojuqů na?

zər.

-o, mənjaʋ na?

-mənjaʋ vaq aie, gəɣəňie,

zəm da. tutfi skəi maf da, jai ňinəŋ afq jaqarənəf
əksəm. tukumə da afq jaqarʁə morin da ɢayaqů
fəkśir morint da śien əmən toʁům giaʁəi. toʁům
giamaq ta cǔa morimb ňi mələm zər yuɹdunt
da, mələm vajərt da cǔa morimf boči aidada tər
čiŋkuaŋ ňi bəy ňi modiləm taqəmůrů, śiŋčəŋəi
julh duqai bat da gənəmə da skəi dozorʁůi iv°i
bat da cǔlmaʁ°n avələr əm durun əm dozorh
əm dozorh baičəm tam, məraʋ tar diorgit da
ou, bohtun bahtən əm am if da. fonqůt da
məsk ambu nan døźim čiškə, glčiŋ glčiŋ oʁůi.
ou, tutof da juan bai oksůn badəri yilamaq ta
morin nuŋudəri qaičim. baijihua, baijihua zəm.
tukumə da skʰi həh yinəŋ sun omə ursun vaq
na, diovr omə da əvəri. ňinəŋ sun fars zəm tičim
juə, uju aʋə ňi səŋkərɣə, su da skəi sas həh əm
durun, skəi samən əlči samdəmačimə həh gurun
yivagən suvdun javm əm durun, mətər əm durun,
yaz aʋə ňi fulaʁůn fəɹgien, səŋkər səŋkər jimə
da tom.

---

"If anything happens, take them out and burn
them."
So she gave her three pieces of hair. So they
lived, in a year the wife gave birth to the thin
boy, and one night the wife started again,
she said to her husband: "Oh, men have no
conscience." "What? What have I done to you?
I live in peace with you, how else should I live?"
"You have forgotten about that. That woman.
Baijihua has already given birth to a son. This
is your unfaithfulness. Can't you think about it?
Can't you go and see her?" "Oh, really?" "Of
course, my elder sister."
The next morning at daybreak the husband
saddled the best horse and, saying that he was
going to water the other horses, he set forth.
When he finished watering the horses, he
drove them home. He himself seemed to have
suspected something, so he rode to the southern
gate of Xincheng, where there was a needlegrass
plain with graves. He was searching through
the bunches of needlegrass, as if hunting for
rabbits. Suddenly he stumbled upon a big tomb.
A human figure slipped in and out, it seemed to
be shining. He stopped ten steps from there and
shouted from the horse:
"Baijihua, Baijihua!" The woman – she looked
dreadful in the daylight, while at night she
looked normal. When she appeared in the
daylight, her hair tangled up, like those crazy
women, or like when during shaman rituals the
women are possessed by ghosts, her eyes red,
with dishevelled hair – she ran out and started
abusing him: "Men have no conscience, you
shoud be ashamed, you married Baiyuxiang and
live with her in joy, so selfish!"
He was getting ready on the horse, waiting what
she would do. She entered the pit and came
out with the child. She threw the child at him:
"Look!" The child fell right on the saddle. He
caught him and galloped home. "The buttocks
of your mother!" cries the woman, "Give me
back my child, where are you taking him? How
shameless, he stole my child!"
He gallopped to his home. She followed him, but
she could not enter the village in the daylight. So
she returned home, but she was watching for his
soul from under the earth. He arrived home and

-ei, χaʁə naⁿ gəɹ lianxin aɋů, girim banəɋů
ərgəⁿ. śi gəɹ baiyüśiaŋəf ɢamf səbjən səlak
banjəm, śi! śi da əʀaн lianxin aɋů jaq, śi da
gətqaɋů jaq,
zəm tom. toʁə da
-ər hut ainəm biɣəye,
zəm morin nuŋut bəɹɣəm yilaɋůʁů na, ər jaq afš
azələm biɣəye, zəm. tof tof da ər jaq śaʀs səm
døźim gənɣə. døźimaq jiv ňi tivəɹf čiškəi. jiv
ňi maχtkəi, śi əmdaⁿ tam ta, zəm. jiv ňi əmdaⁿ
taʁəŋ, tof zəm morin əmən nuŋut da jimaq tuhᵊi.
tukumaq ta giamaq mədar fəkškᵊi.
-əňivəŋ faškəv ňie,
ər həɣə ňi ,
-ɢajədi ɢaš min jif ɢajədi ɢaš, śi yet ɢaməm,
śi yet ɢaməm, urai girim banəɋů jaqə, min jif
ɢammə yavm.
oi fəkškə fəkškə da məzəi boi χanč jimə da nanᵊi
ɢaznt jimə da døźimə da døźim mutəɋůʁů, yinəŋ
suⁿ yedəri døźim mutəmie. daohui boči ňi gənɣə.
ər hut gənɣə da nai fərət alim yilaʁəye, əjaqə
fayiŋ ňi. daʁəm jimaq ta duqa jaqət jiɣə. jimə da
həɣəv ňi qačim:
-oi mamə ňi,
zəm da,
-aie?
-ma ma man,
zəm da.
-oi aie,
zəm da
-maɋů na? zəm da. həɣəi ji ňi, śi mənjaн əʀə,
zəm əmdaⁿ taʁəŋ mənjaн kuantour χaʁəč biɣᵊi.
həɣəd ňi buɣə, ər maf, morindəri uvərəŋ da
fayiŋəv ňi ɢammaq yavʁə. nai fərdəri. tuɣərəŋ da
farnʁᵊi. farnəmaq da ər abbanšq bait oh zəm da
həɣə ňi fatəm qaičim surum, əňi amə ňi qaišqə
surɣə, fatkə ainʁə da ər maf araʀaн məji ərgəⁿ
doškᵊi. tutta bot ɢaməm døźivʁə, ər əm daivəf
ɢašči χoj ojůɋů, tər əm daivəf ɢaščie χoj ojůq,
χoj ojor jaqəi vaq. taʁədə, sunja ňinəŋ oʁᵘi. ər
hut da yaz aнəd bioʁůⁿ toχtomašqə, əm ňinəŋ
dəri əm ňinəŋ ər ňuŋk ujiⁿ om, daivəf ɢajəmə
gum taqərɋů. ər ňuŋkəf taqərɋů.
-o, yemj yemji ňi da bəčəmůʁůye, jaləн dəri
aɹjəmoʁůye. tər əmdan tər baitaɋů baitəf gizərh,
ər baitəf gizərəɋůči om biɣᵊi. ər jovolomf tam ta.
ər bait urai ɢošqo.

called his wife: "Granny!"[7] "What?" "Here you
are!" "What is it?" "The woman's child!"
Indeed, she looked and saw a bald boy. He
passed him to his wife, but as he was alighting
from the horse, Baijihua stole his soul and he
lost consciousness. "What happened?" cried
his wife, pinching him, his parents also started
shouting and pinching, and he cleared up a little.
They took him into the house and were calling
one doctor after another, but they could not help.
It did not seem that he could recover. After five
days dust started to lay on his eyes and mouth,
the ilness was getting more and more serious.
They were calling doctors, but no one new what
to do, no one knew the disease. "Oh, he will die
soon, I should not have told him that day, now
look at the disaster." So his wife was thinking,
and suddenly she remembered the hair her
mother gave her. "I have to bring my mother, if
not, I cannot solve it." She burned the hair – at
that time people were using torches – and her
mother came in five minutes. As she arrived, she
started scolding her: "What did I tell you? Do
not play with human lives. Luckily I came today,
he would have died tomorrow. Why are you
touching peoples' lives, just take care of your
parents-in-law and behave yourself, you have
caused them such a pain, you gawk!"
"Oh enough abusing, can you bring him
to life?" The old woman said: "I rather have
use magic."[8]
She brought rushes, made a human figure of
them and, as if making a scarecrow, she put on
it the clothes of her son-in-law, and on the head
she put his cap. Then she took a spear which was
in the house. She caught a hunting dog they had
there and leashed him. Then the old woman took
a spade and climbed the (…) on the norhtern side
of the house, where she dug a pit. She cut the
head of the dog and buried (it) in the pit. Then
she burned the figure of rushes and buried it too.
Then she gave Baijihua the soul of the dog in
exchange for the soul of her son-in-law.

---

7   It is common between a husband and a wife to call
    each other "old man" and "granny", even if they are
    young.
8   The expression *arʁəv yavəf*- lit. to use the method
    (cf. Mo. *argala*-) is a term designating rituals by
    which disasters and illnesses caused by evil beings
    are cured.

əraŋ bodəm ainəm, diovr dulіⁿ bodomə yilaʁədə
əňiŋə buh finɣə ňi ɢůňint doškᵊi.
-o, χaiš da min əňif diaoləm ɢajə. aqůči ər baitəf
jojiləm mutəqů.
bələn dəŋjən tůa bičie tər ərint skᵊi tiŋtiel
bi vaq na, fars zəm dəŋjən da tiavə, tiavərəŋ
da wufən juŋ da əňi ňi iźinmaq jiɣəi. jimə
da tom:
-bi ai zəɣə, a, nanᵊi ərgənmaq əm ivərə, tə yiɣiⁿ
əmgəri da čimar, kuli bi ər yemj jiɣᵊi, čimar da
bəčəm. śi nanᵊi ərgəmf ainəmie, uɴandaf śieⁿ
giŋuləm, ər baitəf χojəye iškia, śi əraŋ jovolon
tierʁᵊi, urai bandiaos jaqə?
zəm tom.
-toχ jalin ainəmůʁůo, zər.
-ər baitə ňi banjənər bait na?
skəi mamə da,
-ai, χaš da arʁəf yavəvůqůči ojůqů,
zəm da. skəi mamə da skəi olʁůf ɢaškə, olʁůf
ɢajəm skəi ɢaʁəf gələvər skəi olʁᵘⁱ nanəf
aram vaq na, olʁᵘⁱ nanəf arʁə, aram vajəmaq
da χošqůňi utkuf utuvʁə. maʁaɹv ňi ujud ňi
utuvʁə. tukumə da bod ňi bih jadəf tičivm ɢaškə.
bod ňi bih tər əm tiaχ yindaʁůnf χaitəm giaʁə,
tumaq ta ər mamə ta giamaq da čuf gəɹ giaʁə,
yet gənəmie, emirh (unintelligible) tavənəm
gənɣə, gənəmə da əm ulan fətkə. tukumaq ta
ulan fətəmaq ta ulan həzənt yindaʁůn ujuf
čaq čaqalʁə. ulan umɣə. tumə da oɹʁůi nanəf
diškə. dijim ummaq ta, uməm vajəmaq ta afś
azəɹʁəye, yindaʁůn fayiɴəf tər həɣət, baijiχůat
bumaq, χočqoɴə fayiɴəv ňi χůliazəmaq gaškᵊi.
ər mamə. tukumə da, məzəi ajigurun gələmə da
najən əyit χore χore zəm, əraŋ bait biʁə. təraɴ
bait tof zəm ər mamə aram yavʁᵊi. fayiɴəv
ňi χůliazəmaq ɢaškᵊi. tuməda tər mamə da,
χočqoɴə utkuv ňi, qanjiaɹv ňi javmaq ta:
-χore χore, bo naʁən śiňi əvat bie, həh jus śiňi
əvat bie, śamə ňi əvat bie,
zəm da χore, χore zəm da skəi ajigurun gələmə,
mətəraɴ əkəm vaq na? mətəraɴ χoriɹʁədə, bod ňi
gənəm. bod ňi afś azəɹʁəye, amə əňi ňi həɣə ňi
χočqůn dat təfie,
-χore χore, həh jus śiňi əvat bie,
zəm χoriləm təɣᵊi, mamə ňi gəɹ χoriləm təɣᵊi.

After that she did the same as if people make
"χore, χore" to the Grandfather Lord of the
Earth, when the little children get scared.[9] In
that way she exchanged the soul and brought it
back, then she took her son-in-law's shirt, and,
chanting "χore, χore" like when the children get
scared, walked into the house. What did they do
in the house? His parents and wife were sitting
around him and chanting "χore ore, your home
and *kang* is here, your wife and children are
here, your mother and father are here." They all
were sitting and chanting and the old woman
was chanting too, it took about half an hour.
She was slowly walking backwards. When she
lead the soul inside and reached her son-in-
law's bed, she stroked the drum and asked "Have
you come, Chunxi?" and she was vigorously
drumming. Thus she saved the soul of her son-
in-law by exchanging it for the dog's soul and
bringing it back. The next day the old woman
took some medicine out of her coffer and gave
three pills to her son-in-law. When he swallowed
them, he started quickly recovering, after one
week he was like before. When he recovered,
the old woman summoned the whole family and
told her daughter: "We only narrowly saved his
life, this is not fun, you must not mention these
things any more. Be bringing up your children
and serve your parents-in-law." After she told
her all she had to say clearly, she returned to her
work. After she left, they had two little sons.
They were like twins. They were attending
school and when the teacher was explaining one
thing, they understood two, they were extremely
clever. When he was teaching three things, they
learned five.
They quickly finished primary secondary school
and went to Peking for special examinations.
In that times Peking was called *Gemun hecen*[10]
(the Capital). They went there and sat the
examinations for medicine. They both became
outstanding doctors, one in Western medicine,
the other in Chinese medicine. Later the old

---

[9] The causes when the soul (or a part of it) leaves the
body are most frequent among children. Every Sibe
person knows about this topic and so the speaker
used this example to describe what the old woman
was doing. Summoning the soul is a frequent shaman
rituals and the summoning exclamation "χore: χore:"
(cf. Mo. *hurai hurai*) is used during them.

[10] *Gemun hecen* is the Manchu name of Peking.

ɢajəmjih jiɣədə, təri śidən da bangəjoŋ da oʁⁿ̌i.
χoriĸʁə χoriĸʁə, əɹɣə yavm vaq na, sozorumə
χoriĸʁə χoriĸʁə χoriləm ɢajəmjiɣə da χošqǔn dat
yinĸan fierəm vaq na,
-jiɣəi na, čunśi, jiɣə na,
zəm da, pas pas fierəm, χošqǔmb ňi afš
azəɹĸəye, tof zəm da ər yindaĸǔn fayaɴǔv ňi tər
həɣət bumaq ta χošqǔn fayaɴǔv ňi døźivmaq
ɢajəmaq jiɣ°i. tut χošqǔmb ňi jəjoɹɣ°i. tutof ta
jai ňinəŋ da ər mamə da skəi guizədəri oχtuf
čičivmaq ta χošqǔndə ňi yilan vans oχt emivĸə,
tumə da yemivh aməɹ da əm ńinəŋdəri əm ňinəŋ
əm śiŋčit da da bəy ňi oĸǔi. tukumə da da bəy ňi
utdurun χoj oʁⁿ̌i, tukumə da χoj ovm vajəmaq ta
gum χǔlam ɢajəfə gizərəm, saĸənjimaq:
-tə əmgəri ər baitə ararəŋ ərgən døźivĸə, ər
baitabə ivin yovn ojǔqǔ, jai əmdaⁿ jonoroɴ da
biavǔqǔ, jus dazəf χǔazəvm, uɴandaf χojəye
giŋuləm,
zəm da, ut əkəmaq ta, əňi ňi gian gian aɹmbum
vajəmaq ta bəy ňi χaišgəɹ nanᵊi aɹvən bači ňi
veiləmə yavĸ°i. yavĸaməɹ da ju χaĸəč oĸǔye.
ər ju χaĸəč da šuanboɹ. tašqǔt gənəm. tašqǔt da
səf əmkən aɹmbumə ju savm giam. usun gətkuⁿ.
yilaⁿ aɹmbumə sunja savm giam. əraliŋ.
tukumə da taqə da čujuŋdəri biyelɣə, biyelmə
da bəijiŋt juaŋyen kaoluvm gənəmǔɣǔ. ju χaĸəč.
kaolum gənəmaq da əmdan tər ərint gəmuⁿ kəčəⁿ
zəm, əmdan kaolĸəŋ da ər daivəi ərdəmət kaolh
biɣ°i. ju nan gum ɢayaqǔ. diyimin giaĸ°i.
tukumə da əmkən ňi da śiyi javm, əmkən ňi omə
da juŋyi javm.
aməɹ jimə da guizəi anqəv ňi saĸənjid ňi virifə
yavĸ°i, ər guizət ai bie? vaśhim gum oχt biɣ°i.
juŋyi tər χačačin ohto. tut ofə oχtov ňi χaĸəj ňi
gum daif oĸo, gəm ambu daif oĸo, yos anqəv
ňi ju χaĸəjid ňi buɣ°i tukumə da məzəi gufč
jalən jəčənt ər ju nan da gəf biźir daif oĸo. tərəi
śidən da nanᵊi əyi mamə ňi gum təsk aň oĸǔi,
bəčəm tuɣum vašqə, tutof bəyzə ňi bədərəm jih
aməɹ daivəi məji bod ňi anpaiɹχ aməɹ da əzə
ňi uɴandav ňi giɴuləm, həh jus giam, əm jalənt
bayin śieⁿ əraŋ tuɣunum banšk°i.
vačkəi!

woman gave her daughter the keys of her
coffers, and what was inside? Only medicine,
many kinds of Chinese medicine. Both of the
boys were doctors and so the keys got to their
hands and the sons became doctors famous in
our whole world. Many years passed and the old
parents all passed away, the boys started working
in a hospital, married, had children, cared about
their parents and so they lived well and rich for
their whole lives.
Finished!

## bə jaŋənᵊi juvə

ər sunjač ňurt əm bə jaŋəⁿ zəh jaŋən jaŋən dah
biɣə. tukumaq ta ər nunbə ňi uju ňurt buɣᵊi. bə
jaŋən gəvuv ňi taqəqŭʁŭye. bə jaŋəⁿ, bə jaŋəⁿ,
zəm. bə jaŋəⁿ ər nundə ňi əm χaʁač biɣə. daʁəm
jih ərint da ər χaʁəč jaqŭ sə oh biɣᵊi, məzəi
ərvadə. tər ərint da juailan zə oh biɣᵊi. tukumə da
ər bə jaŋən ňi nunmaqə ňi gizərəm:

— ər χaʁəjivə mint ɢajə, bi ɢam gənəm maji
baitəɹkie, zəm. daʁəfkie, zəm. tukumaq ta amə
əňi ňi:
— oʁŭye, χaʁəč ajigə, təňi juailan zə, jaq
mutəqŭo,
zəm da.
— baitaqŭ, ɢam gənəm məji tačifkie.
tut of ɢajəmjih biɣᵊi χandərda. sunjač ňurt ɢam
gənərəŋ da maji maɹʁŭn baitai iškiavm. əm
ňinəŋ da jaŋən taitai ňi da:
— śi yiʁandə əm ašχan ačəm gənəmaq ta muku
əm ašχan ɢajəmaq juə,
zəmaq da,
— sunjač ňurui noroi həzəndə ňi sər bi vaq na,
tədəri ɢajəm juə.
tut tər mavə ňi ərdə yimaq da, jəŋkən jəiŋkən
taitai gizərh soŋkoi da ai yiʁaⁿ ačərəŋəf saqŭ.
əmdaⁿ taʁəŋ da, χuarəⁿ diøɹmbad ňi əm ambu
muʁazn yiʁan dutk biɣᵊi. kuk fiaŋ muʁazn
yiʁaⁿ.
— o ər da mənjaʁ davəli,
gənə, viɣəd ňi uzam ɢajəm juə, ərgəɹji əmənəv
ňi əm ɢaɹmaq ačəvə, tuŋzəv ňi gəɹ ɢam gənəm
səndamaq ta uzamə yavmaškəŋ. ər yiʁan da šu
da ňunʁun əliaŋ daʁəm yavmɛye. yask huzun
biɣəŋəf saqŭ. norət gənɣə. gənəmaq ta jəŋ maji
muku vəidər śidən da, gəɹ əm asχan orun ňi
muku ɢajəm gənɣᵊi, noro dəri. ər da ičə χoɹfh
ərin ňi biɣə na, ər mavə ňi da, aji mavə ňi, ičə
orun χoš banškəv ňi gəɹ taʁə. tukumaq da skəi
ɢaɹ ňi sula omaq səndaʁᵊi. yiʁan viɣəf jafχ
ɢaɹ ňi. skəi yiʁan muɹt tatəmaq ta fəkśimaškᵊi
χandərda, ər mavə ňi əmdan tam, ər yiʁan
tuliajəm tuliajəm fəkśimaq dutkᵊi. mər amčəm.
amškə amškə, yiŋbi χanč jimə śiňi amčəm jafhᵊi.
skəi muku tuŋzᵊi gum tuɣəmaq χŭaʁə, ər yiʁamf
javmaq ta:
— oi. urai doraqŭ ərgəⁿ, oi, ər muku tuŋzəi gum
χŭaɹm, əmdan tandkie,
zəm. tikimaq əmdan škuaɹʁəŋ, ər ifčiv ňi, yilan
śirgə ifčiv ňi čaq škuaɹʁᵊi. əmdan da bəčəmaq

## The story of the Be janggin

Here in the Sixth Banner there was a certain
janggin called Be *janggin*. His younger sister
was given[11] to the First Banner. I do not know
his name, people just call him Be *janggin*. That
sister of Be *janggin* had a son. When she came to
our place (following her husband), the boy was
eight years old, at that time he was thirteen years
old. So this Be *janggin* says to his sister:
"Give me that boy, I will take him with me and
use him a little."
His parents said:
"Better do not, the boy is still small, only
thirteen, he does not know how to work."
"No problem, I will take him with me and teach
him a little."
So he brought him here. After he brought him to
the Fifth Banner, he was using him to make him
do light work. One day the *janggin's* wife said:
"Go, load a moss on a bull and bring it full of
water. There is a spring on the side of the swamp
near the Fifth Banner, bring it from there."
The boy followed the order of the lady and
arrived there, but he did not know which bull he
should load. When he looked around, a big bull
was lying in the middle of the enclosure, a bull
of blue colour.
"That should be him."
So he approached him, grasped his horns and
pulled him out, with one hand he put the saddle
and the yoke on the bull, took the tub and went.
The bull was following him like a dog, he did
not know how strong the bull was. When he
arrived, a young woman came also to the swamp
for water. She seemed to have been just married
and the little guy was looking at her beauty. In the
meantime he loosened his hand with which
he was holding the bull. The bull tore away and
started running. When the boy looked at him, he
was running and flinging. He threw himself after
the bull, he was chasing him and caught him
near the front wall. The tub fell down and broke
into pieces. When he caught the bull: "What
a shameless animal, he even broke the water tub,
I have to beat him!"

---

[11] married

səndah biɣˀi. yiʁamf vam vajəmaq ta bot jim
mutəqůʁůo. jaŋən dəri gələmə, zər.
– ai, uŋqanaqǔči ojůqǔ,
zəm da, mətərbit da yafhəŋ fəkśimašk biɣˀi, boči
ñi, uju ñurči. oi, jaŋən ñi qarč qarč, ər χaʁəč aqǔ.
taitaidəri fienščie, jiʁaqǔ, zəm.
– afš banšk bait oʁůo,
zər. yinənəi mierɣə na, ailiaŋ ərin oh biɣə. mərbit
da boi gurunt
– gənəm tam ta,
zəm. əmdan gənəm taʁəŋ, yiŋbi dat yiʁambə ñi
vaf səndaʁˀi. o, ər yiʁan an bəšk ərə, zəm, češ
əmdan taʁəŋ, skəi muku tuŋzəv ñi ɢaraŋ ɢaraŋ,
tut bod ñi jimə da aɹʁəŋ da:
– o, ər jaq bait čiškə,
zəm da. jaŋən da morin yaɹʁəŋ da mər amčəm
biɣəi. tukumə də čavčaɹ tovət giraŋyeɹ ñi biɣə
na, giraŋyeɹ jaqət døźimə,
– təraliŋə χaʁəč uŋqanʁaye, əvat jiɣə na?
zəm da.
– aqǔ, oi, mər təvalən əm χaʁəč kus kus zəm
dulumə yavʁəŋ,
zəm da,
– ər mavəi yavərəŋ da šu naf fuskulur əm durun.
əza ɢor bat dønjim biɣəye, ər mavəi yavər eiskəv
ñi. boi gurun əmdan taʁəŋ da əm ajigurun dulum
yavmɛye, hərčun aqǔ.
tut uju ñurt gənh. jaŋən ñi da əmdan gənyəŋ da,
jaŋəmf savərəŋ da uŋqanah biɣˀi. tukumə da mər
nunmaqə ñi gizərəm:
– χaʁəč jiɣə na,
zəm da.
– o, aqǔ, aqǔ.
– ɛi, jiɣˀi. bi čavčaɹ tovət fienškədə, iči jim
yilamaqa, śi sam. śi gələmaʁəŋ. gugu ñi, śi əm
gələr. bi ər χaʁəjif ainah zəm tandəqǔ. tər yiʁan
ñi gəɹ bəš da, bəšk davəli. χoš χoš gizərəm, ər
χaʁəjif χoɹtom, ararəŋ da morin ɛmirgit yaɹf
ɢajəmjih χandərda. ɢajəmaq da boi gurunt
avəvm:
– ainaχ zəm yeye bači taqǔrči ojůqǔ. ərəi huzumf
sačie, ərət huzun laft biɣə ərə,
zəm da. set da əm aň dulɣə, jai aňi ñi da ər
qarəmf tükiar aɹvən ñi ər setət jih biɣəi. yüdu ñi.
ər da yüdulmə tükiam biɣˀi, orozəi jəčəmbə. ər
da dolontə ba qarən na, tohu qarən zəm dønškˀi.
tər julgit biɣˀi. tukumaq da əmgəri yüdu ñi jiɣə.
tər ərint da əmdan tükiamə da əlkiki taŋ iźim
nan tükiam biɣˀi. tukumaq da ər χaʁəjif ɢamʁə.
ɢammaq ta ai aravmǔʁǔ, məji morin jaqəiv ñi

He hit him with his fist and broke the bull's three
ribs. The bull was dead in that moment. As the
boy killed the bull, he could not return home,
because he was afraid of the *janggin*.
He thought: I have to run off, and he started
running to his home in the First Banner. The
*janggin* was waiting and waiting and when he
could not see the boy, he asked his wife. She told
him that the boy had not come back.
"What could be the matter?",
he thought. Noon passed, or what time it was,
then he told his wife:
"Go and look for him."
They went and saw that somebody had killed the
bull near the front wall at the gate. Why did he
die, they wondered, and when they looked to the
other side, they noticed a tub broken into pieces.
So they returned home and said:
"The boy did mischief."
The *janggin* mounted a horse and went to chase
him. He had some relatives in the hamlet near
the Chabchal cannal. He stopped there and
asked:
"A boy has run off from my place, did he pass
by?"
"No, no – oh really, a while ago a little boy was
marching by, he was trampling as if kicking
the earth. His pace was heard from afar. My
wife just thought that a little boy was going
somewhere, she did not pay attention to him."
So he went to the First Banner. When he arrived
there, the boy, as he saw him, started running. He
asked his sister:
"Did the boy come here?"
"No, no."
"Oh yes, he did. I was asking in the Chabchal
hamlet and they told me that he was walking in
this direction, so you must know. You are scared.
Don't be scared, sister, I will not beat him in any
case. If the bull is dead, it is dead, I do not care."
He was talking nicely, persuading the boy, and
he barely got him to return with him behind his
saddle. When he brought him back he ordered
the people in the house: "You must not make
him do ordinary small tasks, he has great
strength."
A year had passed and the next year the old
man was sent to watch the post. At these times
they were guarding the Russian border in turns.
I have heard that this was the fortress in Dolonte

danəvm na. tukumə da bolori jaqůn biya tofχont, jaŋən ňi da

– ər χaʁəjit avəvm yavčie, bot gənəmaqa, bod ňi yindəmaq jiki. śi śien tükiamə yila, əm amʁərə. qarəmbə nanət dürivərə.

alim giaf ta, ər maf tükiaʁə. diøvr da, ər bə jaŋən ɢaznči yavʁə zəm dønjimaq ta. oros da dønška. čaŋdi məjigšəmə yilam.

– əzəi qarəmb da dürim gənkie, zəm da. diøvr da taŋ dulur čoaχ ɢajəm jimaq da dürim døškᵊi χandərda. ər mavə ňi məji yazm maŋ biyə na, o, šu ujaqů dürnumačimə śiňi gətk biyᵊi. əmdan gətkəŋ, uňiu, əm ju orozəi čoaχ ta šu gida javmaq gidalm jiyᵊi χandərda. mavə ňi boɹq uviaɹm yimaq da, ju gida javmaq ta, əmdan əhəŋ, skəi ju čoaʁə ňi amš sozurur da taɢaɹjəmaq tuhə na, oi, ər maf šu fanšk χoront da səkəi nanᵊi bətkə dəriŋ ňi əm ɢaɹt əm nanəf javmaq da əmgəri da jiɣə li nanəf fierɣəmaškəŋ. oi, tanʁə, fierɣə, oi, taŋ iźim nandəri ɢoźiⁿ ut nan vaʁᵊi. oros čoaʁə ňi gələmə da burulum yavʁə. bəyiŋ gəɹ bəšk biyɣəye. amʁəm tutkə jih jaq ůrů. tut jai ňinəŋ yinəŋdəri amźie jaŋən ňi jih χandərda. əmdaⁿ taʁəŋ jalu bəšk nan,

– ainʁə,

– diøvr təraliaŋ jiɣəye, zəm.

– o-o-o, qarəm dürivʁaqůŋ da śieⁿ, ər mavəf da ələi ujiləm tamašk biyə. ut azəɹm, əm bar aňi tükiam biyᵊi. tumə da χůliazim gənɣə, nanə. əs gəɹ bədərɣə. ərəi śidən da huis fašqůrh biyə. juanjaqůn yüdui huis vieš turulum avm jih biyə. tumaq ta torʁůtəi badəri moŋə čoaʁəv ňi fidəm ɢaškᵊi. ɢajəm jimaq ta gəɹ yilan duyin bia tükiavm, huizə ňi latəm jim mutəqůʁůo. ər manjus ňi məji ɢůňin əh, oi ər bai banjər gurun ňi ai jaqət baitiŋə, lančipazao nanəf ɢaɹvaŋ tam. ojůqůmə kunduzəi ɢosqůn uva bum. tukumə da səkəi moŋəz ňi fančər da χariya zəmə virimə yafh biyᵊi. ər afš azəɹmůʁů, moŋ čoaχ əkərəŋ da əmgəri huis čoaχ ta jimůʁů, tuttu əmgəri śivə aimandəri čoaχ giaʁᵊi χandərda. jaqůn qůza dəri. ər bə jaŋəmf χůlam ɢammaq ta,

– śi afš azəɹmůʁů, ərəvə, zəm da. tumə da bə jaŋən ňi avəfh biyᵊi:

– oʁůi, mində əm taŋ suzai morin čoaχ, əm taŋ suzai yafhəŋ čoaχ, yilan taŋ čoaχ bumaq ta oʁůi. tükiarə,

or maybe the fortress in Tohu. Over there in the south. So it was his turn. At that time the garrison had to consist of almost a hundred men so he took the boy with him. When he took him, what could he make him do – he just made him take care of the horses. In the autumn, on the fifteenth day of the eighth month, the *janggin* says:

"I will leave this boy in charge here and I will spend the night at home. Keep watching it thoroughly, do not fall asleep! Do not let the fortress be robbed."

The boy agreed and was guarding the post. At night, when it became known that the *janggin* Be had left, the Russians also learned about it. They were collecting new information all the time. They said:

"Let us go and rob the fortress!"

At night more than a hundred soldiers fell upon the fortress. The boy was sound asleep, he woke up only when everything was turned upside down. As he woke up, oh, two Russian soldiers are were just approaching him to stab him with spears. The boy woke up immediately, grasped the two spears, and as he did so, the two soldiers backed off and tumbled. The boy in rage grasped one of the soldier's legs in both hands and started thumping all who were coming. As he was beating around, he killed more than thirty men of the hundred. The Russian soldiers left in fear. There were some Sibe people among the dead, probably because he was still sleepy. Next day the *janggin* came and saw lots of dead people:

"What happened?"

"It happened at night," they said.

"Well, it is good that you did not let the rob the fortress."

From that time he was observing the boy with even greater respect. So they were on guard for the whole year. Then others came and they returned home. At that time the Uighurs rose up. The eighteenth Uighur division turned west and came here. So they ordered the Torghut Mongol soldiers to come here. They came and were guarding for three or four months, so the Uighurs could not get close. But the Manchus are a little mean, they thought: "Why should we keep the people here for nothing?" And they were humiliating them, giving them bitter flour

zəm. tukumaq da

– oʁŭi,

zəm əkərə da ər bə jaŋən da məji čoaʁɐi ərdəmt ɢayaqŭ arvən bi, tukumə ər χaʁəjit gəɹ tačivm. tərəi gəvəvňi da sajiŋa zəm. sajiŋa tər ərint juanduyin zə oʁŭye. juanduyin zəɹ nanət da tačivyə, gənyə, usun śien oʁŭye. tukumə da ju naⁿ əmgəri čoaχ giam čičimŭʁŭ. ər χaʁəč omə da yafhəŋ yavm čaʁaŋ. tumə da əm taŋ suzai yafhəŋ čoaʁəf da ər χaʁəjit buyᵊi. tukumə da χaʁəjit fienjim:

– śi ai javmie,

zəm da.

– o, naχčə, məs dulinki aň skəi qarəmf tükiaʁədə ju nanᵊi giramf əm ɢaɹt əmkən javmaq tandəmaškəŋ usun śien ɢaɹt ačənam. mint təraliŋ aʁŭraf əmkən aram bu,

zəm. o-o-o, skəi uskun sələf huŋkurmaq da nanᵊi əm durun jaq arardə, ɢaɹ aqŭ, əm bətkə aqŭ, əraliaŋ əm bətk nanəliaŋ da aram buh biyᵊi. ujui gum bi, nan əm durun. ər jaqəf əmdan ginlᵊyəŋ da nadənjə sunja gin čiškᵊi. tər ərin gində. tukumə da ər χaʁəjif da

– yafkie,

tukumaq da skəi gənəmaq yiŋyiɹyəŋ da ɢŭɹjai virgi χašə birai nuṇut, ərəi dirh həzənt gənəmaq da yiŋyilyᵊi. vierh həzəndə ňi huis bi. əmdan śivə čoaχ jiɣᵊi zəyəŋ da dulum jim mutəqŭ, tükiaʁə gənyə da ju yilan bia oʁŭi. tərəi śidən bølir om jih. ərəf afš azəɹmuʁŭo? ərəi śidən manjus ňi da gəɹ

– oi, əs ňi əm jaq araqŭ bai banjər gurun, əzəd ňi gəɹ ai gətkun jaq bumŭʁŭo,

zəm da skəi liaŋšə jaq əkəm omə da tər kunduzəi va šüliaχ maizəi uvaf bum bum səndam. əzəňi jəm zəmə χaq χaq ɢosqŭn, aŋət azəm mutəqŭ. urai jadən. čoaχ

– bədərkie, gəɹ ojŭqŭ, bədərəqŭ ba,

kəvəɹ duʁa yüyüm, əraliaŋ ɢošq omaq, tukumaq da əmgəri həfsəmašqə, afš azəlmŭʁŭ, zəm. tukumaq da jaŋən ňi da gizərəm:

– ai, naq, uf azələr uvədə, ərgəmf səlm huizəmaq əm faidan ač,

zəm.

– a, eitəm baʁeš da məzəi uf, eitəm baʁaqŭš da araʁaqŭ.

tukumə da χašə biraf afš dulumŭʁŭo, tə həfsəm.- oi, orʁŭmaq fas χaitəm,

– tukumaq duɹkie.

– a, ja, omŭʁŭo.

and so on. So the Mongols got angry and left. What to do now? Since the Mongolian army left, the Uighurs would come soon. So they mobilized soldiers among the Sibes, from the Eight Banners. They called the *janggin* Be and asked him: "How will you manage it?" The *janggin* ordered: Just give me hundred and fifty mounted soldiers and hundred and fifty foot-soldiers.

This *janggin* Be seems to have been excellent in the military arts, and he was also teaching the boy. The boy's name was Sajingga. Sajingga was fourteen at that time. So he was teaching a fourteen-years-old boy and the boy was making quick progress. Now the two are were preparing to set forth with the army. The boy liked walking most of all, so the hundred-and-fifty foot soldiers were entrusted to him. Then he asked him: What kind of weapon will you use? "Uncle, last year, when I was guarding the post, I was fighting with one human body in each hand, it was just right. Make me a weapon like that."

They cast a thing of melted iron, which looked like a man without hands and one leg, it looked like a one-legged man, it even had a head like a man. When they weighed it, it weighed seventy five pounds. He said to the boy: "Let's go!" So they went and camped west of Ghulja, above the river Kashgar, on its eastern bank. On the western bank the Uighurs were camping. Since the Sibe soldiers had come, they could not cross the river. In this way they were guarding there for two three months. The autumn came. What to do now? At this time the Manchus thought: "These are useless mouths that are doing nothing – why should we give them good food?" And they started giving them wheat flour mixed with bitter flour. When they tried to eat it, it was so bitter, that they could not even put it into their mouths. The soldiers were debating about what to do. Some of them wanted to return, since they were starving, the others thought that they could not leave. In the end Be *janggin* said: "Once our fate is like this, we have to clash with the Uighurs for life or death. If we defeat them, it is

əm ňinəŋ əmgəri da fas χaitəm bəɹɣəm. tumə
da yinəŋdəri ər yilan taŋ čoaʁa, ju janjündə arχ
bi oʁů na, təvat da əm laoye miao biɣ°i. dači
omə guan laoyev ňi gul vəčəm biɣ°i. ɢaznt gəɹ
bim yafh jaqə. uju ňurui bat gəɹ bi, yilač ňurt
gəɹ bi. dučurt gəɹ tər əm laoye miao zəm bi. tər
miaot gənəmaq ta əmgəri yaqůrum hiŋkəɹm,
bəyi cůňimb ňi aləmašk°i. jiŋkən na, χoɹ na, tər
baitəf saqů oʁůye, zər. vajəmə bədərəm jih, jəŋ
yamsqůn bəda jər śidən da, dirh badəri da yev
yečkən tuksuɹmaq jih. taʁə da ambu udun, aʁa
surʁan jiɣə gəsk,
– omoh,
zəm da mətər udun huzunt da duɹh zərə. χašə
bira dulumaq ta yavm. əmdan χašə bira virh
həzənt gənɣəŋ da əm ju duŋlo da juɹɣut yavmaq
dutk°i. ər ju duŋlof da daʁəf da yavmaq dudəm.
yaskə li nan tumən afχa, sačqə, əm diøvr
əkəmaq ta skəi huis sujam mutəqůʁůo mərbit
da burulumašk°i. mər amčəm. yuɹdus davan
gum duluvɣ°i zərə. laft ɢor iźinh biɣ°i. tukumaq
jai ňinəŋ manjus əmdan məjik śiksəm, uňiu,
śivə čoaχ əmkən gələ aqů. əmdan nəɣəmaškəŋ,
suda laft ɢor amčəm yafh χandərda. tər huizəf
šu nanjaňči duluf bədərəvm ɢašk°i χandərda.
tukumə da tər ərint əjəndə ňi baoɹʁa, ər baitəf.
əmdan baoɹʁəŋ da
– o, śivə čoaχ sə am guŋ yiləfh,
zəm da gum čaliŋ bumə, jaŋli bum. əraliaŋ
buh biɣ°i χandərda. tukumaq ta ambandə ňi
javəvmaq da əm miŋan sunja taŋ yan, əm biat
baʁər čaliŋ. ər ňi əm miŋan sunja taŋ ňi yask
jiʁa. ər sajiŋdə ňi miŋan yan, əzəi guŋə ňi
da əraliaŋ bia tom əraŋ baʁəvmie. tukumə da
janjünt ər əjən həsəv ňi vaźivʁə, tukumə da
janjün javə, ərəd ňi tər gəsk ainəmie, zəm da. təri
śidən da gəɹ bə jaŋən ňi amban oh biɣə. amban
omə da veiškə. sajiŋav ňi da jaŋən ofh biɣ°i,
orundə ňi.
jaŋən zəɣəŋ aie, məzəi əm ɢazn oš da əm toksoi
əjən, əmbiš da sunjaŋ. tərəv ňi gəɹ əjən badəri
həs vaźim śəŋjim biɣəye. umai da jəjiedi əjən
badəri jih biɣ°i. tut, ər sajiŋadə ňi əm biya sunja
taŋ yan. ər da skəi manjui məzəi śivə nanəf
ɢaɹvaŋ tam, tut azəɹm. ər da əm juvə, əm suduri.

our fortune, if not, there is no other way."
So they started thinking, how to get over the
Kashgar river.
"Let us make rafts of grass and cross."
"All right, that will do."
And for the whole day they were preparing
and binding the rafts. In the afternoon the three
hundred soldiers and two officers got an idea.
Nearby was a temple of Laoye.[12] At that time
people were regularly worshipping Guan Laoye,
in Chabchal as well. In the First Banner there
was one, the Third Banner too. In the Fourth
Banner there also was one temple of Laoye. So
they went to the temple and were bowing and
prostrating, praying for their plan. Today it is
not known whether this is true or not. Then they
returned and in the evening, just when they were
eating dinner, very black clouds came from the
east and overcast the sky. A storm with rain and
ice drift came.
"We succeeded,"
they said and crossed the river with the help of
the wind.
After they crossed the Kashgar river, they
proceeded further.
As they were on the western bank of the Kashgar
river, two lanterns were going in front, and all
were following the two lanterns. All of them
were fighting and slashing, it continued the
whole night and in the end the Uighurs lost their
foothold and started withdrawing. They pursued
them, crossing the whole Yuldus Daban, they
got very far. The next day the Manchus were
gathering information and, alas, there was not
a single Sibe soldier. When they started to search
for them, they were already far away. They were
pursuing the Uighurs all the way to Nanjiang
and brought them back. Then they made an
announcement to the Emperor and the Emperor
said:
"The Sibe soldiers gained great merit"
and he ordered to give all of them a salary and
rewards. In this way he rewarded them. The
amban got one thousand and five hundred yuans

---

[12] Laoye (= Chin. Grandfather) – Guan Laoye, Guan
Gong, a taoist deity which was especially popular
among the Manchus and was worshipped mainly
as a protector and helper in military matters. In the
Mongolian areas, following the Manchu system, this
deity was identified with Gesar Khan.

as a monthly salary. One thousand and five hundred, that is a lot of money. Sajingga was appointed thousand yuan every month for his merit. The Emperor's orders were passed on to the General,[13] but he replied: "Why should I give him so much?" At that time the Be *janggin* was promoted to the rank of an *amban*. Sajingga became *janggin* in his place.

What does it mean, a *janggin*? In Chabchal it is the commander of one village, something like a bailiff. He used to be appointed by the Emperor's order, or sometimes commanded there from the Emperor's court. So Sajingga got five hundred yuans per month. This was because the Manchus did not like our Sibe people. This is one tale, one history.

---

[13] The General of the Ili area was the most important Manchu military official in the Jungarian region.

# VOCABULARY

| | |
|---|---|
| ač(ə)-/aš- | to meet |
| ačəf-/ačəv(ə)- | to load |
| ačən(ə)- | to match, to be correct |
| adan(ə)- | to participate |
| adaš(ə)- | to resemble |
| afanti | Effendi (a character from Uyghur folklore) |
| afqa | sky |
| afś, afš | how |
| agə | elder brother |
| aʁa | rain |
| aʁŭⁿ | elder brother |
| aʁŭra | weapon |
| ai | what |
| aič(i)- | to move |
| ailiaŋ, ailiɴ | what kind of |
| aimaⁿ | tribe, ethnic group |
| ain(ə)-, an(i)-, aiqa | if |
| aiźiⁿ sər | Golden Spring (toponyme) |
| aitiɴ | when |
| aji, ajik/ajig(ə) | small |
| ajiguruⁿ | children |
| al(ə)-/aɹ- | to tell |
| ali-, ɛli- | to wait |
| aliⁿ | mountain |
| am, ambu | big |
| ambamə | uncle (father's brother) |
| ambaⁿ | amban (Manchu official) |
| amč(ə)-/amš- | to chase, to reach |
| amə | father |
| aməɹ | after |
| amirh, ɛmirh | north, side, back side |
| amnə- | to imitate |
| amrə- | to rest |

204

| | |
|---|---|
| amš | to the back, to the north |
| amtiŋ | sweet, tasty |
| amχ-/ amʁ(ə)- | to sleep |
| aɴ | mouth |
| a$^n$ | why |
| aň | year |
| an(ə)- | to push |
| an$^ə$q | key |
| antq | what |
| antqəl(ə)- | to be too polite |
| aɴəɹ | family member, person |
| aodu$^n$ | firm, stable, secure |
| aoju$^n$ | lightening |
| aq(ə)- | to worry |
| aq$^ŭ$ | no, not, absent |
| ar(ə)- | to do, to make, to write |
| araraɴ, ararəɴ | hardly |
| arχ | way to do |
| arsla$^n$ | lion |
| arvə$^n$ | form, apearance |
| aɹč | stuck in an upright position |
| aɹdəv(ə)-/aɹdəf- | to do something involuntarily |
| aɹh | spotted, coloured |
| aɹjə- | to split off, to part |
| aɹvə$^n$ | work, duty |
| as | net |
| asχa$^n$, asqə$^n$ | young |
| asir(e)-/azər(ə)- | to preserve |
| ašχa$^n$ | moss |
| ašta | young man |
| av(ə)-/af- | to fight |
| avəf-/avəv(ə)- | to order |
| avəɹ-avəl(ə)- | to hunt |
| azə- | to put in one's mouth |
| azəl(ə)-/azəɹ- | to arrange, to behave, to settle |
| | |
| ɛli- | to wait |
| ɛmiɹ | male animal (mostly about a rooster) |
| ɛn(i)- ɛn(ə)- | to do what (vicarious verb) |
| ɛtə- | to save |
| | |
| ba | place |
| babəli | lullaby |
| baχ/baʁ(ə)- | to hit (the mark), to reach |
| baχtə- | to fit into |
| baʁən(ə)-, banə- | to ba able, to succeed in, to find |

| | |
|---|---|
| bai | in vain |
| bail | merit |
| bailə- | to rejoice |
| baiš-/baič(ə)- | to check |
| bait | matter, thing |
| baitaqᵘ | no matter, no problem |
| baitəɹ-/baitəl(ə)- | to use |
| baitiŋ- | necessary, useful |
| baivůqᵘ | unnecessary, no need |
| bakši | master (Mong.) |
| banč-, banj(ə)- | to live |
| bandiaos | gawk |
| bangəjoŋ | half an hour (Chin.) |
| baňiχa | thank you |
| banjən, banjiⁿ | life |
| baoɹ-/baol(ə)- | to report |
| bayiⁿ | rich |
| bazar | market (Uig.) |
| beš-/bəč(ə)- | to die |
| bəda | food |
| bədər(ə)- | to return |
| bəijiŋ | Peking |
| bələⁿ | ready |
| bən(ə)- | to deliver, to escort |
| bənšəⁿ | ability (Chin.) |
| bəɹh-/bəɹɣ(ə)- | to prepare |
| bəri | bow |
| bətk | foot, leg |
| bəy | body, self |
| bi 1. | I (1ˢᵗ sg. pronoun) |
| bi 2. | is (existential copula) |
| bi- | to be |
| bia-, biɛ- | to lok for, to ask |
| bia, biya | month, moon |
| biak śiaɴəⁿ | pale, colourless |
| bierh-/bierɣ(ə)- | to collect, to keep |
| bigaⁿ | wild |
| bioʁůⁿ | dust, sand |
| biɹ-/bil(ə)- | to stroke |
| bira | river |
| bitkə | book, document |
| biyeɹ-/biyel(ə)- | to graduate |
| bo | house, home |
| bo/məs | we (1. pl. pronoun) |
| bobo | bread (children´s expression) |
| bohtoⁿ, bohtuⁿ bahtəⁿ | bumpy |

| | |
|---|---|
| boɹq | abruptly, vehemently, completely |
| boɹʁŭ$^n$ | clean, cleanliness |
| bot-/bod(ə)- | to think |
| bølir, bolori | autumn |
| bu- | to give |
| bučun(u)- | to argue |
| buja$^n$ | forest |
| burul(u)- | to retire |
| | |
| čaʁaɹ-/čaʁalə- | to like |
| čaɣaŋ | liking |
| čai | tea |
| čalabu$^n$ | difference |
| čaləf-/čaləv(ə)- | to differ |
| čaliŋ | salary |
| čaŋdi | often |
| čaɴ | full |
| čaq | in a broken way, into parts |
| čaqaɹ-/čaqal(ə)- | to cut to pieces |
| čaqaš-/čaqajə- | to be broken |
| čaqŭr | shaman ladder, black birch |
| čavaɹ | bowl |
| čavčaɹ | Chabchal |
| čɛ | behind, further |
| čeňinj | the day before yesterday |
| češ, čeś | over, further |
| čəksə | yesterday |
| čik | suddenly |
| čimar | tomorrow |
| čiŋkuaŋ | situation |
| čir čir | a pointy object, a stitching pain |
| čira 1. | strict, firm |
| čira 2. | face |
| čiśkə, čiškə | sparrow, little bird |
| čiš-/čič(i), tič(i)- | to come forth |
| čoaχ, čŭaχ | soldier |
| čoʁo | teapot |
| čoqo | hen |
| čorʁo | neck |
| ču | spade |
| čujuŋ | middle school (Chin.) |
| čuk(ə)- | to be exhausted |
| | |
| da 1. | root, base |
| da 2. | particle |
| da maf | mythical ancestor of the clan |

| | |
|---|---|
| da- | do have connection to |
| dačі | originally |
| daχ-/daʁə- | to follow |
| daif | doctor |
| daɹji | connection |
| daɹvə | beside, aside, next to |
| daɹvət | besides |
| | |
| daməɴ | tobacco |
| damjiⁿ | scale beam |
| dan(ə)- | to take care |
| daohui | backwards (Chin.) |
| dart | trembling (onom.) |
| dat | next to, close to and some others |
| davaⁿ | mountain pass (Mong.) |
| davəli | particle |
| dazə-/das- | to repair, to rouge |
| dəɣəmə | aunt (mother's sister) |
| dəⁿ | high |
| dəŋjəⁿ | lamp |
| dər | cushion; table |
| dərgi | upper; eastern |
| dərif- | to begin |
| dəvər | boiling (onom.) |
| dəvərgəⁿ | whelp |
| dəy(i)- | to fly |
| dianχůa | telephone (Chin.) |
| dⁱaoɹ-/dⁱaol(ə)- | to send by order |
| dⁱeɹ-/dⁱel(ə)- | to chase |
| dⁱetti | immediately |
| dih | fourty |
| dⁱøf | fox |
| dⁱorgidə, diorgut | inside |
| dⁱøɹmba | middle |
| dⁱovr, dⁱøvr | night |
| dirh | east |
| diš | to the east |
| diš-/dij(i)- | to burn |
| dišk | fuel |
| diur(i)-, dür(i)- | to fight over something |
| diyimiŋ | top (at an examination, Chin.) |
| domdoqǔⁿ | buttterfly |
| donš-/donj(i)-, dønš-/ønj(i), doɴdoɴ | hard |
| dienj(i)- | to hear, to listen |
| doo- | to land |
| dor | custom, law |

208

| | |
|---|---|
| doraqᵘ | ill-bred |
| doʁŭr- | to roll |
| døš-/døź(i)-, doš-/dož(i)- | to enter |
| dozorh | needlegras |
| dᵘaɹ | strophe (Chin.) |
| dučur (duič ňur) | the Fourth village in Chabchal |
| dulin | middle |
| dulinki, dulinᵊi | past |
| dunda- | to eat (of pigs) |
| duŋlo | lantern |
| duɴa | watermellon |
| duqa | gate |
| duɹ-/dul(u)- | to pass |
| duʁa | intestines |
| düri | craddle |
| durun | form, shape |
| durvo | fly |
| dut-/dud(ə)-, dud(u)- | to lie, to rest |
| duyin | four |
| | |
| eisk | pace, sound |
| eit(ə)- | to save |
| emi- | to drink |
| eŋ | the interjection of nodding |
| ere | the interjection of the sigh |
| erk, ɛrk | liquor, alcohol |
| | |
| əčə | uncle |
| ədəri | from now |
| əɣəliŋ | ugly, wicked |
| əh | bad, evil |
| əh(ə)-, ək(ə) | to do what (vicarous verb) |
| əhśien | evil power, demon |
| əjən | lord |
| ək | that one (pronoun) |
| əkčin | riverbank |
| əksə- | to hurry |
| əli | still more |
| əlkiki | allmost |
| əɹči | one type of a ritual specialist |
| əɹdən | light |
| əɹɣə | slowly |
| əm, əmkən | one |
| əmbat | at one place, i.e. together |
| əmbič | or |
| əmdan | once |

| | |
|---|---|
| əməŋ | saddle |
| əmfalə<sup>n</sup> | moment, short time |
| əmgəri | already, once |
| əmzaq | alone |
| ənduri, əndür, əndüri | deity |
| ənəŋ | today |
| əňi | mother |
| ər | this, he/she/it (3. sg pronoun) |
| əraliɴ, əraliŋ, əraɴ | thus, in this way |
| ərbit | here |
| ərɣə- | to take a rest |
| ərdə | morning |
| ərdəm | knowledge |
| ərəču<sup>n</sup> | hope |
| ərgə<sup>n</sup> səlm | for life and death |
| ərɣə<sup>n</sup>, ərgə<sup>n</sup> | life |
| ərgəɹji | small saddle |
| əri<sup>n</sup> | time, hour |
| ərsu<sup>n</sup> | ugly |
| ərt | early |
| əs | they (3. pl. pronoun) |
| əš-/əj(ə)- | to remember |
| ət(ə)- | to win |
| əvat, ərvadə | here |
| əvə<sup>n</sup> | bread |
| əvəri | normal |
| əvəš-/əvəj(ə)- | to break down |
| əyi | grandfather, old man |
| əyu<sup>n</sup> | elder sister |
| əyunnu<sup>n</sup> | sisters |
| əza | relatively many/much |
| | |
| fa | window |
| fa- | to shout |
| faida<sup>n</sup> | eyebrows |
| faχ | ball, pill |
| faɹ- | to leaven (Chin.) |
| famdor | tomato |
| fanč(ə)- | to be angry |
| fanča<sup>n</sup> | small coin (Chin.) |
| fanjəŋ | in fact (Chin.) |
| faqar | trousers |
| farn(ə)- | to faint |
| farʁů<sup>n</sup> | dark, dusky |
| fars | quick movement (onom.) |
| fas | raft |

| | |
|---|---|
| fašk, fašq | buttocks |
| fašqůr(ů)- | to uprise |
| fat(ə)- | to pinch |
| favə$^n$ | law |
| fayaNů, fayiŋ | soul |
| feiančaobi | magic power (Chin.) |
| fə | old |
| fəjərgit | below |
| fəjil, fəji.ɹ | under |
| fəkś(i)- | to run |
| fər | bottom |
| fə.ɹgie$^n$ | red |
| fərgoško | extraordinary |
| fət(ə)- | to dig |
| fətər- | to dig, to stoke |
| fəy- | to boil |
| fiaNqalə$^n$ | low |
| fiaŋ | youngest child |
| fiča- | to blow |
| fidə- | to move by order |
| fienš-/fienj(i)- | to ask |
| fier(ə)- | to beat |
| fiet(ə)- | to fart |
| fih | brains |
| finh | hair |
| fioʁůlů$^n$ | short |
| fišk | Buddha |
| fita | airtight |
| fiźi$^n$ | dense |
| fot | an implement used during burial rituals |
| foliŋə | talkative |
| fonq | hole |
| foq foq | consistence of a dried apple or cucumber |
| foro$^n$ | peak |
| fo.ɹχ | bag |
| fosχů$^n$ | downwards |
| fulaʁů$^n$ fə.ɹgie$^n$ | scarlet, deep red (often used for human face) |
| fulaʁů$^n$ | reddish |
| fulo | more, excessive |
| fus | through |
| fuskulu- | to kick |
| | |
| gəf | name |
| gəɣə | elder sister |
| gə.ɹ | still |
| gə.ɹ-, gəl(ə)- | to be afraid |

| | |
|---|---|
| gəɹšk | awful, awesome |
| gəmuⁿ | capital |
| gən(ə)- | to go there |
| gənčeɹ | spoon |
| gənkəndi | suddenly |
| gəs, gəsk, gəskə | as big as |
| gət- | to wake up |
| gətkuⁿ | clever |
| gətqaqǔ | bad, useless |
| gia | street (Chin.) |
| gia- | to take |
| giaⁿ | matter, need |
| gida | spear |
| gidaɹ- | to stab with a spear |
| giliŋ giliŋ | shiningly, cleanly, totally |
| giⁿ | scale |
| ginl(ə)- | to weigh |
| giŋ(ň)in | light blue |
| giŋuɹ- | to care, to show respect |
| gir(i)- | to be shy |
| giraⁿ | bone |
| giraŋ | skeleton |
| giraŋyeɹ | relatives |
| giriⁿ | Kirin (toponyme) |
| giršk | shameful |
| gizər(ə)- | to speak |
| gizuⁿ | word |
| glčiŋ glčiŋ | shiny |
| guanśi | relationship |
| gučᵘ | friend |
| guə- | to avoid |
| gufč | all, whole |
| gugu | aunt (father's sister) |
| guida- | to last |
| guis | coffer |
| gul- | to peer |
| gul, gulgul | often |
| gum, gəm | all |
| guŋ | merit (Chin.) |
| guŋčaŋdaŋ | the Communist Party (Chin.) |
| guŋzuo | work (Chin.) |
| guoguo | shoes (children's expression) |
| gurh | wild animal |
| guri- | to move |
| guruⁿ | state, people |
| gurunbo | state |

| | |
|---|---|
| ɢaft(ə)- | to shoot with bow and arrows |
| ɢaitai | suddenly |
| ɢam- | to take |
| ɢaňiŋ | strange |
| ɢaɹ | hand |
| ɢaraŋ ɢaraŋ | ragged |
| ɢarʁə$^n$ | branch |
| ɢaɹvaɴ | bad |
| ɢasχ | wild bird |
| ɢaš-/ɢaj(ə)- | to bring |
| ɢayaq$^{\mathring{u}}$ | outstanding |
| ɢazn | village, homeplace |
| ɢor | far, distatnt |
| ɢoɹmisχu$^n$ | elongated, oblong |
| ɢosqů$^n$ | bitter |
| ɢošq | terrible |
| ɢoźi$^n$ | thirty |
| ɢ$^{\mathring{u}}$a | another, different, other |
| ɢůč(i)- | to smoke, to draw in |
| ɢůɹja | the city of Ghulja |
| ɢůɹmaʁə$^n$ | rabbit |
| ɢůňi- | to think, to miss |
| ɢůňi$^n$ | thought, mind |
| ɢůňiχaq$^{\mathring{u}}$ | unexpectedly |
| | |
| hamt(ə)- | to defecate |
| haɴś | part of the winter period in the Chinese agricultural calendar |
| hɛm(i)- | to bear, to stand |
| həfs(ə)- | to consult |
| həh | woman |
| hərču$^n$ | awareness |
| hərgə$^n$ | script, letter |
| həs | order |
| hət-/həd(ə)- | to fold |
| həzə$^n$ | edge, rim |
| hiŋkəɹ- | to kowtow |
| hirgi- | to wander |
| huis | Uighur |
| huŋkur- | to melt |
| hut | soul (of a dead person) |
| huzu$^n$ | strength |
| | |
| χač, χajə | loving, close, love |
| χači$^n$ | type, kind |
| χafs(ə)- | to report |

| | |
|---|---|
| χaʁəč | boy, son |
| χairiⁿ | regretful |
| χaiš | rather (Chin.) |
| χait(ə)- | to bind |
| χaliⁿ | tree |
| χaɹʁůⁿ | warm, hot |
| χaɹt-/χaɹdə- | to touch, to importune |
| χam | excrements |
| χamtə- | to defecate |
| χaň(i) | little, at least |
| χanč | close |
| χaq | bitter |
| χasq | scissors |
| χašə bira | the Kashgar river |
| χateⁿ | sharp, burning |
| χatqůⁿ | salted |
| χazəq | Kazakh |
| χočqůn, χošqůn | son-in-law |
| χof | coffin |
| χoj | nice |
| χojəye | properly |
| χoɹ | lie, fake |
| χoɹt(ə)- | to cheat |
| χoňiⁿ | sheep |
| χoril(ə)- | to invite by prayer |
| χoroⁿ | grandeur |
| χorʁůⁿ | enclosure |
| χos | corner |
| χoš | well, nicely |
| χotuⁿ | town, city |
| χoźiⁿ | paper |
| χůa | in a tearing way |
| χůalar χůalar | a great waterstream, an extrovert and talkative character |
| χᵘaliazuⁿ | peace |
| χůaɹ- | to cut into halves |
| χᵘarəⁿ | courtyard |
| χᵘazə-/χᵘas- | to grow up |
| χůdůⁿ | quickly |
| χůla- | to call |
| χůlias-/χůliaz(ə)- | to change |
| χůɹʁa | to steal |
| χůzuⁿ | strength |
| | |
| ičaɴ | proper, agreeable |
| ičaqů | unpleasant, improper |

214

| | |
|---|---|
| ičə | new |
| iči | to here |
| if | grave |
| ifči | ribb |
| inč | sixty |
| indi | not yet (particle) |
| inji- | to laugh |
| inšk | laugh |
| irgən | citizen, people |
| iśte | right |
| iš-/iź(i)- | to suffice |
| iškⁱa- | to arrange |
| išta-, śⁱta- | to be late |
| iv(i)- | to play |
| iza- | to gather |
| izanč | Isanju (name of a deity) |
| iźin(ə)- | to reach |
| | |
| ja | easy, cheap |
| jadən | very, extremely |
| jaf-/javə- | to hold, to catch |
| jaft-/javd(ə)- | to hurry up [so as] to manage |
| jai | second, next |
| jalən | joint, world |
| jaliⁿ | sake |
| jalu | full |
| jam | violet, orange |
| janjüⁿ | general (Chin.) |
| jaŋəⁿ | military official (Chin.) |
| jaŋli | reward (Chin.) |
| jaq, jaq jamuⁿ | thing |
| jaqər(ə)- | to dawn |
| jaqůči | eighth |
| jaqůⁿ | eight |
| jaqůnč | eighty |
| jašqaⁿ | letter |
| jat | spear |
| jazm | pumpkin |
| jə- | to eat |
| jəčəⁿ | border |
| jəjiedi | directly (Chin.) |
| jəjoɹ- | to solve (Chin.) |
| jəŋ | just |
| jəŋkəⁿ, jiŋkəⁿ | real(ly) |
| jəyiⁿ | edge |
| ji | child |

| | |
|---|---|
| ji- | to come |
| ji jii | to urinate (children's expression) |
| jil | anger |
| jiɹʁaⁿ | sound |
| jinčüeⁿ | the Golden Spring (toponyme) |
| jiʁa | money |
| jiram | thick |
| jiri | pair |
| jon(o)- | to mention |
| jovoloⁿ | suffering |
| ju | two |
| juaⁿ | ten |
| juht(ə)- | to venerate |
| juʁǔⁿ | way, path |
| jüjü | clothes |
| juləⁿ | an epic poem |
| juɹh, juɹbi | southern side, front side |
| junguo | China (Chin.) |
| juŋyi | Chinese medicine (Chin.) |
| juś | forwards/towards the south |
| jus | children |
| juš | to the south |
| juvə | story |
| | |
| kaolu- | to examine (Chin.) |
| kara | black (horse) |
| kəčəⁿ | wall |
| kəməⁿ | level |
| kənəŋ | maybe (Chin.) |
| kənɣunjə- | to suspect |
| kəskə | cat |
| kəvəɹ | stomach |
| kimiⁿ | revenge |
| kira- | to look aside |
| kokor- | to huddle |
| kuantour | bold (Chin.) |
| kuk | blue, gray (of animals) |
| kuli | fortunately |
| kus | heavy pace (onom.) |
| kuźi | knife |
| | |
| laft | many, much |
| lahčə- | to separate, to |
| laɹ-/lal(ə)- | to be hungry |
| lam | Buddhist monk (Mong.) |
| lančipazao | messy (Chin.) |

| | |
|---|---|
| laoχaⁿ | old man (Chin.) |
| lat(ə)- | to stick |
| leik(ə)-, liek(ə)- | to hang |
| li | PART. |
| li | sweat |
| li- | to open |
| liaŋšə | crops (Chin.) |
| liaŋxin | conscience, kindness (Chin.) |
| liaoča | pitchfork (Chin.) |
| loχ | sword |
| lom | Buddhist ritual |
| lous | tower, building |
| luk | firmly, inseparably |
| lüs | donkey |
| | |
| maf | ancestor, old man |
| maχt(ə)- | to throw |
| maʁaɹ | cap |
| mais | wheat |
| maitoɹ- | to beat with a stick |
| maɹʁůn | a little |
| maɹt(ə)- | to rub |
| mamə | grandmother, old woman |
| man(ə)- | wear through |
| manč/manj(u) | Manchu |
| maŋ | difficult |
| maŋiⁿ | lower deity |
| maɴ | difficult |
| maɴus | monster |
| mašqůⁿ | slim, skinny (lit. Ma. mačuhůn) |
| mašqůⁿ | thin |
| mavəɹ- | to wipe |
| məda- | to turn, to return |
| mədəri | sea |
| məɣəjəⁿ | swine |
| məih | snake |
| məiməňi | every, each |
| məji, maji | little |
| məjig | message |
| məjigšə- | to collect information |
| məmə | sexual organ |
| mənjaɴ | indeed, yes, true, the same |
| mər | exactly this |
| məɹ-/məl(ə)- | to water (animals) |
| məraɴ | exactly thus |
| mərbit | exactly here |

| | |
|---|---|
| mərgə$^n$ | clever, wise |
| məs | we (1pl. pronoun, incl.) |
| məsk | thus much |
| mətər | exactly that one |
| mətəraɴ | exactly that way |
| mətərbit | exactly there |
| miao | temple, shrine |
| mier(ə)- | to bend |
| miʁa$^n$ | piglet |
| miŋa$^n$ | thousand |
| mit(ə)- | to cut |
| mo | wood |
| modil(ə)- | to know by intuition (Chin.) |
| moχt | short |
| mo$^n$ | our (excl.) |
| moň | monkey |
| moŋ | Mongolian |
| moŋu$^n$ | silver |
| moqsa$^n$ | a wooden stick |
| mori$^n$ | horse |
| muduri | dragon |
| muʁazn | bull |
| muku | water |
| muɹt | by sidling |
| mutə- | to be able to, to master, to overcome |
| | |
| na 1. | earth |
| na 2. | interrogative particle |
| nadə$^n$ | seven |
| nadənč | seventy |
| naχčə | uncle (mother's brother) |
| naʁə$^n$ | kang |
| najə$^n$ | the Earth god |
| nan ňi | lit. his/its person, the person |
| na$^n$ | person, man |
| nanjaŋ | Southern Xinjiang (Chin.) |
| naq, naqa, naqə | stop it, let it be |
| narʁů$^n$ | narrow, fine |
| nazə- | to sob |
| nəɣə- | to require |
| nəkəlie$^n$ | subtle, lowly |
| nənəm | first, before |
| nienšku$^n$ | a sharp smell (i.e. of fish) |
| ňilmaʁů$^n$ | the Realm of the dead |
| ňimaχ | beetle |
| ňimʁa | fish |

| | |
|---|---|
| ňiŋu$^n$ | six |
| ňuŋňe$^n$ | green |
| niungnie$^n$ | green |
| ňoʁů$^n$ | greenish |
| ňoʁů$^n$ ňuŋňe$^n$ | deep green |
| ňonʁů$^n$ | dog |
| ňoɴů$^n$ | sand |
| nor | swamp |
| ňumzu$^n$ | belt |
| nu$^n$ | younger sister |
| ňunʁu$^n$ | dog |
| ňuňu | baby |
| ňuŋk | illness |
| nuŋš | upwards |
| nuŋut | above, on |
| ňur | banner, village |
| | |
| o- | to become, to be possible |
| of-/ov(ə)- | to wash |
| oh | armpit |
| oksů$^n$ | pace |
| oɹh | rushes |
| oɹʁů$^n$ | dry |
| oɹχ-/oɹʁ(ů)- | to dry |
| om | lake |
| onč$^u$ | wide, widely |
| ongoɹ | before, ago |
| oɴ(ů)- | to forget |
| ori$^n$ | twenty |
| oros | Russian |
| oru$^n$ | daughter-in-law |
| orχ | grass |
| oyuɴ | important |
| oχt | medicine |
| | |
| paqa | of a short stature |
| paraɴ | talk (Uig.) |
| pas | sound of beating |
| | |
| qač(i)-, qaiš-/qaič(i)- | to shout |
| qafči- | to squeeze |
| qanjiaɹ | jacket |
| qaqa | hot (children's expression) |
| qar | black (horse) |
| qarə$^n$ | watchpost |
| qarmə- | to protect |

| | |
|---|---|
| qoms | little, few |
| qor | injury |
| qors(o)- | to weep |
| qotoŋ | a sound of a falling object |
| qᵘariaɴ | beautiful |
| qǔčir(ə)- | to dig |
| qǔza | banner |
| | |
| sa- | to know |
| sač(ə)- | to cut |
| saf | shoes |
| saft-/savdə- | to drop |
| saʁənč | girl, daughter |
| saʁər(ə)- | to catch cold |
| saʁǔrǔⁿ | cold, coldly |
| saⁱt/sɛt/set | old |
| saməⁿ | shaman |
| saⁿ | ear |
| saq | a description of intertwinned branches etc. |
| sarɢaⁿ | wife |
| sarɢaš(ə)-, sarš(ə)- | to walk around |
| sas | fool |
| sat-/sad(ə)- | to be tired |
| sav- | to see |
| savdəⁿ | drop |
| sə, zə | age, year of age |
| sə-, zə- | to say |
| səbjəⁿ | joy, pleasure |
| səf | teacher |
| səjəⁿ | cart |
| səkt(ə)- | spread |
| səlačuqa, səlak | pleasant, joyful |
| sənda- | to put |
| səŋkər | dishevelled |
| sər(ə)- | to pay attention |
| sər(i) | water source |
| səsk | chin |
| set | old man, old (for animate beings) |
| set(ə)- | to grow old |
| skəi /səkəi | that one |
| so- | to put off |
| so | you (pl.) |
| solo | free, free time |
| soɴ(ǔ)- | to cry |
| soŋkoi | according to |
| soo | trough |

| | |
|---|---|
| soqᷰ | skin, leather |
| soʁů$^n$ suye$^n$ | bright yellow |
| soʁů$^n$ | yellowish |
| sozor(u)- | to back |
| su/šu | ultimately (PART.) |
| suduri | history |
| suɣə$^n$ śiaɴə$^n$ | very white, snowwhite |
| suɣe$^n$ | whitish |
| suja- | to procede |
| sula | free, loose |
| suɹʁo | apple |
| su$^n$ | milk |
| sunja | five |
| sunjači | fifth |
| sunjaŋ | bailiff (Chin.) |
| sur | soul of a dead person |
| sur(u)- | to shout |
| surɣun(u)- | to tremble |
| surʁa$^n$ | frozen rain |
| susai, suzai | fifty |
| susχa | whip |
| susχaɹ- | to whip |
| suvdu$^n$ | air, wind |
| suyen | yellow |
| | |
| śalaq | futile |
| samdə- | to shamanize |
| śamə | your father |
| śa$^n$ | whistling sound |
| śaq śaq | futile (onom.) |
| śars | a quick movement |
| śerh | crotch |
| śeri$^n$, śieri$^n$ | wedding |
| śi | you (2. sg) |
| śiaŋə$^n$ | white, steam |
| śidə$^n$ | between |
| śidər χodur | in agreement |
| śie$^n$ | good, well |
| śik | urine |
| śiks(ə)- | to check |
| śiliŋ | dew, slobber |
| śinaq | mourning |
| śiŋčəŋ | name of a village |
| śiŋči | Sunday, week |
| śiŋčiliu | Saturday |
| ś$^i$qa | horsehair |

| | |
|---|---|
| śiram(ə) | later, in future (1) and |
| śirgə | thread |
| śit(ə)- | to urinate |
| śiumɣun | finger |
| śivə | Sibe |
| śiyi | Western medicine |
| śomoχoɹt | Mill Valley (toponyme) |
| śønś-/śønj(i)- | to chose |
| śoɹ- | to invite |
| śoro | jujube |
| sorq | awl |
| śorʁ(ǔ)- | to rub |
| śoɹʁo | left |
| śumi$^n$ | deep |
| | |
| šaɴbaɹ- | to work (Chin.) |
| šašqaɹ- | to slap |
| škuaɹ- | to hit with one's fist |
| šuanboɹ | twins (Chin.) |
| šülia- | to mix |
| šu$^n$ | sun |
| | |
| ta- | to see, to look |
| taɢaɹjə- | to stumble |
| taχ-/taq-/taq(ə)- | to know, to recognize |
| taʁaɹ | sack |
| tais | platform (Chin.) |
| taitai | lady (Chin.) |
| tana | pearl |
| tant-/tand(ə)- | to beat |
| taŋ | hundred |
| taqǔr(u)- | to order |
| tarχ-/tarʁ(ǔ)- | to grow fat |
| tarʁǔ$^n$ | fat, fleshy |
| taš-/tač(i)- | to learn |
| taškie$^n$ | religion |
| tašqǔ | school |
| tat(ə)- | to pull |
| tavənə-, tafšə- | to climb, to ascend |
| tə | now |
| tə- | to sit |
| tək(ə)- | to do that (vicarious verb) |
| təkši$^n$ | plain, equal |
| təňi | recently |
| tər | that |
| təraliaŋ, təraliŋ, təraɴ | in such way |

| | |
|---|---|
| təsk | that much, that big |
| təvat | there |
| tiaf-, tiav(ə)- | to light |
| tiaχ | burnt, spotted |
| tier(ə-) | to plant |
| tiki- | to lift |
| tiɳtiel | torch |
| tiørχ-/tiørʁ(ů)- | to circle |
| tiuɹgut | outside |
| tivəl(ə)/tivəɹ- | to embrace |
| tivmo | stick |
| to- | to abuse |
| tof 1. | hut |
| tof 2. | precisely |
| tofχoⁿ | fifteen |
| toχto- | to remember |
| toʁ(ů)- | to saddle |
| tohu | name of a watchpost |
| tokso | village |
| tømiⁿ | thick |
| toro | peach |
| torʁůt | Torghut (ethnonyme) |
| tůa | fire |
| tuɣun(u)- | to live |
| tuh-/tuɣ(ə)- | to fall |
| tükia- | to guard |
| tuks | cloud |
| tuksuɹ- | to ger overcast |
| tukum- tumə | thus |
| tuliaš-/tuliaj(ə)- | kick up |
| tuməⁿ | ten thousand |
| tuɳz | bucket |
| tuɴaɹ- | to encounter |
| turguⁿ | reason |
| türⁱ | winter |
| tuta- | to stay |
| tuza | help, advantage |
| tuza- | to drop |
| tůχtaⁿ | initial |
| | |
| uča | waist |
| uči | door |
| učuɹ-/učul(u)- | to sing |
| učuⁿ | song |
| udaⁿ | slow, slowly |
| uduⁿ | wind |

| | |
|---|---|
| uf | fate |
| uf-/uv(ə)- | to descend |
| uɣumə | aunt |
| uɣuri | all |
| ujandaqů | excessively |
| ujən | heavy |
| ujilə-, ujələ- | to respect |
| uju | head |
| ujui | first |
| uksur | ethnicity |
| ulaf-/ulav(e)- | to hand down |
| ulan | pit |
| uluf-/uluv(e)- | to feed |
| uluk | soft |
| um(e)-, um(u)- | to burry |
| umai | at all |
| unča- | to sell |
| unčᵘ | different |
| uŋqan- | to escape |
| ůɴaⁿ | ancestor |
| uɴanda | elder |
| urai, ərai | how |
| ursuⁿ | bad, ugly |
| uśikun, ušhun | wet |
| uśiχa, ušχa | star |
| uskuⁿ | raw |
| usuⁿ | much |
| uškuⁿ | wet |
| ut 1. | how much, how many |
| ut 2. | thus |
| ut(u)- | to put on |
| utkᵘ | clothes |
| uva | flour |
| uviaɹ- | to turn, to translate |
| uyaⁿ | liquid |
| uyiⁿ | nine |
| uyinč | ninety |
| uza- | to pull, to carry |
| uzat | sad |
| uźiⁿ | heavy |
| | |
| va | smell, taste |
| va- | to kill |
| vaš-/vaj(ə)- | to finish |
| vans | ball, pill |
| vaq, vaqa | not |

| | |
|---|---|
| vaś-/vaź(i)- | to descend |
| və | who |
| vəč(ə)- | to offer, to sacrifice |
| vəid(ə)- | to measure, to scoop |
| veiɣu$^n$ | living |
| veilə- | to work |
| vəɹgie$^n$ | pig |
| vəra | buttocks |
| vešhu$^n$ | upwards |
| vierh | east |
| vieš | eastwards |
| vih | tooth |
| vir(i)- | to leave |
| vuyuk | light |
| | |
| ya | what, which |
| yaf-/yav(e)- | to go |
| yafhəŋ | on foot |
| yaχčə$^n$ | puppy |
| yam | which |
| yam(kə$^n$) | which one |
| yamsqů$^n$ | evening |
| yaɴk | smear |
| yaqs(ə)- | to close to lock |
| yaqůr(u)- | to bow, to kowtow |
| yaɹ-/yal(e)- | to ride |
| yas | leye |
| yask, yaskə | how much |
| yaya | every |
| yazm | sleep |
| yeči$^n$ | black |
| yemj, yamji | night |
| yenjir | doll |
| yet | where |
| yeye | every |
| yi-/ye- | to get up, to stand up |
| yiɣə | goose |
| yiɣi$^n$ | husband |
| yiʁa$^n$ | cow, cattle |
| yila- | to stand |
| yila$^n$ | three |
| yilə- | to lick |
| yiɹʁa | flower |
| yind(ə)- | to stay overnight |
| yindaʁů$^n$ | dog |
| yinəŋ, ňinəŋ | day |

| | |
|---|---|
| yinəŋdəri | everyday |
| yinʁaⁿ | drum |
| yiŋbi | front wall (Chin.) |
| yiŋyiɹ- | to camp (Chin.) |
| yiqaⁿ | Chinese |
| yivagəⁿ/yivaʁəⁿ | evil spirit, demon |
| yivəŋ | swarming (onom.) |
| yoloq | soft, smooth |
| yono | funny |
| yos 1. | lock |
| yos 2. | custom |
| yovn | fun |
| yozuɹ- | to lock |
| yüdu | sequence, order (Chin.) |
| yüdul- | to take turns |
| yuh | wolf |
| yuɹduⁿ | opportunity |
| yuɹdus | name of a mountain pass |
| yüyü- | to starve |

# REFERENCES

BLOOMFIELD, L., 1933, *Language*. George Allen & Unwin Ltd., London.

BOLDYREV, B. V., 1976, *Kategorija kosvennoj prinadležnosti v tunguso-man'čžurskih jazykah*. Izdateľstvo „Nauka", Moskva.

CEVEL, Y.A., 1996, *Mongol helnii tovc' tailbar tol'* [Stručný výkladový slovník mongolštiny]. Ulaanbaatar.

CINCIUS, V. I., 1975, *Sravniteľnyj slovar' tunguso-man'čžurskih jazykov*. Izdateľstvo „Nauka", Moskva.

*DONJINA-I SABUHA DONJIHA EJEBUN* [Notes of what Donjina saw and heard], 1994, *Xinjiang renmin chubanshi*. Urumqi.

GLEASON, H. A., 1967, *An Introduction to Descriptive Linguistics*. New York.

GORELOVA, L. M., 1988, The Sibe Dialect of Manchu Language as Interpreted by Russian and Foreign Linguists. In: *Indian Journal of Linguistics – A Soviet Approach*. Calcutta, 300–317.

GORELOVA, L. M., 2002, Manchu Grammar. Brill, Leiden–Boston–Köln.

HAENISCH, E., 1986, *Mandschu Grammatik*. Leipzig.

HEJI, WANG XIAOMU, 1998, *Šolokon manju-nikan gisun kamcibuha bithe* [Brief Manchu-Chinese Dictionary]. Beijing.

HOCKETT, F., 1967, *A course in Modern Linguistics*. New York.

*HOIFA KARUN-I JASIGAN* [Letter from the Hoifa fortress], 1985, Xinjiang renmin chubanshi. Urumqi.

HOPPE, T., 1995, *Die Ethnischen Gruppen Xinjiangs: Kulturunterschiede und interethnische beziehungen*. Hamburg.

IVANOVSKIJ, A. O., 1895, *Man'čžurskaja hrestomatia*. Sankt-Peterburg.

JAHONTOV, K. S., 1992, *Kniga o Šamanke Nisan'*. Peterburskoe Vostokovedenie, Sankt-Peterburg.

JANG, TAEHO, 2008, *Xibo yu yufa yanjiu* [Sibe Grammar]. Kunming.

JANHUNEN, J., 1991, *Material on Manchurian Khamnigan Evenki*. Helsinky.

JANHUNEN, J. 1993. The teens in Jurchen and Manchu revisited. *Mémoires de la Société Finno-Ougrienne* 215: 169–184. [Festschrift für Raija Bartens].

JANHUHEN, J., 1996, *Manchuria, an Ethnic History*. The Finno-ugrian Society, Helsinki.

JIN NING, 1993, *Sibe-English Conversations*. Wiesbaden.

JIN NING, 1991, The Sibe-Manchu legend of Blackening the Face. In: *Aetas Manjurica* 2, 147–173.

KAŁUŻYŃSKY, S., 1987, *Dis Sprache des Mandschurischen Stammes Sibe aus der Gegend von Kuldscha*. Warszawa.

KAŁUŻYŃSKY, S., Charakteristika sibinskogo jazyka. In: *Problemy jezykow Aziji a Afryki*, Warszawa 1987, 195–210.

KAPIŠOVSKÁ, V., 2003, Spatial orientation of the Mongols and its reflection in Mongolian. In: *Mongolica Pragensia* 3, 76–122.

KUBO, T., ZHUANG SHENG, 2011, *Shibe go no kiso* [Basic Sibe], Tokyo.

LAVRILLIER, A., 2006, S'orienter avec les riviers chez les Evenks du Sud-Est siberien. Un system d'orientation spatial, habitual et rituel. In: *Etudes Mongoles et Siberiennes, Centralasiatiques et Tibetaines*, 95–138.

LATTIMORE , O., 1934, *The Mongols of Manchuria*. New York.

LI SHULAN, 1985, Xibo yu de zhuangci [Imitatives in Sibe]. In: *Minzu yuwen* [Nationality Languages] 5, 12–25.

LI SHULAN, 1986, Xibo yu huayu cailiao [Materials of oral Sibe]. In: *Minzu yuwen* [Nationality Languages] 5, 76–79.

LI SHULAN, ZHONGQIAN, WANG QINGFENG, 1984, *Xibo yu kouyu yanjiu* [Study of Colloquial Sibe]. Zhongya minzu chubanshe, Beijing.

LI, GERTRAUDE ROTH, 2000, *Manchu – A Textbook for Reading Documents*. Honolulu.

LI YONGHAI, ZHAO ZHIZHONG, BAI LIYUN, 1989, *Manju gisun jaqūn tanggū hacin – Xiandai manwen babai ju* [Eight Hundred Sentences of Modern Manchu]. Zhongya minzu xueyuan chubanshe, Beijing.

MANJU – NIKAN YONGGIYANGGA BULEKU BITHE – MAN-HAN DA CIDIAN (*Large Manchu-Chinese Dictionary*), 1993. Beijing.

MIS'IGDORZ', GO., 1976, *Mongol, manz' bic' giin helnii haricaa* [The Relationship Between the Mongolian and Manchu Literary Languages]. Ulaanbaatar.

MÖLLENDORFF, P. G. VON, 1892, *A Manchu Grammar with Analysed Texts*. American Presbyterian Mission Texts, Shanghai.

NORMAN, J., 1974, A Sketch of Sibe Morphology. In: *Central Asiatic Journal* 18, 159–174.

OBERFALZEROVÁ, A., 1986, *Subjekt u slovesných jmen v mongolštině*. M.A. Thesis, FF UK, Praha.

OBERFALZEROVÁ, A., 2002, *Metaforická řeč a myšlení mongolských nomádů*. PhD. Thesis, Univerzita Karlova.

*OČERKI SRAVITELNOJ MORFOLOGII ALTAJSKIH JAZYKOV*, 1978, Izdateľstvo „Nauka", Leningrad.

PETROVA, T. I., 1967, *Jazyk orokov – uľta*. Izdateľstvo „Nauka", Moskva.

POPPE, N., 1960, *Vergleichende Gramatik der Altaischen Sprachen (Teil 1 – Lautlehre)*. Wiesbaden.

POPPE, N., 1955, *Introduction to Mongolian Comparative Studies*. Suomalais-ugrilainen seura, Helsinki.

QICHESHAN (Kičešan), 2011, *Shuai luo de tong tian shu: Xinjiang xibozu saman wenhua yicun diaocha* [The Declining World Axis Tree: Research of the Remnants of Sibe Shaman Culture]. Minzu chubanshe, Beijing.

RAMSTEDT, G. J., 1957, *Einführung in die Altaische Sprachwissenschaft – I. Lautlehre*. Helsinky.

RAMSTEDT, G. J., 1957, *Vvedenije v altajskoe jazykoznanie* (Introduction to Altaic Linguistics). Moskva.

RHOADS, EDWARD J. M., 2000, *Manchus and Han – Ethnic Relations and Political Power in Late Qing and Early Republican China*, 1868–1928, University of Washington Press, Seattle and London.

*SAMAN JARIN* [Shaman prayers], 1990, Xinjiang renmin chubanshi. Urumqi,.

SANŽEEV, G. D., 1963, *Sravniteľnaja grammatika mongoľskih jazykov*. Izdateľstvo „Nauka", Moskva.

S'ARIBU, 2000, *Manju suduri bithei deji* [A Selection of Manchu Literary Texts]. Ulaanbaatar.

SECHENBAATAR, B., 2003, *The Chahar dialect of Mongol, a Morphological Description*. Helsinki.

*SIBE GISUN ISAMJAN* [Sibe language dictionary], 1991, Xinjiang renmin chubanshe. Urumqi.

*SIBE „MANJU" GISUN-I BULEKU BITHE* [Dictionary of the Sibe "Manchu" Language], 1987, Xinjiang renmin chubanshe. Urumqi.

*SIBE UKSURAI AN TACIN* [The Sibe ethnography], 1989, Xinjiang renmin chubanshe. Urumqi.

*SIBE UKSURAI IRGEN SIDEN JUBE* [Sibe folktales] I–IX, 1984–2000. Urumqi.

*SRAVNITEL'NO-ISTORIČESKAJA GRAMMATIKA TJURKSKIH JAZYKOV* – Fonetika, 1984. Izdateľstvo „Nauka", Moskva 1984.

*SRAVNITEL'NYJ SLOVAR' TUNGUSO-MAN'ČŽURSKIH JAZYKOV* (A Comparative Dictionary of the Manchu-Tungus Languages), 1975–1977, Izdatel'stvo 'Nauka', Leningrad.

SUNIK, O. P., 1982, *Suščestvitel'noje v tunguso-man'čžurskich jazykach*. Izdateľstvo „Nauka" Leningrad.

SUNIK, O. P., 1962, *Glagol v tunguso-man'čžurskih jazykah*. Izdateľstvo „Nauka", Leningrad.

TODAEVA, B. H. 1985, *Jazyk Mongolov Vnutrennej Mongolii – očerk dialektov*. Izdateľstvo „Nauka", Moskva.

VACEK, J., LUVSANDORDŽ, DŽ., LUVSANDŽAV, ČOJ., 1977, *Učebnice mongolštiny – hovorový styl*. Praha. [Textbook of Spoken Mongolian]

VACEK, J., 2002, Emphasizing and Interrogative Enclitic particles in Dravidian and Altaic. In: *Mongolica Pragensia* 2, 151–185.

WANG XIAOHONG, GUO MEILAN, 1985, Xibo yu kouyu yinwei xitong [Fonological structure of spoken Sibe]. In: *Manyu yanjiu* [Manchu language studies] 1, 48–53.

WU YUANFENG, ANJUN, ZHAO ZHIQIANG, 1985, *Sibe uksura-i šolokon suduri* [Short history of the Sibe nationality]. Xinjiang renmin chubanshi. Urumqi.

YAMAMOTO, K., 1969, *A Classified Dictionary of Spoken Manchu*. Tokyo.

ZAHAROV, I., 1875, *Polnyj man'čžursko-russkij slovar'*. (Full Manchu-Russian Dictionary) Tipografija imperatorskoj akademii nauk, Sanktpeterburg.

ZAHAROV, I., 1879, *Grammatika man'čžurskago jazyka*. Tipografija imperatorskoj akademii nauk, Sanktpeterburg.

ZHU KELIN, BOYA, QICHESHAN, 1990, *Xibo zu yanjiu* [Studies of the Sibe nationality]. Urumqi.

# SUMMARY

The Sibe language, nowadays spoken by more than ten thousands of Sibe poeple in the Xinjiang Uighur autonomous province in China, deserves special attention of linguists for several reasons. For Manchurologists it is its position as an oral variety of Manchu that makes it particularly important. Spoken Sibe seems to be relatively close to the literary language and thus its knowledge facilitates the understanding of literary Manchu.

The present work was intended to give a description of the grammar of spoken Sibe as it functions in everyday communication. Therefore I did not take literary Manchu as a basis for this description, although remarks on similarities differences between the two idioms appear throughout the text.

The grammar of spoken Sibe is largely similar to that of oral forms of Mongolian and the difference between spoken Sibe and literary Manchu is comparable to the difference between classical Mongolian and the modern Mongolian dialects. In the description of the Sibe grammar I point out some typical analogies with Khalkha Mongolian, which may bring the described grammatical features closer to readers familiar with Mongolian. For the same reason I mostly used the grammatical terminology that was introduced by Poppe for Mongolian but proved to be fully suitable for spoken Sibe as well.

The present description focuses on the part of Sibe lexicon which is inflected according to two main patterns – the nominal and verbal inflection. These two basic parts of speech are firmly established for most Altaic languages, which makes it possible to go into greater detail in the description. Other parts of speech, both uninflected and those displaying certain morphological regularities, are left for further investigation.

The described grammatical features are illustrated by examples gathered during fieldwork, which demonstrate practical function of the grammar. Appended are two longer texts recorded by Mr. Kicengge in 1996 in Chabchal, which are intended as samples of genuine usage of the language in its cultural context.

sibe gisun oci enenggi sinjiyang de banjire emu tumen funcere sibe uksurai baitalara gisun inu. sibe anggai gisun de udu oyonggo holbobun bi. mini bodorode, manju gisun sibkire urse de oci, sibe gisun serengge manjui anggai gisun i emu gisun mudan duwali seci geli ombi. uttu ofi, sibe gisun be bahanaci, manju bithei gisun be tacire ulhirede umesi tusa ombi.

mini ere leolen be araha oyonggo gvnin oci, inenggidari baitalara sibe anggai gisun i gisun kooli be narhvn ejeme tucibuhe. ere turgunde manju bithei gisun be ten obuhakv, sibe anggai gisun be ten obume arahabi. damu araha dorgide, ememu bade sibe anggai gisun jai manju gisun siden i acanara acanarakv babe duibulebume ejehebi.

sibe anggai gisun i gisun kooli oci monggo anggai gisun i gisun kooli de hanci bihebi. geli sibe gisun jai manju bithei gisun i siden i calabun oci, monggo anggai gisun jai monggo bithei gisun siden i calabun de amba muru acanambi. ere turgunde, monggo gisun be bahanara gucusa de ulhirede ildungga obuki seme leolen i dorgide sibe anggai gisun i gisun kooli be araha bade, monggo anggai gisun i gisun kooli de acanara babe ejehebi. uttu ofi geli sibe gisun i gisun kooli be leolerede, nicolas poppe i monggo gisun i gisun kooli be ejere jalin banjibuha cohotoi baitalara gisun be juwen gaime baitalahabi.

ere mudan i leolen de, gibsun jai aššasun sere juwe oyonggo gisun meyen i gisun kooli be ejeme arahabi. ere juwe hacin gisun meyen i kvbulin be altai gisun i sibkisi sa emgeri umesi šumin i sibkime duleke turgunde, sibe gisun dorgide geli ere jergi hacin meyen be narhvn leoleme mutembi. gvwa hacin gisun meyen be ere mudan i leolen de ejeme gisurehekv, sirame i sibkire nashvn de werihebi.

sibe anggai gisun i gisun kooli be banjin dorgide yargiyan i absi baitalara be tuwabure jalin, sibe niyalma i irgen siden de baitalara gisun jai jube be gisun tuwakvn obume baitalame ejehebi. leolen i šošohon de kicengge agu i 1996 aniya de cabcal de genefi irgen siden deri isabume singgebume gaiha juwe jube be acabume ejehebi. ere juwe jube i dolo, sibe uksurai banjire durun, suduri, tacihiyan jai da gisun mudan i šumin gvnin be umesi getuken i iletulehe seme bodofi, leolen i šošohon de gingguleme ejehebi, geren tacihasi jai sibkisi sai hvlarade tusa ojoro be erembi.

VERONIKA ZIKMUNDOVÁ

# SPOKEN SIBE
## MORPHOLOGY
## OF THE INFLECTED
## PARTS OF SPEECH

Published by Charles University in Prague
Karolinum Press
Ovocný trh 3–5, 116 36, Prague 1, Czech Republic
http://cupress.cuni.cz
Prague 2013
Editor vice-rector prof. PhDr. Ivan Jakubec, CSc.
Cover by Jan Šerých
Layout by Kateřina Řezáčová
Typeset by Karolinum Press
Printed by Karolinum Press
First Edition

ISBN 978-80-246-2103-6